Contemporary Descriptions of Early Musicians

Books by David Whitwell

The Sousa Oral History Project
The Art of Musical Conducting
The Longy Club: 1900–1917
La Téléphonie and the Universal Musical Language
Extraordinary Women
A Concise History of the Wind Band
Essays on the Modern Wind Band
Essays on Performance Practice
A New History of Wind Music
The College and University Band
The Early Symphonies of Mozart
Music of the French Revolution
Stories from the Podium

On Composers
Wagner on Bands
Berlioz on Bands
Chopin: A Self-Portrait
Liszt: A Self-Portrait
Schumann: A Self-Portrait in His Own Words
Mendelssohn: A Self-Portrait in His Own Words

On Education
Philosophic Foundations of Education
Foundations of Music Education
Music Education of the Future

Aesthetics of Music

Aesthetics of Music in Ancient Civilizations
Aesthetics of Music in the Middle Ages
Aesthetics of Music in the Early Renaissance
Aesthetics of Music in Sixteenth-Century Italy, France and Spain
Aesthetics of Music in Sixteenth-Century Germany, the Low Countries and England
Aesthetics of Baroque Music in Italy, Spain, the German-Speaking Countries and the Low Countries
Aesthetics of Baroque Music in France
Aesthetics of Baroque Music in England

The History and Literature of the Wind Band and Wind Ensemble Series

Volume 1 The Wind Band and Wind Ensemble Before 1500
Volume 2 The Renaissance Wind Band and Wind Ensemble
Volume 3 The Baroque Wind Band and Wind Ensemble
Volume 4 The Wind Band and Wind Ensemble of the Classical Period (1750–1800)
Volume 5 The Nineteenth-Century Wind Band and Wind Ensemble
Volume 6 A Catalog of Multi-Part Repertoire for Wind Instruments or for Undesignated Instrumentation before 1600
Volume 7 Baroque Wind Band and Wind Ensemble Repertoire
Volume 8 Classical Period Wind Band and Wind Ensemble Repertoire
Volume 9 Nineteenth-Century Wind Band and Wind Ensemble Repertoire
Volume 10 A Supplementary Catalog of Wind Band and Wind Ensemble Repertoire
Volume 11 A Catalog of Wind Repertoire before the Twentieth Century for One to Five Players
Volume 12 A Second Supplementary Catalog of Early Wind Band and Wind Ensemble Repertoire
Volume 13 Name Index, Volumes 1–12, The History and Literature of the Wind Band and Wind Ensemble

Ancient Voices

Ancient Views on Music and Religion
Ancient Views on the Natural World
Ancient Views on What Is Music
Contemporary Descriptions of Early Musicians
Early Views of Music and Ethics
Early Thoughts on Performance Practice
Music Performance in Ancient Societies

Renaissance Voices

Essays on Renaissance Philosophies of Music
Renaissance Men on Music

www.whitwellbooks.com

David Whitwell

Ancient Voices
Views on Music by Ancient and
Medieval Writers

Contemporary Descriptions of Early Musicians

Edited by Craig Dabelstein

WHITWELL PUBLISHING • AUSTIN, TEXAS, USA

Ancient Voices: Views on music by ancient and medieval writers
Contemporary Descriptions of Early Musicians
Dr. David Whitwell

WHITWELL PUBLISHING
AUSTIN, TX 78701
WWW.WHITWELLPUBLISHING.COM

© 2013 by David Whitwell
All rights reserved. First edition 2013

Based on essays written between 2000 and 2005.

Composed in Bembo Book.
Published in the United States of America.
All images used in this book are in the public domain except where otherwise noted.

ISBN-13: 9781936512751

Cover design by Daniel Ferla

Contents

	Acknowledgement	ix

Part 1 In Ancient Societies

1	On Early Performers	3
2	On Early Singers	15
3	On the Ancient Rhapsodist	39
4	Women Performers of the Ancient World	47
5	On Ancient Conductors	59
6	On the Aulos	71
7	On the Ancient Trumpet	83

Part 2 In Medieval Europe

8	On the Medieval Trumpet	93
9	On the Jongleur	99
10	On the Minstrel	109
11	On the Troubadours	121
12	Music of the French Romances	141
13	On the Minnesingers	147
14	On the Goliards	163
	Bibliography	169
	About the Author	179
	About the Editor	181

Acknowledgments

I am indebted to my friend and colleague, Craig Dabelstein, for his help in preparing this book for publication.

David Whitwell
Austin, Texas

PART I
IN ANCIENT SOCIETIES

On Early Performers

WE BEGIN THIS BOOK with an essay in which we present a broad sampling of descriptions of ancient players and singers. It seems to us a fitting introduction for the reader will notice many values which we honor today were already in place at the time of some of the oldest surviving literature.

Some of our earliest information about actual musicians is found in tributes and eulogies by their contemporaries. One, upon retiring, observes,

> May I never touch a lyre again or carry the instrument of the music I made of old. Let young men love the lyre-string, but I, instead of holding the plectrum, support my shaky hands on a staff.

These words were spoken by a retiring lyre player named Eumpolpus as he symbolically laid his instrument on a tripod as an offering to Phoebus, an alternative name for Apollo, the ancient Greek god of music. This is found in a poem by Macedonius, dating from the early Christian years, and is one of several which give us the actual names of ancient Greek performers.[1] Another poem by this same poet memorializes an elderly panpipe player.

> I, Daphnis the piper, in my shaky old age, my idle hand now heavy, dedicate, now I have ceased from the labors of the fold, my shepherd's crook to rustic Pan. For still I play on the pipes, still in my trembling body my voice dwells unshaken. But let no goatherd tell the ravenous wolves in the mountains of the feebleness of my old years.[2]

A poem by Agathias Scholasticus, is very rare, being written in honor of a deceased *female* singer and lyre player.

> Alas! alas! this earth covers the tenth Muse, the lyric chanter of Rome and Alexandria. They have perished, the notes of the lyre; song hath perished as if dying together with Joanna. Perchance the nine Muses have imposed on themselves a law worthy of them—to dwell in Joanna's tomb instead of on Helicon.[3]

The poet, Paulus Silentiarius, wrote a poem in honor of a deceased lyre player, which includes an interesting association of music and grammar.

> Damocharis passed into the final silence of Fate; alas! the Muses' lovely lyre is silent; the holy foundation of Grammar has perished. Sea-girt Cos, thou are again in mourning as for Hippocrates.[4]

---

[1] *The Greek Anthology*, trans. W. R. Paton (Cambridge: Harvard University Press, 1939), I, vi, 83.

[2] Ibid., I, vi, 73.

[3] Ibid., II, vii, 612.

[4] Ibid., I, vii, 588.

The reader may be surprised by the association here of music and grammar, but it is a topic often mentioned by ancient writers. Usually the observations speak about the rules of grammar being based on the practice of music, in reference to accents, pauses and cadences. One authority, Arthur Pickard-Cambridge, has written at length about the use of music in the ancient Greek theater.[5] He believed that the aulos player was a permanent member of the drama company and also wore costumes. He mentions one for which there is considerable documentation, the famous aulos player, Kraton of Chalkedon. This book is recommended for those who may wish to seek further clues about the relationship of music and grammar. To either encourage or discourage the reader, as the case may be, here is a sample of his argument which deals with his belief that the aulos had specific relationships with the meter of the text.

> It has been made plain that the anapaests of the parabasis were accompanied by the [aulos], as also, in all probability, were any tetrameter speeches delivered by an actor while the chorus or a semi-chorus was dancing, and in particular the epirrhema and antepirrhema of the parabasis, which were commonly in trochaic or iambic tetrameters.[6]

The reference to the aulos player wearing costumes is also mentioned by Socrates in his description of the typical virtuoso. He is discussing imposture in this passage, which explains the last line, that is, 'dress like a great player, but don't actually play in public and expose yourself for what you are.'

> Suppose a bad aulos player wants to be thought a good one, let us note what he must do. Must he not imitate good players in the accessories of the art? First, as they wear fine clothes and travel with many attendants, he must do the same. Further, seeing that they win the applause of crowds, he must provide himself with a large claque. But, of course, he must never accept an engagement, or he will promptly expose himself to ridicule as an incompetent player and an impostor to boot.[7]

The dress of the artist is also mentioned in one of the comedies of the great ancient Greek playwright, Aristophanes. As Aristophanes mentions here, the ancient poet was nearly always a musician; poetry was sung and not read.

> Besides, it is bad taste for a poet to be coarse and hairy. Look at the famous Ibycus, at Anacreon of Teos, and at Alcaeus, who handled music so well; they wore head-bands and found pleasure in the lascivious dances of Ionia. And have you not heard what a dandy Phrynichus was and how careful in his dress? For this reason his pieces were also beautiful, for the works of a poet are copied from himself.[8]

---

5   Sir Arthur Pickard-Cambridge, *The Dramatic Festivals of Athens* (Oxford: Clarendon Press, 1953), 164, 218, 300ff.
6   Ibid., 162.
7   'Memorabilia,' I, *Memorabilia and Oeconomicus*, trans. E. C. Marchant, (Cambridge: Harvard University Press, 1953).
8   *The Thesmophoriazusae*, 161.

The dress of the artist is mentioned again by the Roman Emperor, Julian (331–363 AD), but he says that only foolish people would judge the artist by how he dresses. Most people, he believed, would judge the artist by whether he performed 'inspired music.'

> If one were to judge the best of two musicians, and were to clothe him in the raiment suited to his art, and were then to bring him into a theater full of men, women, and children of all sorts, varying in temperament and age and habits besides, do you not suppose that the children and those of the men and women who had childish tastes would gaze at his dress and his lyre, and be marvelously smitten with his appearance, while the more ignorant of the men, and the whole crowd of women, except a very few, would judge his playing simply by the criterion of pleasure or the reverse; whereas a musical man who understood the rules of the art would not endure that the melodies should be wrongly mixed for the sake of giving pleasure, but would resent it if the player did not preserve the modes of the music and did not use the harmonies properly, and conformably to the laws of genuine and inspired music? But if he saw that he was faithful to the principles of his art and produced in the audience a pleasure that was not spurious but pure and uncontaminated, he would go home praising the musician, and filled with admiration because his performance in the theater was artistic and did the Muses no wrong. But such a man thinks that anyone who praises the purple raiment and the lyre is foolish and out of his mind.[9]

This topic is closely related to a phenomenon often observed today, an audience who responds to the *performance* rather than to the *music*. In this regard we find the fifth century poet, Sidonius, critical of those choirs who, through good singing, make bad compositions appear good.[10] And Cicero (106–43 BC) mentioned the same thing with respect to the orator, that the audience can be enthusiastic about the orator even though the speech itself was devoid of content.

> Thus, for example, if the wind instrument when blown upon does not respond with sound, the musician knows that the instrument must be discarded, and so in like manner the popular ear is for the orator a kind of instrument; if it refuses to accept the breath blown into it, or if, as a horse [refuses to move] to the rein, the listener does not respond, there is no use of urging him. There is however this difference, that the crowd sometimes gives its approval to an orator who does not deserve it, but it approves without comparison. When it is pleased by a mediocre or even bad speaker it is content with him; it does not apprehend that there is something better; it approves what is offered, whatever its quality; for even a mediocre orator will hold its attention, if only he amounts to anything at all, since there is nothing that has so potent an effect upon human emotions as well-ordered and embellished speech.[11]

We know the names of some more performers from ancient Greece. One, an aulos player named Ismenias, is known from a compliment by Zeno:

> The wise man does all things well, just as we say that Ismenias plays all melodies on the aulos well,[12]

---

9   *The Works of the Emperor Julian*, trans. Wilmer Wright (London: Heinemann, 1913), I, 299.

10 *Sidonius Poems and Letters*, trans. W. B. Anderson (Cambridge: Harvard University Press, 1965), II, 445.

11 *Brutus*, li, 192.

12 Quoted in Diogenes Laertius, *Lives of the Eminent Philosophers*, trans. R. D. Hicks (Cambridge: Harvard University Press, 1950), II, 229.

This same player is mentioned rather disrespectfully, for his lowering himself to play popular entertainment music, by another aulos player, Dionysodorus, who comments that no one will ever hear him play, like Ismenias, on ships or at the fountain in the town square![13]

In a lost play called *The Harper*, by Menander, a character speaks of someone playing a musical instrument, 'He is very fond of music, and always practicing tunes in luxurious ease.'[14] We assume he was being portrayed as a good player.

Because Aristotle was so rational a man, he very rarely discusses actual performances. As disappointing as this is, it remains clear that he was paying attention. He recognized the difference between the musical and the unmusical performance[15] and he noticed that quality of birth or wealth was not the factor that resulted in a good player.[16] In various places, Aristotle mentions the institution of the chorus, how it is supported[17] and how the conductors should be elected.[18] The breadth of observations which he lists in his 'Problemata,' in a chapter devoted to music, is very impressive. Among them are,

> A sound made by a chorus travels farther than that of a solo singer.
> Most people prefer hearing music they already know.
> Most people prefer to hear an accompanied singer, rather than a solo singer.
> Low notes which are out of tune are more noticeable than high notes which are out of tune.
> A large chorus keeps better time than a smaller one.

He also must have observed the work of good performers, for he gives as one reason why children should indeed actually learn to perform music that, 'it is difficult, if not impossible, for those who do not perform to be good judges of the performance of others.'[19]

We can assume there were many fine performers who were poet/singers who accompanied themselves on an instrument. Ovid (43 BC–17 AD) describes such a professional singer and gives us a rare reference to a musician 'tuning up,' with a specific indication of some kind of harmony. When he begins to sing, he appeals to Jove for inspiration.

> And when he had tried the chords by touching them with his thumb, and his ears told him that the notes were in harmony although they were of different pitch, he raised his voice in this song:
> From Jove, O Muse, my mother—for all things yield to the sway of Jove—inspire my song! Oft have I sung the power of Jove before; I have sung the giants in a heavier strain, and the victorious bolts hurled on the Phlegraean plains. But now I need the gentler touch, for I would sing of boys beloved by gods, and maidens inflamed by unnatural love and paying the penalty of their lust.[20]

---

[13] Ibid., I, 399.
[14] Quoted in Athenaeus, *Deipnosophistae*, XII, 510.
[15] *Coming-to-be and Passing-away*, II.6.
[16] *Politica*, 1283a.
[17] *Atheniensium Respublica*, 56.2.
[18] *Politica*, 1299a.17.
[19] Ibid., 1340b.25.
[20] Ovid, *Metamorphoses*, X, 143.

It is fairly rare in the literature of ancient Greece to read of a poor or bad player. One such case is mentioned by Diogenes (third century AD), a musician whose audiences always got up and left, whom Diogenes named 'Rooster.'[21] Perhaps Diogenes may have heard a number of unsuccessful performers, because after an observation regarding the 'incessant toil' required to be a musician, he adds that if instead they had 'transferred their efforts to the training of the mind, certainly their labors would not have been [so] unprofitable or ineffective.'[22]

Cicero (106–43 BC) mentions an aulos recital, which he is quick to point out the audience did *not* like. The incident is worthy of mention for the comment made by the teacher of this unhappy player, 'Play for me and for the Muses.'[23]

On the other hand we know the names of some famous instrumentalists of the early Roman period, including Nero's teacher, Terpnos, the kithara player. Nero also rewarded the kitharode player, Menecrates, with a palace and estate. The emperor Vespasian (69–79 AD) gave huge cash gifts to the lyre players Terpnus and Diodorus.[24] Another kitharode player, Anaxeron, was not only honored by a monument erected in a public square in his birthplace, but was given the tax income of four cities by Mark Anthony.

Canus, the most famous aulos player of the first century AD made the interesting statement that if the audiences only knew how much pleasure he received from playing, instead of paying him, he would be required to pay them.[25] The rhetorician and biographer, Flavius Philostratus,[26] recounts a visit by a traveler named Apollonius to this aulos player. In describing to him the kinds of music he played, Canus provides a list of types of music which would seem familiar today: music for those who are sad; music for celebration; music for lovers; and music for religious usage.

> [The purpose of my music is] that the mourner may have his sorrow lulled to sleep by the pipe, and that they that rejoice may have their cheerfulness enhanced, and the lover may wax warmer in his passion, and that the lover of sacrifice may become more inspired and full of sacred song.[27]

Upon further questioning, Canus admits it is the music itself which accomplishes these ends, not the aulos 'constructed of gold or brass and the skin of a stag, or perhaps the shin of a donkey.' Finally, Canus provides a very rare glimpse into the basic technique of playing the aulos.

---

[21] Diogenes, *Lives of the Eminent Philosophers*, II, 49.

[22] Ibid., II, 73.

[23] Cicero, *Brutus*, xlix, 187.

[24] Suetonius, *Lives of the Caesars*, VIII, xix.

[25] Alfred Sendrey, in *Music in the Social and Religious Life of Antiquity* (Rutherford: Fairleigh Dickinson University Press, 1974), 411.

[26] Philostratus, *The Life of Apollonius of Tyana*, V, xxi.

[27] Aelianus, in *On the Characteristics of Animals*, XII, 44, mentions another use of the aulos in Libya: 'This is the aulos music which throws mares into an amorous frenzy and makes horses mad with desire to couple. This in fact is how the mating of horses is brought about.'

> ... namely reserves of breath ... and facility with the lips consisting in their taking in the reed of the pipe and playing without blowing out the cheeks; and manual skill I consider very important, for the wrist must not weary from being bent, nor must the fingers be slow in fluttering over the notes.

During the early years of the Christian Era we have fewer references to performers because the Church controlled literature and discouraged interest in the arts. But we have a few descriptions of performers, beginning with the emperor Julian's (b. 332 AD) reference to the 'swift fingers' of a player of the water organ. Perhaps we might be surprised at the virtuoso repertoire pieces that might have been heard on this instrument at this time.

> I see a new kind of reeds. Are they, perchance, the wild product of some strange brazen soil? They are not even moved by our winds, but from a cave of bull's hide issues a blast and passes into these hollow reeds at their root. And a valiant man with swift fingers stands touching the notes which play in concert with the pipes, and they, gently leaping, press the music out of the pipes.[28]

Another reference by the emperor Julian clearly suggests that the solo singer of epic poetry, who sang of great men and deeds, was still familiar at this time.

> For you are already surfeited with them, your ears are filled with them, and there will always be a supply of composers of such discourses to sing of battles and proclaim victories with a loud clear voice, after the manner of the heralds at the Olympic games.[29]

The early Church father, Paulinus of Nola (354–431 AD), mentions a fine player of the lyre, 'a musician strumming the strings of the lyre with fluent quill.'[30] He also describes a skilled harpist and panpipe player, by way of creating a metaphor for the workings of God. The description of the panpipe player is particularly interesting in its suggestion that the instrument may have been played more like a modern harmonica, rather than as a series of single pipes.

> Think of a man playing a harp, plucking strings producing different sounds by striking them with the one quill. Or again the man who rubs his lips by blowing on woven reeds; he plays one tune from his one mouth, but there is more than one note, and he marshals the different sounds with controlling skill. He governs the shrill-echoing apertures with his breathing and his nimble fingers, closing and opening them, and thus a tuneful wind with haste of airy movement successively passes and returns along the hollow of the reed, so that the wind instrument becomes alive and issues forth a tune unbroken. This is how God works. He is the Musician who controls that universal-sounding harmony which he exercises through all the physical world.[31]

---

[28] Julian, in *The Greek Anthology* (London: Heinemann, 1925), III, 365.

[29] Julian, 'The Heroic Deeds of Constantius,' in *The Works of the Emperor Julian*, trans. Wilmer Wright (London: Heinemann, 1913), I, 209.

[30] *The Poems of St. Paulinus of Nola*, trans. P. G. Walsh (New York: Newman Press, 1975), Poem 27, 93ff.

[31] Ibid., Poem 27, 72.

There are also sufficient references to suggest that art music performed by solo instrumentalists was also still in evidence. One such example is given by Marcellinus, in his description of the private music of the emperor Valentinian (364–375 AD).

> He assumed the privilege, when he returned home after a dinner, of having a flute player play soft music before him.[32]

Martianus Capella (5th century AD), although writing in a poetic allegorical style, appears to reflect ensembles performing in multi-part harmony at this time.

> Immediately a sweet new sound burst forth, like the strains of auloi; and echoing melodies, surpassing the delight of all sounds, filled the ears of the enchanted gods. For the sound was not a simple one, monotonously produced from one instrument, but a blending of all instrumental sounds creating a full symphony of delectable music.[33]

When accounts of performance resume after the dark ages one finds the same kinds of performers as before, lending the impression that similar musical activities continued throughout the centuries from which we have so little extant literature. This is also the period known as the pre-Renaissance, because of the dramatic flowering of all the arts. Accordingly, in the following quotation from the twelfth-century French romance, *Roman de Horn*, although we have the same kind of poet-singer, and in this case a harpist, that one finds during the early Christian Era, now we notice the enthusiasm of the account, the rapt attention of the listeners and, for the first time, the appearance of 'architectural form.' This obviously expert harpist first performed a kind of instrumental prelude, then he sang the basic song and then concluded by performing the song in an instrumental version.

> Then he took the harp to tune it. God! whoever saw how well he handled it, touching the strings and making them vibrate, sometimes causing them to sing and at other times join in harmonies, he would have been reminded of the heavenly harmony. This man, of all those that there are, causes most wonder. When he has played his notes he makes the harp go up so that the strings give out completely different notes. All those present marvel that he could play thus. And when he has done all this he begins to play the aforesaid lai of Baltof, in a loud and clear voice, just as the Bretons are versed in such performances. Afterwards he made the strings of the instrument play exactly the same melody as he had just sung; he performed the whole lai for he wished to omit nothing.[34]

We see the poet-singer, now accompanying himself on a rote, in another twelfth-century French romance, *The Lay of the Thorn*. Here we have a visiting singer–rote performer from Ireland and again the author, Marie de France, is careful to mention the contemplative listeners, 'no one let his mind wander from the song,' and indeed we observe that the listeners did

---

[32] Ammianus Marcellinus, *Constantius et Gallus*, trans. John C. Rolfe (London: Heinemann, 1935), II, 583.

[33] *Martianus Capella and the Seven Liberal Arts*, trans. William Harris Stahl and Richard Johnson (New York: Columbia University Press, 1977), 351.

[34] An Anglo-Norman work, in French, quoted in Christopher Page, *Voices and Instruments of the Middle Ages* (London: Dent, 1987), 4.

not resume conversation until after the performance. We should also point out that some phrase such as 'the tables were cleared' before the performance is very frequently found in early literature, an obvious clarification by the author that the after dinner performance was not entertainment music such as was heard during the meal.

> After supper, when the tables were removed, the King seated himself for his delight upon a carpet spread before the dais, his son and many a courteous lord with him. The fair company gave ear to the 'Lay of Alys,' sweetly sung by a minstrel from Ireland, to the music of his rote. When his story was ended, forthwith he commenced another, and related the Lay of Orpheus; none being so bold as to disturb the singer, or to let his mind wander from the song. Afterwards the knights spoke together amongst themselves.[35]

Another Romance[36] by this writer describes a lay as 'sweet to hear, and the tune thereof lovely to bear in mind.' That this phrase suggests that music is remembered and does not just 'disappear' when the performance is finished is an important observation and departure from the ancient official Church dogma.

In the famous English twelfth-century poem, *Beowulf,* one finds several singing poets who accompany themselves. First there is the elderly harpist, Scylding, whose performance first brought delight, first soothed and then brought sadness to his listeners.

> The gray-haired Scylding,
> much tested, told of the times of yore.
> Whiles the hero his harp bestirred,
> wood-of-delight; now lays he sang
> of sooth and sadness.[37]

In another place we are told, 'Oft minstrels sang blithe'[38] and in still another a minstrel fills the hall with joy.[39] This last reference is particularly interesting for the phrase 'song *and* music.' This phrase, and similar ones found in the bible, mean by 'music' the use of instruments, as seems clear here.

> Then song and music mingled sounds
> in the presence of Healfdene's head-of-armies
> and harping was heard with the hero-lay
> as Hrothgar's singer the hall-joy woke
> along the mead-seats, making his song
> of that sudden raid on the sons of Finn.

---

35 *French Mediaeval Romances from the Lays of Marie de France,* trans. Eugene Mason (London: Dent, 1924), 140ff.

36 'The Lay of Graelent,' in Ibid., 148.

37 'Beowulf,' trans. Francis Gummere in *Epic and Saga*, vol. 49, *The Harvard Classics* (New York: Collier), XXVII.

38 Ibid., VII.

39 Ibid., XVI.

A thirteenth-century French epic, *Hervis de Metz*, includes a performance by a fiddle-singer and again the poet stresses the presence of a contemplative listener.

> Hervis says: 'Noble minstrel, you are welcome!'
> He had him brought to the banquet, and after the meal he
> began to play the fiddle at once and to sing *sons d'amours*
> in a beautiful and sweet way; Hervis, courteous and
> noble, listened to him.[40]

One of the tales in the *Gesta Romanorum* involves an impromptu performance after a banquet with a very rare reference to actual applause.

> She commanded the instrument to be brought, and began to touch it with infinite sweetness. Applause followed the performance, 'There never was,' said the courtiers, 'a better or a sweeter song.'

A visiting knight, named Apollonius, then volunteers to perform.

> Apollonius retired for a few moments, and decorated his head; then re-entering the Triclinium, he took the instrument, and struck it so gracefully and delightfully that they unanimously agreed, it was the harmony not of Apollonius, but of Apollo.
> The guests positively asserted, that they never heard or saw anything better.[41]

The late Middle Ages was also the period of the troubadours and some of them earned outstanding reputations as performers, as the reader will find in a following chapter. We also have at this time a series of important music treatises which make a few interesting observations on performances and performers. The most interesting to us is the *Micrologus* (ca. 1026–1028 AD) by Guido of Arezzo (the first treatise to introduce a staff of lines and spaces for notation) for it makes important psychological comments from the perspective of the listener. First, there is this curious reference to cadences:

> The previous notes, as is evident to trained musicians only, are so adjusted to the last one that in an amazing way they seem to draw a certain semblance of color from it.[42]

Another interesting suggestion has to do with the psychological relationship of the speed of notes at the cadence.

> Towards the ends of phrases the notes should always be more widely spaced as they approach the breathing place, like a galloping horse, so that they arrive at the pause, as it were, weary and heavily.[43]

---

[40] Quoted in Page, *Voices and Instruments of the Middle Ages*, 31.

[41] *Gesta Romanorum*, Ibid., II, 251ff. Later in this same tale the daughter again 'sang to an instrument, with such a sweet and ravishing melody, that Apollonius was enchanted.'

[42] *Hucbald, Guido, and John on Music*, trans. Warren Babb (New Haven: Yale University Press, 1978), 139.

[43] Ibid., 175.

There is a point of view that the origin of accents is found in the unconscious raising of the pitch of the voice by early man, in states of fear or excitement. A comment by Guido seems to admit a similar psychological effect for him as a listener when he hears the repetition of a melodic note.

> We often place an acute or grave accent above the notes, because we often utter them with more or less stress, so much so that the repetition of the same note often seems to be a raising or lowering.[44]

He concludes his discussion with the aesthetic qualification that, in the end, taste must rule.

> Do everything that we have said neither too rarely nor too unremittingly, but with taste.[45]

The treatise, *On Music* (ca. 1100 AD) by John, formerly known as 'John Cotton,' was intended for a Church choir school. His viewpoint follows the strict old Church mathematical dogma, which always found concern with the use of accidentals. The following passage reminds us of a famous observation by Gustav Mahler, 'Tradition is the last bad performance.'

> We do know most assuredly that a chant is often distorted by the ignorance of men, so that we could now enumerate many corrupted ones. These were really not produced by the composers originally in the way that they are now sung in churches, but wrong pitches, by men who followed the promptings of their own minds, have distorted what was composed correctly and perpetuated what was distorted in an incorrigible tradition, so that by now the worst usage is clung to as authentic.[46]

Finally, there is an important contribution to the discussion of the relationship of Nature and performance contributed by John of Salisbury (twelfth century), which focuses on the communication of feelings. He is discussing poetry and presents two fragments of poems by Horace,[47] which again reminds us that the best performance traditions were maintained for long periods of time. Here Salisbury reminds his readers that in poetry the voice is merely a surrogate for the emotions. This is also, of course, the entire point of music. He makes the point that Nature supplies the emotions in music and the performer must communicate these emotions in order to be understood. It is the hallmark of the arrival of Humanism and the Renaissance.

> Nature first adapts our soul to every
> Kind of fate: she delights us, arouses our wrath,
> Or overwhelms and tortures us with woe,
> After which she expresses these emotions
> Employing the tongue as their interpreter.

---

44 Ibid.

45 Ibid., 177.

46 Ibid., 104.

47 Horace's quotation may be found in *De Arte Poetica liber*, ed. F. Vollmer (Leipzig, 1925), 108–111, 102, 103.

So true is this principle that a poet must never forsake the footsteps of nature. Rather, he should strain to cleave closely to nature in his bearing and gestures, as well as in his words:

> ... If you expect me to weep, then first
> You yourself must mourn ...

Likewise, if you want me to rejoice, you yourself must first be joyful.[48]

This advice Salisbury offers his contemporary poet-singers is also, we hasten to add, very good advice for all performers today.

---

[48] *The Metalogicon*, trans. Daniel McGarry (Berkeley: University of California Press, 1955), 36, 51. Born of humble parents in southern England, John went to Paris in 1136, where he studied with Peter Abelard, Gilbert de la Porree, William of Conches and others. With the aid of Bernard of Clairvaux he became Archbishop of Canterbury, where he became an intimate counselor of, and witnessed the murder of, Thomas Becket.

On Ancient Singers

*Voice is a kind of sound characteristic of what has soul in it;
nothing that is without soul utters voice.*[1]

Aristotle

THIS ESSAY IS CONCERNED WITH THE SOLO VOICE. A separate book will discuss the choral organizations which were so much a part of the ancient world and were also associated with the solo singers. The earliest period for which we have a body of information about the solo singer is the seventh and sixth centuries BC and a group of poets who are known as 'lyric poets.' The name lyric poet is coined to reflect the fact that this poetry was sung. We must remember that even though we speak here of a very ancient period, the late Bronze Age, in the long span of man this is still a very recent period. The true origin of this type of sung literature is too distant to be known. Gregory Nagy, in his brilliant book on the work of these lyric poets, gives a lengthy hypothesis on the development of both poetry and prose from earlier song forms.[2] He also makes the interesting suggestion that the retention of melody with poetry, as in the case of these lyric poets, may have been in part for the purpose of aiding the memory of the performer.

> Melody can be an important feature in the mnemonics of oral tradition in song, as we know from the studies of folklorists who scrutinize the transmission and diffusion of song: melody helps recall the words.[3]

Our knowledge of these lyric poets is frustrated by the fact that the extant body of their work is very incomplete. For Archilochus, for example, we have not a single complete poem and for all of them we have numerous fragments, sometimes fragments consisting of only a single word. A large number of these fragments survived in the wrappings of mummies, resulting in the irony of our debt to the dead, not the living, for their preservation, as Davenport points out.

---

[1] *De Anima*, 420b.5.

[2] Gregory Nagy, *Pindar's Homer* (Baltimore: Johns Hopkins University Press, 1982), 38ff.

[3] Ibid., 50. The logic of this lies in the fact that both music and emotions are primarily in the right hemisphere of the brain and in the clinical evidence that emotions are the key to recall.

We have brief quotations by admiring critics; and we have papyrus fragments, scrap paper from the households of Alexandria, with which third-class mummies were wrapped and stuffed. All else is lost. Horace and Catullus, like all cultivated readers, had Archilochos complete in their libraries. What the living could not keep, the dead and the dullest of books have preserved.[4]

The most important of these poets are:

- Archilochus (first half of the seventh century BC) was a very creative person. He invented the iambic verse, wrote the first animal fable and is the author of the oldest fragment of a love lyric in Greek.[5] A professional soldier (his name means, 'First Sergeant'), we are not surprised at the barracks eroticism of some of his poetry.[6]

- Sappho (ca. 640–550 BC) is said by Plutarch[7] to be the first to introduce the mixolydian, which the ancients heard as melancholic. An early writer said she was a harp player from Mytilene in Lesbos. An early writer says she was the first to use the pectis.[8]

- Alkman (ca. 640–600 BC) was a slave and choral conductor. Chamaeleon says Alkman 'led the way as a composer of erotic songs.'[9]

- Alcaeus (ca. 640–550) together with Sappho and Ibycus, specialized in lyric love poetry.

- Stesichorus of Himera (ca. 610–550 BC) was the creator of the epic hymn.

- Anacreon of Teos (ca. 550–500 BC) was surpassed only by Sappho in the lyrical quality of his poetry.[10]

- Ibycus of Rhegium (ca. 550–500 BC) specialized in choral odes.

- Simonides (b. ca. 556 BC) was considered by Pindar to be a mere imitator.[11]

- Pindar (b. ca. 518 BC) wrote the largest variety of forms[12] among these poets and is widely respected as the most talented.

- Bacchylides, a contemporary of Pindar, and nearly as talented. He was known to ancient writers for his erotica.

---

[4] Guy Davenport, *Archilochos, Sappho, Alkman* (Berkeley: University of California Press, 1980), 2. Plutarch, in 'Concerning Music,' lists some additional lyric poets whose works are now lost to us: Thamyras the Thracian, Demodocus the Corcyraean, and Phemius of Ithaca.

[5] Ibid., 5.

[6] Ibid., 3.

[7] Quoted in Plutarch, 'Concerning Music.'

[8] Menaechmus of Sicyon, quoted in Athenaeus, *Deipnosophistae*, XIV, 635.

[9] Chamaeleon, quoted by Archytas of Mytilene, quoted by Athenaeus, *Deipnosophistae*, XIII, 600.

[10] Critias, quoted by Athenaeus, in Ibid., XIII, 600.

[11] Plutarch, in 'Apophthegms of Kings and Great Commanders,' relates that when Simonides wanted Themistocles to render an unjust sentence, the latter replied, 'You would not be a good poet if you should sing out of tune; nor I a good governor, if I should give judgment contrary to law.'

[12] Epinikia, enkomia, hymns, paeans, hyporchemes, dithyrambs, prosodia, partheneia, skolia, and dirges.

This body of literature was performed in public by the solo singer with lyre (*kitharoidos*), the solo singer with aulos[13] (*auloidos*) and by both professional and non-professional choirs (*khoros*). According to Athenaeus, these singers traditionally had few facial expressions, but were more active with the feet, 'both in marching and in dance steps.'[14]

Although contests in instrumental and vocal music were more ancient, it was the festivals held in connection with the Olympiad for which most of the extant lyric poetry was composed.[15] These particular festivals began in 582 BC when the traditional Python festival in honor of Apollo was transformed into one given in the third year of each Olympiad. Two years later the Isthmian festival of Poseidon, in celebration of Spring, began to be held in the second and fourth year of each Olympiad. During these years the festival of the Neiman Zeus was also held. The fourth of these festivals, and the most ancient, dating from 776 BC, was the Olympian festival of Zeus, held each four years according to a lunar cycle.[16] The honoring of the athletes through the music of these lyric poets seems to have preceded somewhat the tradition of their being honored by statues, the earliest sculptors being documented from about 520 BC.[17] In these public athletic festivals the performance of music centered on competition, called *krisis*, judged by adjudicators called, *kritai*.

We have a glimpse of the rigid training the professional singer/lyre players received as boys in *The Clouds* by Aristophanes. Those were the days, he says, when students were quiet and had discipline. They studied only the best music and the student who showed disrespect for the music by improvising was repaid for his efforts with lashes from the whip!

> CHORUS. Applaud the discipline of former days,
>   On your I call; now is your time to show
>   You merit no less praise than you bestow.
> DICAEOLOGOS. Thus summon'd, I prepare myself to speak
>   Of manners primitive, and that good [old] time
>   Which I have seen, when discipline prevail'd.
>   And modesty was sanctioned by the laws,
>   No babbling then was suffer'd in our schools;
>   The scholar's test was silence. The whole group
>   In orderly procession sallied forth
>   Right onwards, without straggling, to attend
>   Their teacher in harmony; though the snow
>   Fell on them thick as meal, the hardy brood

---

[13] The aulos was the double-pipe familiar in Greek vases. Although it was clearly a reed, and probably a double reed, instrument, much English literature persists in calling it a flute. Where we quote, we preserve this usage —- in respect to the author, not his error.

[14] Athenaeus, *Deipnosophistae*, I, 22.

[15] Not all Odes were performed at the festival; some were performed in procession, some in banquets at the palace, and some in serenade at the homes of the victors.

[16] Additional information on these festivals can be found in Richard C. Jebb, *Bacchylides* (Hildesheim, Georg Olms Verlagsbuchhandlung, 1967), 35, and Nagy, Op. cit., 116ff.

[17] Jebb, *Bacchylides*, 37.

> Breasted the storm uncloak'd: their lyres were strung
> Not to ignoble melodies, for they were taught
> A loftier key, whether to sing the name
> Of Pallas, terrible amidst the blaze
> Of cities overthrown, or wide and far
> To spread, as custom was, the echoing peal.
> There let no low buffoon intrude his tricks,
> Let no capricious quavering on a note,
> No running of variations high and low
> Break the pure stream of harmony; no Phrynis
> Practicing wanton warblings out of place—
> Woe to his back that so was found offending!
> Hard stripes and heavy would reform his taste.[18]

The tradition of singing with the aulos, on the other hand, is credited by Plutarch to Clonas, 'an elegiac and epic poet' who also invented the *Prosodia*, a processional song sung with the aulos. He also mentions that some writers give credit, instead, to Ardalus the Troezenian. Finally, to be thorough, Plutarch passes on the opinion of some that it was a mythical player called Olympus, to whom this credit should go.

Apparently the performance skills of the aulos players gradually began to usurp the attention of the public, as we notice several writers, Plato among them, vigorously complaining over liberties being taken by the aulos player. Pratinas, in 500 BC for example, reminded his listeners that the Muse had ordained that the song should be the mistress and the aulos the servant, and not the other way around![19]

We regard most of the Odes written for the Olympiad festivals as being art music. Excepting the processional works, they do not seem functional in nature and neither do they seem to have entertainment for their aim. On the contrary we believe these works were listened to. Pindar mentions the listener in a poem in which he also comments on his work being carefully written.

> And touched your ears with fine-wrought melody ...[20]

We read several times of the importance of the poet being inspired. In Pindar for example,

> Pisa too enjoins
> My speech, for from her bidding come to men
> The songs inspired of heaven.[21]

---

[18] *Clouds*, 961ff.
[19] Jebb, *Bacchylides*, 46.
[20] Ode for Pytheas of Aegina, Winner of the Youth's Pankration.
[21] Ode to Theron of Acragas, Winner of the Chariot Race.

Pindar drew a distinction between original genius and imitation. He accused Simonides of imitation, observing the true poet has a *fertile* mind, whereas those who have only *learned* chatter like crows.[22]

Regarding the musical nature of the odes, Plutarch writes that it was Archilochus (seventh century BC) who invented the idea of playing interludes on the lyre during a song, whereas the ancients (!?) played only during the singing.[23] Pindar suggests that his odes had an instrumental prelude for the purpose of giving the singers the pitch.

> And the singers heed your bidding,
> When on the vibrant air your prelude strikes,
> To guide the harmonies of choral song.[24]

The adjectives most often used by the poets to describe this lyric poetry are 'rich' and 'sweet.' Pindar, on five occasions, even calls the effect 'honey-sweet,' as in the following example:

> … and if some spell to charm his soul
> Lay in the honeyed sweetness of my songs …[25]

In another poem in which Pindar uses this description, he adds the important qualification that the serious composer is not one who composes for money nor is a mere hired craftsman.

> For then the Muse had not yet bowed to love of gain,
> Or made herself a hireling journeyman;
> Nor in the market clad in masks of silver
> Did honey-tongued Terpsichore barter
> Her gentle-voiced and sweetly-sung refrains.
> But now she bids us pander to that word
> The Argive spoke, too sadly near the truth:
> 'Money, money makes [the] man' said he
> By goods and friends alike deserted.[26]

We know from these odes that the lyre or aulos player did not merely accompany note for note the vocal part, but rather played an independent role.[27] The independent instrumental and vocal parts argue for some form of harmony, an argument strengthened by several descriptions of the result being 'blended.' Pindar, for example, writes,

---

[22] Quoted in Jebb, *Bacchylides*, 15.
[23] Plutarch, in 'Concerning Music.'
[24] Ode for Hieron of Aetna, Winner of the Chariot Race.
[25] Ode for Hieron of Syracuse. In his Ode for Diagoras of Rhodes, Winner of the Boxing Match, Pindar refers to his music as 'the sweet fruit of the mind.'
[26] Ode for Xenocrates of Acragas, Winner of the Chariot Race.
[27] Athenaeus, *Deipnosophistae*, V, 180, says they also functioned as 'leaders,' or conductors, especially when dance was included.

> Not for him sounds the blended harmony,
> Under the roof-trees echoing to the lyre,
> Of children's lips in soft refrain.[28]

And certainly harmony must have been what Bacchylides meant when he described the music as,

> the blended strains of flutes and lyres.[29]

Finally, Chappell points out several early Greek harpists who were known to play chords on their instrument.[30]

Interestingly enough, we even find in one of these early poets an awareness of the irony that art composed for posterity may *not* enjoy wide popularity with the masses.

> And this is what everyone will say: 'These are the words of Theognis of Megara, whose name is known among all mortals,'
> But I am not yet able to please all the townspeople.[31]

In conclusion, we find in these odes all the important characteristics of art music which one would find in any age: music which is inspired, carefully written, for the common joy for mankind and listened to by a receptive audience.

There are rare references to solo singers who officiated in the ancient Greek religious cult ceremonies. The fifth century BC historian, Thucydides, in describing the ceremonies in honor of Apollo by the Ionians mentions women singing and dancing and includes some verses in which the old singer wishes to be remembered.

> Well, may Apollo keep you all! and so,
> Sweethearts, good-bye—yet tell me not I go
> Out from your hearts; and if in after hours
> Some other wanderer in this world of ours
> Touch at your shores, and ask your maidens here
> Who sings the songs the sweetest to your ear,
> Think of me then, and answer with a smile,
> 'A blind old man of Scio's rocky isle.'[32]

---

[28] Ode for Hieron of Aetna, Winner of the Chariot Race. The translation of Pindar's Ode for Aristocleides of Aegina, Winner of the Pankration, actually uses the word, 'chord.'

> Of song grant, of my skill, full measure. Strike,
> O daughter of the lord of cloud-capped heaven,
> Chords to his honor.

[29] Ode for Automedes of Philius, Victor in the Pentathlon at Nemea.

[30] W. Chappell, *The History of Music* (London: Chappell), I, 149.

[31] Quoted in Nagy, *Pindar's Homer*, 375.

[32] Thucydides, *The Peloponnesian War* (New York: Modern Library, 1951), 202.

Another great fifth century BC historian, Herodotus, recalls a tale of a ghost singer at the time the armies of Xerxes were devastating the countryside of Attica.

> They saw a cloud of dust, such as might have been raised by an army of 30,000 men on the march, coming from the direction of Eleusis, and were wondering what troops they could be, when they suddenly heard the sound of a voice. Dicaeus thought he recognized the Iacchus song, which is sung at the Dionysiac mysteries, but Demaratus, who was unfamiliar with the religious ceremonial of Eleusis, asked his companion whose voice it was. 'Sir,' Dicaeus answered, 'without any doubt some dreadful disaster is about to happen to the king's army. There is not a man left in Attica; so the voice we heard must clearly be a divine voice coming from Eleusis to bring help to the Athenians …
>
> While Demaratus was speaking, the cloud of dust, from which the mysterious voice had issued, rose high into the air and drifted away towards Salamis, where the Greek fleet was stationed. By this the two men knew that the naval power of Xerxes was destined to be destroyed.[33]

The philosophers who came later appear to have associated musicality with the lyric poets, as we can see in three anecdotes.

Theocritus (third century BC) reveals an acute awareness of the qualities of fine musicianship. In 'Idyll VII,' he has a singer confess,

> Everyone says, the best singer, although I am slow to believe them
> Truly, for in my opinion I cannot begin to compete with
> Noble Sicelidas, who is from Samos, or even Philetas,
> Not in Musicianship! Sooner a bullfrog might rival a cricket.

Another epigram suited for a statue, now in the form of a memorial to the Muses by a lyric poet named Xenacles, also emphasizes musicianship.

> Goddesses, on pleasing all nine of you intent,
> Xenacles erected this marble monument.
> The title of musician nobody refuses
> Him. Respected for his wit, he thanks the Muses.[34]

Finally, Diogenes Laertius tells an anecdote about Arcesilaus which mentions work songs sung unmusically by brick makers.

> A certain dialectic, a follower of Alexinus, was unable to repeat properly some argument of his teacher, whereupon Arcesilaus reminded him of the story of Philoxenus and the brickmakers. He found them singing some of his melodies out of tune; and so he retaliated by trampling on the bricks they were making, saying, 'If you spoil my work, I'll spoil yours.'[35]

---

33 Herodotus, *The Histories*, VIII, 68.

34 Theocritus, 'Epigram X.'

35 Quoted in Diogenes Laertius, *Lives of the Eminent Philosophers*, trans., R. D. Hicks (Cambridge: Harvard University Press, 1950), I, 413.

The musical accomplishments of many of the more recent Roman emperors is surprising.[36] Caligula (12–41 AD) received an education which included both vocal and instrumental music and used to perform in private concerts before the aristocracy. Caligula once asked a famous singer, Apelles, whether he considered himself or Jupiter the greater. When the singer unfortunately hesitated in his answer, Caligula had him scourged, but complimented his voice as being attractive even in his cries of pain! We are also told that 'if anyone made even the slightest sound while his favorite was dancing, he had the person dragged from his seat and scourged him with his own hand.'[37]

But the cruelty of Caligula was nothing compared to Nero (37–68 AD), the most debauched and cruel of the emperors. Nero murdered his own mother—after numerous attempts, three times by poison; once by having constructed a special bed which would collapse on her; once by urging her to go for a boat ride in a boat that would sink and, when all these failed, by paid assassin—when age twenty-two! Suetonius provides a long list of other people Nero murdered among whom was his wife Poppaea.[38] Tacitus suggests it may have been because she had a lover who was a flute player and singer from Alexandria.[39]

But he loved music, poetry and the theater and in addition to playing the water-organ and bagpipe, he also played the kitharode, giving concerts on the Tiber and in Naples, and composed some comic songs. But mainly, he thought of himself as a singer and in order to be able to accompany himself as a singer, he studied the lyre with the foremost teacher of his time, Terpnos, as is described by Suetonius.

> Having gained some knowledge of music in addition to the rest of his early education, as soon as he became emperor he sent for Terpnus, the greatest master of the lyre in those days, and after listening to him sing after dinner for many successive days until late at night, he little by little began to practice himself, neglecting none of the exercises which artists of that kind are in the habit of following, to preserve or strengthen their voices. For he used to lie upon his back and hold a leaden plate on his chest,[40] purge himself by the syringe and by vomiting, and deny himself fruits and all foods injurious to the voice. Finally encouraged by his progress, although his voice was weak and husky, he began to long to appear on the stage, and every now and then in the presence of his intimate friends he would quote a Greek proverb meaning, 'Hidden music counts for nothing.' And he made his debut at Naples, where he did not cease singing until he had finished the number which he had begun, even though the theatre was shaken by a sudden earthquake shock. In the same city he sang frequently and for several successive days. Even when he took a short time to rest his voice, he could not keep out of

---

[36] Ibid., 392ff.

[37] Suetonius, *Lives of the Caesars*, Book IV, lv.

[38] Suetonius, *The Twelve Caesars* (New York: Penguin, 1989), 233.

[39] Tacitus, *The Annals*, XIV, 61.

[40] This information comes from Pliny the Elder, *Natural History*, XXXIV, xliv, 167, who says,

> Nero, whom heaven was pleased to make emperor, used to have a plate of lead on his chest when singing songs *fortissimo*, thus showing a method for preserving the voice.

sight but went to the theater after bathing and dined in the orchestra with the people all about him, promising them in Greek, that when he had wetted his whistle a bit, he would ring out something good and loud.[41]

Nero also entered contests in singing with lyre and Suetonius' account of his participation provides rare information about these contests.

> Nero was greatly taken too with the rhythmic applause of some Alexandrians, who had flocked to Naples from a fleet that had lately arrived, and summoned more men from Alexandria. Not content with that, he selected some young men of the order of knights and more than five thousand sturdy young commoners, to be divided into groups and learn the Alexandrian styles of applause (the called them 'the bees,' 'the roof-tiles,' and 'the bricks'), and to ply them vigorously whenever he sang …
>
> Considering it of great importance to appear in Rome as well, he repeated the contest of the Neronia before the appointed time, and when there was a general call for his 'divine voice,' he replied that if any wished to hear him, he would favor them in the gardens; but when the guard of soldiers which was then on duty seconded the entreaties of the people, he gladly agreed to appear at once. So without delay he had his name added to the list of the lyre players who entered the contest, and casting his own lot into the urn with the rest, he came forward in his turn, attended by the prefects of the Guard carrying his lyre, and followed by the tribunes of the soldiers and his intimate friends. Having taken his place and finished his preliminary speech, he announced through the ex-consul Cluvius Rufus that 'he would sing Niobe'; and he kept at it until late in the afternoon, putting off the award of the prize for that event and postponing the rest of the contest to the next year, to have an excuse for singing oftener …
>
> Not content with showing his proficiency in these arts at Rome, he went to Achaia, as I have said, influenced by the following consideration. The cities in which it was the custom to hold contests in music had adopted the rule of sending all the lyric prizes to him.[42] These he received with the greatest delight, not only giving audience before all others to the envoys who brought them, but even inviting them to his private table. When some of them begged him to sing during dinner and greeted his performance with extravagant applause, he declared that 'the Greeks were the only ones who had an ear for music and that they alone were worthy of his efforts.' So he took ship without delay and immediately on arriving at Cassiope made a preliminary appearance as a singer at the altar of Jupiter Cassius, and then went the round of all the contests.
>
> To make this possible, he gave orders that even those which were widely separated in time should be brought together in a single year, so that some had even to be given twice, and he introduced a musical competition at Olympia also, contrary to custom. To avoid being distracted or hindered in any way while busy with these contests, he replied to his freedman Helius, who reminded him that the affairs of the city required his presence, in these words: 'However much it may be your advice and your wish that I should return speedily, yet you ought rather to counsel me and to hope that I may return worthy of Nero.'
>
> While he was singing no one was allowed to leave the theatre even for the most urgent reasons. And so it is said that some women gave birth to children there, while many who were worn out with listening and applauding, secretly leaped from the wall, since the gates at the entrance were closed, or feigned death and were carried out as if for burial. The trepidation and anxiety with which he took part in the contests, his keen rivalry of his opponents and his awe of the judges, can hardly be cred-

---

41 Suetonius, *Lives of the Caesars*, Book VI, xxff

42 Ibid., VI, xii.

ited. As if his rivals were of quite the same station as himself, he used to show respect to them and try to gain their favor, while he slandered them behind their backs, sometimes assailed then with abuse when he met them, and even bribed those who were especially proficient.

Before beginning, he would address the judges in the most deferential terms, saying that he had done all that could be done, but the issue was in the hands of Fortune; they however, being men of wisdom and experience, ought to exclude what was fortuitous. When they bade him take heart, he withdrew with greater confidence, but not even then without anxiety, interpreting the silence and modesty of some as sullenness and ill-nature, and declaring that he had his suspicions of them.

In competition he observed the rules most scrupulously, never daring to clear his throat and even wiping the sweat from his brow with his arm. Once indeed, during the performance of a tragedy, when he had dropped his scepter but quickly recovered it, he was terribly afraid that he might be excluded from the competition because of his slip, and his confidence was restored only when his accompanist swore that it had passed unnoticed amid the delight and applause of the people. When the victory was won, he made the announcement himself; and for that reason he always took part in the contests of the heralds. To obliterate the memory of all other victors in the games and leave no trace of them, their statues and busts were all thrown down by his order, dragged off with hooks, and cast into privies.[43]

Returning to Rome, Nero organized an appropriate welcoming procession in honor of his victories in the singing contests.

He entered that city with white horses through a part of the wall which had been thrown down, as is customary with victors in the sacred games. In like manner he entered Antium, then Albanum, and finally Rome; but at Rome he rode in the chariot which Augustus had used in his triumphs in days gone by, and wore a purple robe and a Greek cloak adorned with stars of gold, bearing on his head the Olympic crown … while the rest were carried before him with inscriptions telling where he had won them and against what competitors, and giving the titles of the songs … His car was followed by his claque … All along the route victims were slain, the streets were sprinkled from time to time with perfume, while birds, ribbons, and sweetmeats were showered upon him. He placed the sacred crowns in his bed chambers around his couches, as well as statues representing him in the guise of a lyre player; and he had a coin too struck with the same device. So far from neglecting or relaxing his practice of the art after this, he never addressed the soldiers except by letter or in a speech delivered by another, to save his voice; and he never did anything for amusement or in earnest without an elocutionist by his side, to warn him to spare his vocal organs and hold a handkerchief to his mouth. To many men he offered his friendship or announced his hostility, according as they had applauded him lavishly or grudgingly.[44]

Nero's musical activities after he returned to Rome are covered extensively by Tacitus. It seems apparent that Tacitus considered the performance of music to be something done by slaves. Therefore, in all his accounts of Nero's performances he points over and over to the disgrace associated with an emperor engaging in such public performances.

---

[43] Ibid., VI, xx.

[44] Ibid., VI, xxff.

He had long had a fancy for driving a four-horse chariot, and a no less degrading taste for singing to the harp, in a theatrical fashion, when he was at dinner. This he would remind people was a royal custom, and had been the practice of ancient chiefs; it was celebrated too in the praises of poets and was meant to show honor to the gods. Songs indeed, he said, were sacred to Apollo, and it was in the dress of a singer that that great and prophetic deity was seen in Roman temples as well as in Greek cities …

Still, not yet wishing to disgrace himself on a public stage, he instituted some games under the title of 'juvenile sports,' for which people of every class gave in their names. Neither rank nor age nor previous high promotion hindered any one from practicing the art of a Greek or Latin actor and even stooping to gestures and songs unfit for a man. Noble ladies too actually played disgusting parts, and in the grove, with which Augustus had surrounded the lake for the naval fight, there were erected places for meeting and refreshment, and every incentive to excess was offered for sale. Money too was distributed, which the respectable had to spend under sheer compulsion and which the profligate gloried in squandering. Hence a rank growth of abominations and of all infamy. Never did a more filthy rabble add a worse licentiousness to our long corrupted morals … Last of all, the emperor himself came on the stage, tuning his lute with elaborate care and trying his voice with his attendants. There were also present, to complete the show, a guard of soldiers with centurions and tribunes, and Burrus, who grieved and yet applauded …

In the year of the consulship of Caius Laecanius and Marcus Licinius a yet keener impulse urged Nero to show himself frequently on the public stage. Hitherto he had sung in private houses or gardens, during the Juvenile games, but these he now despised, as being but little frequented, and on too small a scale for so fine a voice.[45]

In another place, Tacitus explains how the Senate, in an attempt to keep Nero off the stage, voted to award him first prize in a singing contest in advance of the contest itself.

The Senate, as they were now on the eve of the quinquennial contest, wishing to avert scandal, offered the emperor the 'victory in song,' and added the 'crown of eloquence,' that thus a veil might be thrown over a shameful exposure on the stage. Nero, however, repeatedly declared that he wanted neither favor nor the Senate's influence, as he was a match for his rivals, and was certain, in the conscientious opinion of the judges, to win the honor by merit. First, he recited a poem on the stage; then, at the importunate request of the rabble that he would make public property of all his accomplishments (these were their words), he entered the theater, and conformed to all the laws of harp playing, not sitting down when tired, nor wiping off the perspiration with anything but the garment he wore, or letting himself be seen to spit or clear his nostrils. Last of all, on bended knee he saluted the assembly with motion of the hand, and awaited the verdict of the judges with pretended anxiety. And then the city populace, who were wont to encourage every gesture even of actors, made the place ring with measured strains of elaborate applause. One would have thought they were rejoicing, and perhaps they did rejoice, in their indifference to the public disgrace.

All, however, who were present from remote towns, and still retained the Italy of strict morals and primitive ways; all too who had come on embassies or on private business from distant provinces, where they had been unused to such wantonness, were unable to endure the spectacle or sustain the degrading fatigue, which wearied their unpracticed hands, while they disturbed those who knew their part, and were often struck by soldiers, stationed in the seats, to see that not a moment of time passed with less vigorous applause or in the silence of indifference. It was a known fact that several knights, in struggling through the narrow approaches and the pressure of the crowd, were trampled

---

45 Tacitus, *Annals*, IX, 14ff and XV, 33.

to death, and that others while keeping their seats day and night were seized with some fatal malady. For it was still worse danger to be absent from the show, as many openly and many more secretly made it their business to scrutinize names and faces, and to note the delight or the disgust of the company.[46]

Tacitus also mentions examples of Nero's behavior toward his rival artists. He tried to prevent the publication of the poems of Lucanus.[47] An aristocrat who sang at some games instituted at Nero's birthplace was actually murdered by Nero.[48] Near the end of his reign he also had murdered a popular actor, Paris, whom he thought might receive too much of the applause at a planned festival. Once, after giving the order that only he could wear a special dye of purple, he saw a lady in the audience of one of his recitals dressed in this material, pointed her out to his agents, who dragged her out and stripped her on the spot.[49]

During the great fire in Rome in 64 AD, a fire which Tacitus infers Nero may have had set in order to create a new city named for himself, Nero,

> at the very time when the city was in flames, appeared on a private stage and sang of the destruction of Troy, comparing present misfortunes with the calamities of antiquity.

As he faced his own death, his sorrow was not for Rome. Rather, through his tears he muttered, 'Dead! And so great an artist!'[50] He died at age thirty-one.

While first-hand accounts of solo art singer are rare from the early centuries of the Christian era, there is an occasional clue which suggests this form of music may have still been widely practiced. In one first-century poem, for example, we read of such a poet-singer who, upon his death, left a library of twenty-five cases of music!

> Eutychides the lyric poet is dead. Fly, ye people who dwell under earth; Eutychides is coming with odes, and he ordered them to burn with him twelve lyres and twenty-five cases of music. Now indeed Charon has got hold of you. Where can one depart to in the future, since Eutychides is established in Hades too?[51]

Some of the extant first-century poems offer insights into the musical practice of these solo art singers. An anonymous poem of the first century, found on the statue of a famous lyre player, Eunomus, is particularly interesting for its reference to the performance of 'an elaborate piece' on the lyre. This poem relates a famous story of a cricket which plays a role in the poet's performance.

---

46 Ibid., XVI, 4.
47 Ibid., XV, 49.
48 Ibid., XVI, 21.
49 Suetonius, *Lives of the Caesars*, VI, xxxii.
50 Suetonius, *Twelve Caesars*, 243.
51 Lucilius, quoted in *The Greek Anthology*, trans. W. R. Paton (Cambridge: Harvard University Press, 1939), IV, 133.

Thou knowest, Apollo, how I, Eunomus the Locrian, conquered Spartis, but I tell it for those who ask me. I was playing on the lyre an elaborate piece, and in the middle of it my plectron loosened one chord, and when the time came to strike the note I was ready to play, it did not convey the correct sound to the ear. Then of its own accord a cicada perched on the bridge of the lyre and supplied the deficiency of the harmony. I had struck six chords, and when I required the seventh I borrowed this cicada's voice; for the midday songster of the hillside adapted to my performance that pastoral air of his, and when he shrilled he combined with the lifeless chords to change the value of the phrase. Therefore I owe a debt of thanks to my partner in the duet, and wrought in bronze he sits on my lyre.[52]

Aside from that nice fable, we have a number of additional poems which provide very interesting insights regarding the performance of early Roman singers. According to Juvenal, professional singers were sometimes employed by aristocratic wives to come to their homes for private recitals.

>   If your wife has musical tastes, she'll make the professional
> Singers come when she wants. She's forever handling
> Their instruments, her bejeweled fingers sparkle
> Over the lute, she practices scales with a vibrant
> Quill once employed by some famous virtuoso—
> It's her mascot, her solace, she lavishes kisses on it,
> The darling object.
>   A certain patrician lady,
> Whose lutanist protege was due to compete in
> The Capitoline Festival, made inquiry of Janus
> And Vesta, offering wine and cakes, to find out
> If her Pollio could aspire to the oakwreath prize
> For the best performance. What more could she have done
> If her husband was sick, or the doctors shaking their heads
> Over her little son? She stood there at the altar,
> Thinking it no disgrace to veil her face on behalf of
> This cheapjack twangler. She made the proper responses
> In traditional form, and blanched as the lamb was opened.
> Tell me now, I beg you, most ancient of deities,
> Old Father Janus, do such requests get answered? There must
> Be time to spare in heaven. From what I can see
> You Gods have nothing on hand to keep you occupied.[53]

In another place, Juvenal mentions the singer who performs recitals describing and praising the exploits of former leaders and generals. Juvenal starts to tell the story of one of the earlier Greek battles, and then says, 'O well, the rest,'

> You can hear when some tame poet, sweating under the armpits,
> Gives his wine-flown recital.[54]

---

[52] Ibid., IX, 584.

[53] Juvenal, *Satire* VI, 379ff.

[54] *Satire* X, 178.

Calpurnius Siculus has left us a lengthy poem, rich in musical detail, which is an example of an ode in honor of, and intended to please, one of the emperors—in this case, Nero.

Meliboeus
Why, Corydon, the silence and that frequent frown?
Why sit in an unusual place, beneath this plane-tree
By which a noisy brook chatters? You like the moist
Bank? And the nearby river's breath freshens the day?

Corydon
For long, O Meliboeus, I have been pondering songs
Not of the woodland note but such as can proclaim
A golden age and celebrate the God [Nero] himself
Who governs nations and cities and toga'd peace.

Meliboeus
Sweet is your music nor does contrary Apollo
Despise you, young man, but great Rome's divinities
Are fit for no such ballad as Menalcas' sheepfold.

Corydon
Such as it is, although it smacks of the backwoods
To sharp ears and is famous only in our village,
Still my uncouthness, if not for the polished art
Of song, at least wins credit for its dedication.
Beneath this same rock which the mighty pine-tree shades
My brother Amyntas practices the same as I,
Whose time of life brings our two birthdays close together.

Meliboeus
Do you no longer stop the boy from joining reeds
And ties of fragrant wax, whom often you've forbidden
With fatherly concern to play on the light hemlock?
Corydon, more than once I've heard you saying this:
'Break your reeds, boy, and turn your back on empty Muses.
Instead go gather beechnuts and red cornel-cherries;
Drive flocks to milking-pails and loudly through the town
Cart milk for sale. Whatever will your pipe bring in
To ward off hunger? Certainly there's no one hums
My songs but windy echoes among yonder crags.'

Corydon
I did say that, Meliboeus, I own, but long ago.
Now times are different and we have a different God.
Hope smiles more …
I'd surely now be lodging cheap at the world's end -
Ah, grief!—and as a hired hand with Iberian flocks
Whistling useless on a pipe of seven reeds,
No one among the thornbrakes there would care at all
For my Muse. Perhaps even God himself would never lend me
A ready ear to hear, I fancy, the far-distant

Lengthy murmur of my prayers at the world's end.
But if no better tune has claim upon your ears
Or other songs than ours perhaps attract you more,
May today's page of verse be polished by your file? ...
So, if you can forgive my nervousness, I'll try
Perhaps those reeds which skilled Iollas yesterday
Gave me and said, 'This panpipe can propitiate
Wild bulls and play the sweetest tunes to our Faunus.
Tityrus owned it, who was first among these hills
To sing a modulated tune on Hybla's oat.'

Meliboeus
By striving to be Tityrus you're aiming high,
Corydon. He was a sacred bard who could on oaten
Pipe outsound the lyre, at whose music wild beasts
Would fawn and frisk ...

......

Then please begin; I'm with you. But be careful that
No high-pitched pipe of frail boxwood blows the notes
It's used to voicing for you when you praise Alexis.
These, rather, are the reeds to go for. Finger now
The tenor pipes that sang woods worthy of a consul.
Begin and don't wait. Look, here comes your brother Amyntas.
He shall sing second, alternating with your verses ...

Corydon
With Jove he should begin, whoever sings of heaven,
Whoever shoulders Atlantean Olympus' weight ...

Amyntas
There's peace by his permission on my hills, and thanks
To him, look, no one stops me if I like to sing
Or foot the slow grass thrice, and I can ply for dances
And I can keep my songs in writing on green bark
And snarling trumpets no more deafen our reed-pipes.[55]

With the expectation for such formal praise imposed on court poets, one can understand that Statius (45–96 AD) wondered if he were up to the task, when invited to perform for the first time at the table of the emperor Domitian.

But I, on whom Caesar has now for the first time bestowed
The joy of a sacred dinner, to mount to my Prince's table,
How can my lyre make known my devotion, discharge
My gratitude?[56]

---

55 Calpurnius Siculus, *Eclogue IV*.

56 Statius, *Silvae*, IV, 4.2.

This same poet has left two rather dark poems, which nevertheless have interesting musical content. First, the grim and pessimistic poem, *Thebaid*, in which evil gods arrange for the murder of sleeping Thebans, including a musician.

> Alert Ialmenus, now never to see the dawn,
> had played his lyre to the last stars, singing the paean
> of Thebes. The god pressed his weakened neck to the left,
> and his head lay heedlessly against the lyre.
> Agylleus thrust a sword through his chest and impaled
> his right hand, ready-poised on the hollow lyre-shell,
> his fingers quivering on the strings.[57]

Another dark, but beautiful, poem, Statius wrote on the occasion of the death of his father.

> Father, grant me yourself from Elysian springs
> A dour command of grieving song, the beat
> Of an ominous lyre. It is not permitted to stir
> The Delian caves or initiate Cirrha's accustomed work
> Without you. Whatever Apollo lately ordained
> In Corycian shade, or Bacchus upon Ismarian hills,
> I have unlearned. Parnassus' woolen band has fled
> My hair, I have been aghast at defunctive yew
> Stealing among the ivy, the bays—unnatural!—parching.
> Yet I, inspired, had set myself to extol the deeds
> Of great-hearted kings, to equal in singing lofty Mars.
> Who makes my barren heart decay? And who, the Apollo
> In me quenched, has drawn cold clouds before my lacking mind?
> The goddesses stand dismayed about the seer, and sound
> No pleasant music with fingers or voice. Their leader leans
> Her head on her silent lyre ...
> ......
>
> Only Apollo's choir would be there; I would duly
> Praise you, father, and bind on you the poet's leafy prize.
> I myself, as priest of the shades and of your soul,
> With wet eyes would lead a dirge, from which neither Cerberus
> With all his mouths nor Orpheus' spells could turn you away.
> And there, as I sang your character and deeds, perhaps
> You had not rated mine lower than Homer's mighty speech ...
> ......
>
> I shall not bring to my father's pyre as tribute
> The funeral music the swan transmits when surer of his doom;
> Nor that with which the winged Tyrrhenian Sirens tempt
> The sailors most sweetly from dismal cliffs; nor Philomela's
> Groaning complaint, her lopped murmur, to her cruel sister:
> Bards know these things too well. Who, by the grave has not

---

57 Statius, *Thebaid*, X, 304.

> Recounted all the Heliads' boughs and their wept buds;
> And Phrygian flint; and him who ventured against Apollo,
> When Passas rejoiced that the boxwood flute deceived his trust?
>
> Let Pity, that has forgotten man, and Justice, recalled
> To heaven, and Eloquence in twofold language lament,
> And Pallas, and learned Apollo's Pierian escorts;
> Those who draw out their epic verse in six-feet meter;
> And those who find their toil and renown in the lyre …[58]

Relatively little Greek poetry is extant from the early Christian era, much of it being merely epigrams or material collected from tombstones. Among this fragmentary literature we can still find poems commemorating the lyric poets, the great poet-musicians of the seventh and sixth centuries BC. This tribute to Alcman, by Antipater of Thessalonica, is interesting for its suggestion that such material was internationally known by an early date.

> Do not judge the man by the stone. Simple is the tomb to look on, but holds the bones of a great man. Thou shalt know Alcman the supreme striker of the Laconian lyre, possessed by the nine Muses. Here resteth he, a cause of dispute to two continents, if he be a Lydian or a Spartan. Minstrels have many mothers.[59]

Another tribute to the same lyric poet is somewhat more humorous.

> Alcman the graceful, the swan-singer of wedding hymns, who made music worth of the Muses, lieth in this tomb, a great ornament to Sparta, or perhaps at the end he threw off his burden and went to Hell.[60]

A few poems from first-century tombs have preserved for us the names of performers, as in the case of this flute player.

> Orpheus won the highest prize among mortals by his harp, Nestor by the skill of his sweet-phrased tongue, divine Homer, the learned in lore, by the art of his verse, but Telephanes, whose tomb this is, by the flute.[61]

One poem honors a first-century lyre player named Plato who seems to have been a specialist in the performance of earlier music.

> When Orpheus departed, perchance some Muse survived, but at thy death, Plato, the lyre ceased to sound. For in thy mind and in thy fingers there yet survived some little fragment at least of ancient music.[62]

---

[58] Statius, *Silvae*, V, 3.
[59] *Greek Anthology*, VII, 18.
[60] Leonidas of Alexandria, in Ibid., VII, 19.
[61] Nicarchus, Ibid., VII, 159.
[62] Leontius Scholasticus, Ibid., VII, 571.

We have a tragic poem of the second century which refers to the suicide of a musician, but also provides interesting detail of the several musical instruments he played during his career.

> Clytosthenes, his feet that raced in fury now enfeebled by age, dedicates to thee, Rhea of the lion-car, his tambourines beaten by the hand, his shrill hollow-rimmed cymbals, his double-flute that calls through its horn, on which he once made shrieking music, twisting his neck about, and the two-edged knife with which he opened his veins.[63]

As everyone knows, the final centuries of the Roman Empire were characterized by a general decline in culture. One fourth century AD writer, Ammianus Marcellinus, apparently held music as partly to blame, for he reports,

> the Roman palaces, formerly famous for disseminating sciences, now resound with the singing and playing of instruments. Where formerly the philosophers were welcome, there are now singers and music teachers in their place; everywhere one could hear music, but the libraries, the depositories of knowledge, were silent as the graves.[64]

For the musician, one of the most interesting aspects of the New Testament is how remarkably different it is in its description of music from that found in the Old Testament. Reflecting the stern attitudes of the early Church fathers and their warnings against pagan entertainment, in particular the theater, we find in the New Testament as well the admonition, 'Let there be no … silly talk, nor levity.'[65] Thus, it is no surprise that there is only one reference to any kind of entertainment music, and this is connected to the important moral story of the prodigal son.[66]

The distinction between the Old and New Testaments is particularly noticeable regarding the use of music in the religious service. The Old Testament has numerous references to the role of singers in the Jewish service, but the vocal form, 'Hymn,' appears only in the New Testament. There are a number of recommendations that hymn singing should be a part of the future observances of the Christians.[67] In one of these cases, singing is specifically recommended when the singer himself *feels cheerful*.[68] But there are only two instances in the New Testament of persons singing hymns in the present tense.[69] One of these is Jesus, which is very significant. But for this reference, together with the singing of the angels at Jesus' birth,

---

[63] Philippus of Thessalonica, in Ibid., VI, 94. The reference to the aulos 'with horn' describes a bell of animal horn which had begun to be used to increase volume in Rome after the first century AD.

[64] Ibid., 391.

[65] Ephesians 5:4.

[66] Luke 15:25.

[67] Romans 15:9, I Corinthians 14:15, 26, Ephesians 5:19, and Colossians 3:16 and James 5:13.

[68] James 5:13.

[69] Matthew 26:30, which includes Jesus singing, and Acts 16:25, which describes Paul singing in prison.

the early church fathers might have left music out of the New Testament entirely. It has been widely remarked that while the Old Testament is filled with accounts of instruments in the service, there are none whatsoever in the New Testament.

The writings of the Church philosophers of the first five centuries generally speak of the purpose of hymn singing as simply for praising God, in the manner of the language of the Old Testament. Among the extant works of a man known as Dionysius the Pseudo-Areopagite we find two new explanations which are quite interesting. The first is a variant of the 'divine connection' numerous early philosophers attributed to music in large part, we believe, because of similarities music shares with religion, but not the other arts. In the case of both religion and music, the principal mysteries cannot be seen,[70] but the effect on the observer is apparent to all. Dionysius writes that the first purpose of hymn singing is to create a kind of divine connection, to prepare the participant to be able to communicate with God. The second purpose, he seems to suggest, is that the singing of unison hymns brings a unity, a 'consensus,' in the congregation itself.

> The sacred description of the divine songs, whose purpose is to praise all the divine words and works of God and to celebrate the holy words and works of godly men, forms a universal hymn and exposition of divine things, conferring on those who recite it in a divine and holy fashion a power capable of receiving and distributing all the mysteries of the hierarchy.
>
> Thus, when the chant resuming most holy things has harmoniously prepared the faculties of our souls for the rites to be celebrated a little later, and when it has established through the unison of the divine songs a consensus regarding divine things, ourselves, and others, as if in one harmonious chorus of sacred things ...[71]

From the sixth century we begin to read of a much broader use of hymns and psalms outside the Church by the faithful. Gregory of Tours mentions the singing of hymns during meals, replacing the traditional entertainment music.[72] He also recalls that after a great flood, Gregory the Great ordered the faithful to sing psalms for three days, including in the streets, as a means of asking the forgiveness of God.[73] Adomnan also describes singing hymns and praises as they led a visitor through the streets.[74]

There are several references during this period to the singing of hymns throughout the night. Gregory of Tours mentions two instances of the singing of hymns throughout the night. One instance was for the reception of the relics of St. Julian and and the other was by

---

70 Only the instruments of performance of each can be seen.

71 Dionysius the Pseudo-Areopagite, *The Ecclesiastical Hierarchy*, III, ivff., trans. Thomas Campbell (Washington, D.C.: University Press of America, 1981).

72 Gregory of Tours, *The History of the Franks*, VIII, iii, trans. Lewis Thorpe (Harmonsworth: Penguin Books, 1974).

73 Ibid., X, i.

74 Adomnan, *Life of Columba*, trans. Alan Anderson and Marjorie Anderson (London: Nelson, 1961), 14a.

Mallulf, Bishop of Senlis upon hearing of the death of Chilperic.[75] Gregory the Great writes of the brothers' singing psalms as one of their own was actually dying, recalling the ancient Greek myth of the importance of departing to music.[76]

One of the factors which helped establish the new Church during the first centuries was the retelling of the miracles of Jesus, stories such as the restoring of life to persons, accomplishments which no pagan god could claim. Thus, perhaps to keep the momentum continuing, one encounters numerous stories of miracles during the subsequent years. By the period of which we speak these tales of miracles begin to include music. Admonan, for example, tells of an occasion when the singers were spared, but the non-singers were killed.

> This also seems to be a thing that should not be passed unnoticed: that certain lay people of the same blessed man [Columba], though they were guilty men and blood-stained, were through certain songs of his praises in the Irish tongue, and the commemoration of his name, delivered, on the night in which they had sung those songs, from the hands of their enemies who had surrounded the house of the singers; and they escaped unhurt, through flames, and swords, and spears. A few of them had refused to sing, as if valuing little the singing of the holy man's commemoration, and miraculously those few alone had perished in the enemies' assault.[77]

This same writer tells of another miracle by which St. Columba, a man with a normal speaking voice, could, when he sang a hymn, be heard more than a mile away, 'so clearly that they could distinguish every syllable in the verses that he sang.'[78] The Venerable Bede tells of an occasion when St. Cuthbert spent the entire night, standing up to his neck in the sea, singing hymns, two otters came to his rescue.

> When daybreak was at hand, he went up on to the land and began to pray once more, kneeling on the shore. While he was doing this, there came forth from the depths of the sea two four-footed creatures which are commonly called otters. These, prostrate before him on the sand, began to warm his feet with their breath and sought to dry him with their fur.[79]

Isidore (560–636 AD), Bishop of Seville, is the only writer known today representing Gothic Spain. His twenty-volume *Etymologiarum*, which is really the first encyclopedia, has the goal of presenting all the information a Christian needs to know

The performance of music, Isidore organizes into three types: *harmonica*, *organica*, and *rhythmica*. By *harmonica* he means vocal music, and he reminds us that singing still belonged as much to the actor as to the singer.

---

75 Gregory of Tours, *The History of the Franks*, VI, xlvi.

76 Gregory the Great, 'Dialogue Four,' trans. Odo Zimmerman (New York: Fathers of the Church, 1959). The continuation of belief in this myth is why Jesus, in his first miracle of raising a girl from death, enters a house and cries 'Get those flutes out of here!'

77 Admonan, *Life of Columba*, 10a.

78 Ibid., 40a.

79 Bede, 'Life of St. Cuthbert,' in *Two Lives of Saint Cuthbert*, trans. Bertram Colgrave (New York: Greenwood Press, 1969), 191.

> Harmonica is the modulation of the voice, it is the affair of comedians, tragedians, and choruses and all who sing. It produces motion of the mind and body, and from this motion sound. From this sound comes the music which in man is called voice.[80]

He also introduces the word *Symphonia* here, by which he means harmony in the modern usage. He also maintains that 'melody' comes from the Greek, *mel* [honey] reflecting the 'sweetness' of music.

Finally, he presents the most extensive discussion of texture by any early writer to this date, in a catalog of the various qualities of the human voice.

> Sweet voices are fine, full, loud, and high.
> Penetrating voices are those which can hold a note an unusually long time, in such a way that they continuously fill the whole place, like the sound of trumpets.
> A thin voice is one lacking in breath, as the voice of children or women or the sick. This is as it is in string instruments, for the finest strings emit fine, thin sounds.
> In fat voices, as those of men, much breath is emitted at once.
> A sharp voice is high and thin, as we see in strings.
> A hard voice is one which emits sound violently, like thunder, like the sound of an anvil whenever the hammer is stuck against
> the hard iron.
> A harsh voice is a hoarse one, which is broken up by minute, dissimilar impulses.
> A blind voice is one which is choked off as soon as produced, and once silent cannot be prolonged, as in crockery.
> A pretty voice [*vinnola*] is soft and flexible; it is so called from *vinnus*, a soft curling lock of hair.
> The perfect voice is high, sweet, and loud: high, to be adequate to the sublime; loud, to fill the ear; sweet, to soothe the minds of the hearers.
> If any one of these qualities is absent, the voice is not perfect.[81]

The most interesting comment in this list is the last—that the high voice is associated with the sublime, closer to Heaven, as it were. But we must remember that instrumental music of the entire Middle Ages was characterized by high sounds, for it was only in the sixteenth century that the technology became available to produce the bass instruments. Thus, for these people it is possible that the most aesthetically pleasing register was one placed higher than that which we would find pleasing today.

The second category of performance, by the way, *organica*, includes all instrumental music, except percussion. 'Organ,' he says, 'is the generic name of all musical vessels.'[82] The third category, *rhythmica*, is the percussion instruments.

---

[80] *Etymologiarum*, III, xv, trans. W. M. Linsay, quoted in Oliver Strunk, *Source Readings in Music History* (New York: Norton, 1950), III, xx.

[81] Ibid.

[82] Ibid., III, xxi. One of several such references, giving an entire new view of two-part 'organum.'

By the ninth to the eleventh centuries one begins to find music treatises which include some interesting observations on early singers. Aurelian of Reome in the preface to his *Musica Disciplina* (ca. 843 AD) refers to St. Bernard as 'the archsinger of the entire Holy Church.' Aurelian makes the interesting observation that present day singers know the rules, but are nevertheless lacking as musicians.

> I know that very noble singers are found, but I confess that I have seen none skilled in this art save you alone; for some of our musicians know many rules of music, yet nowhere, I think, is a musician found like the old ones.[83]

Aurelian, in another place, gives a much more detailed explanation of the role of Reason in good musicianship. We must observe that some of these thoughts, faulty logic and all, are voiced even today and continue to obscure the fact that the real essence of music has nothing to do with Reason. He begins by asking the question, 'What is the difference between a musician and a singer?'

> There is as much difference between a musician and a singer as there is between a grammarian and a mere reader, or between physical skill and intellect. For physical skill obeys like a servant, but reason rules like a mistress, because the hands of the worker labor in vain, unless work grows out of the intellect. Every art and discipline has naturally a more honorable character than a handicraft, which is performed by hand and toil. For it is a much greater thing to know what someone does than to do what someone knows ...
>
> Musician and singer seem to differ as much as teacher and pupil. For example, the former creates poems, the latter analyses them; and the least little thing that the pupil accomplishes with time-consuming labor, the teacher discusses and empties of difficulty in the space of a single moment through the skill of his aptitude. And the singer seems to stand before the musician like a prisoner before the judge. Whoever has any notion of music, however small it may be, can understand this fairly well. As we have said in the foreword, very noble singers are found, yet nowhere, in my opinion, is a musician found like the old ones.[84]

Aurelian discusses the aesthetic quality of the human voice, based on the model of Isidore of Seville which we have presented above, but now extended to fifteen classes.

> The first of the voices is the hyperlydian kind, which is the newest and the highest; the hypodorian is the second and is the lowest of all.
> The third kind is song and it is an inflection of the voice. The sound is simple and sound precedes song.
> The fourth is arsis, that is, a lifting up of the voice, i.e., a beginning.
> The fifth is thesis, which is a putting down of the voice, i.e., and end.
> The sixth kind is where there are sweet voices. Sweet voices are those that are thin and intense, loud and high.
> The seventh is where there are clear voices, which sustain fairly long, so that they fill all the place around, like a trumpet.

---

[83] Ibid., 3.
[84] Ibid., VII.

> The eighth is where there are thin voices, as are those in infants or of strings.
> The ninth is fat [*pinguis*], as are the voices of men.
> The tenth is where the voice is sharp, thin, and high, as in strings.
> The eleventh is where there is a hard voice that is emitted violently, like hammers on an anvil.
> The twelfth kind is where the voice is rough; a rough voice is one that is hoarse and is dispersed through minute and dissimilar sounds.
> The thirteen kind is that in which the voice is blind; a voice is called blind when it stops as soon as it is emitted.
> The fourteenth kind is where the sound is tremulous [*vinnola*]; a tremulous voice is a flexible voice; it is called *vinnola* from *vinno*, that is, a lock of hair gently curled.
> The fifteenth kind is where the voice is perfect; a perfect voice is high, sweet, and loud.
> If any of these qualities is lacking, the voice will not be perfect.[85]

John, formerly known as 'John Cotton,' wrote a treatise, *On Music* (ca. 1100 AD), intended for a choir school. In this treatise there are two very interesting reflections. First, he observed that the physical status of the singer can affect the performance, pointing to 'singers weighed down by weariness' singing flat and those of 'high spirits' singing sharp.[86]

Second, we find a curious observation on the relationship of the character of the singing voice with scale-steps. It is a regret that he does not elaborate on this idea which he calls 'obvious.'

> It is obvious that men with harsh and intractable voices avoid semitones as much as possible, while those who have flexible voices relish them greatly—so much so that they sometimes produce them even where they should not be made.[87]

---

[85] Ibid., V, 13.

[86] *Hucbald, Guido, and John on Music*, trans. Warren Babb (New Haven: Yale University Press, 1978),

[87] Ibid., 137.

On the Ancient Rhapsodist

THE PREVIOUS ESSAY was concerned with ancient singers. It is appropriate that this one follow it in order, because the rhapsodists were also a kind of singer. There is abundant evidence that in ancient Greece lyric poetry, if not all poetry, was *sung*. Poetry was sung before the time of Plato (427–347 BC) and continued to be sung at least as late as Petrarch in the fourteenth century.

There is a surviving book by Plato called *Ion*, which is a discussion between Socrates and a professional rhapsodist. In this work Socrates associates the rhapsodist with poets and several times mentions that this poetry was sung. For example, in *Ion*, Socrates says, 'but you rhapsodists and actors, and the poets whose verses you sing …'

The oldest rhapsodist we know of was the author of the oldest extant Greek literature, the poet named Homer. The rhapsodists who followed him performed *from memory* before an audience the *Iliad* and the *Odyssey*. At that time there was as yet no written form of the Greek language and so it is because of the rhapsodists and their incredible feats of memory that Homer was passed across the generations until such time as his work could be written down. This is confirmed in another book by Plato, the *Symposium*.[1] In this book the subject of the rhapsodists is introduced in the following dialog.

> NICERATUS. My father was anxious to see me develop into a good man and as a means to this end he compelled me to memorize all of Homer; and so even now I can repeat the whole of Iliad and the Odyssey by heart.
> ANTISTHENES. But have you failed to observe that the rhapsodists too, all know these poems?
> NICERATUS. How could I, when I listen to their recitations nearly every day?[2]

In *Ion,* no doubt to demonstrate for the reader the incredible memory of the rhapsodists, Socrates gives the rhapsodist a test of his memory with a little pop quiz. Socrates asks,

> Tell me then, what Nestor says to Antilochus, his son, where he bids him be careful of the turn at the horse race in honor of Patroculus.

Ion immediately responds from memory,

> Bend gently in the polished chariot to the left of them, and urge the horse on the right hand with whip and voice; and slacken the rein. And when you are at the goal, let the left horse draw near, yet so that the nave of the well-wrought wheel may not even seem to touch the extremity; and avoid catching the stone.[3]

---

[1] The Greek word *symposion*, usually translated as 'banquet,' meant literally 'drinks-party.'

[2] *Banquet*, III, trans. O.J. Todd, *Anabasis*, Books IV–VII (Cambridge: Harvard University Press, 1947)

[3] *Ion*, trans. Benjamin Jowett.

A modern book gives an excellent summary of what we have so far mentioned and attempts to give us the setting for one of these performances.

> On an average night in the late Greek Dark Ages, a community, probably the wealthiest people, would settle in for an evening's entertainment. The professional story-teller would sing the stories of the Trojan War and its Greek heroes; these songs would be the Greek equivalent of a mini-series, for the stories were so long that they would take days to complete. The Greeks believed that the greatest of these story-tellers was a blind man named Homer, and that he sung ten epic poems about the Trojan War, of which only two survived (although the Greeks seem to have known them) … Whatever the compositional history of the poems, they were set down into writing within a few decades of their composition; the growing urbanization of Greek society led to the rediscovery of writing (learned from the Phoenicians this time), and the Homeric poems were committed to writing very quickly.[4]

Extraordinary though it seems, the basic role of these rhapsodists seems well documented. What we do not know is the precise nature of what they were doing vocally. Clearly, 'recitation' is not the correct word. But did they actually sing? From our perspective today, it staggers the imagination to think of someone composing music for the entire *Odyssey*. We are reminded of an occasion in 1628 when the great Monteverdi had to set one thousand lines of text to music for a horse ballet. He confesses in a letter than when he could no longer find 'emotional variety, I tried to change the instrumentation.'[5]

But, of course, we are wrong to think of music and notation from our perspective. During the period of ancient Greece of which we speak there was no notation system for music at all, and they did not even have names for the individual pitches. And there was no notational system in Egypt for several thousand years before that! And yet, as we know from the Egyptian tomb paintings, that music went on without notation, with singers, instrumentalists, ensembles, conductors and audiences applauding. But how did they do all this without notation? Well, we still do quite a bit without notation. As Couperin pointed out in the seventeenth century, 'the fact is we write a thing differently from the way in which we execute it.'[6] And even today we still have no notational symbols whatsoever, none at all, to notate emotions—which is the whole point of music!

So what could the ancient Greek poet-singers have been doing? We think it might have been possible that they had a system by which they learned, orally, to equate certain musical patterns, or melodic figures, with the sounds of speech. It is possible that Roger Bacon (1220–1292) was in touch with some passed down information, now lost to us, which might have suggested this and might have, therefore, accounted for his writing the following:

---

[4] Richard Hooker, *Bureaucrats & Barbarians, The Greek Dark Ages* (1996). We found this online at http://richard-hooker.com/sites/worldcultures/MINOA/MINOA.HTM

[5] Letter to Alessandro Striggio (February 4, 1628), quoted in *The Letters of Claudio Monteverdi*, trans. Denis Stevens (Cambridge: Cambridge University Press, 1980), 390.

[6] Couperin, *L'Art de toucher*.

> For accent is a kind of singing; whence it is called accent from *accino, accinis* [I sing, thou singest], because every syllable has its own proper sound either raised, lowered, or composite, and all syllables of one word are adapted or sung to one syllable on which rests the principal sound.[7]

If there was a system such as Bacon implies, where 'every syllable has its own sound,' then one can imagine the *text* of the Odyssey 'composing' the music for itself.

The fact that when the Greeks finally evolved a notational system, at the end of the ancient period and well after the period of Plato and Aristotle, it was a system based on alphabet letters and may in itself be a clue to an earlier tradition of music being based on text exactly as Bacon suggests. But even these examples survive in such few numbers that it is really impossible to determine the theory behind the notation.

One theory about the neumes found in the earliest Western European notation, and usually taken as the beginning of modern notation, is that they were formed from these Greek notational letters of one thousand years earlier. One source points out that the *podatus* looks like the upside down letter 'J.'[8] Others suggest the neumes were only memory aids for the singer of otherwise non-notated music.[9] This view would certainly have a link with the memory-centered profession of the rhapsodists. We have still another opinion about the neumes. We think the neumes symbolize on paper the hand motions which were being employed by the conductor one sees on the walls of the ancient Egyptian tomb paintings.[10] Whatever kind of information he was providing the performers in the context of otherwise non-notated Egyptian music, we believe these hand signals continued in use and were eventually paraphrased, or echoed, by neume notation.

Apart from the above speculation, we do have a few clues to the rhapsodists' vocal technique which have been passed down and have found a place in later literature. All of these clues speak of something mid-way between speech and singing. We begin with the most recent one because it actually includes a stylistic label.

It seems clear that in the birth of what became opera, the initial direction the Camerata took was in quest of the opinion that some held that the ancient Greek tragedies were actually sung at the time. The famous works by Sophicles and Euripides came only a generation earlier than the extant discussion in Socrates of the rhapsodists experience and as a result one cannot help but wonder how closely the technique of the rhapsodists resembled what the actors were doing in singing these famous dramas. This is mentioned by Jacopo Peri, in the Foreword to *Euridice* (1601), and our interest is in his choice of words here.

---

[7] *The Opus Majus of Roger Bacon*, trans. Robert Burke (New York: Russell & Russell, 1962), I, 259.

[8] 'Neumes' at http://www.skypoint.com/members/waltzmn/Neumes.html

[9] Willi Apel, *Harvard Dictionary of Music* (Cambridge: Harvard University Press, 1953), 488. He says that the neumes otherwise cannot be deciphered.

[10] Willi Apel, in Ibid., without explanation calls these neumes, 'cheironomic neumes.' This word is also used by some scholars to identify the conductor in the tomb paintings, a 'chironomist.'

> Seeing that dramatic poetry was concerned and that it was therefore necessary to imitate speech in song (and surely no one ever spoke in song), I judged that the ancient Greeks and Romans (who, in the opinion of many, sang their tragedies throughout in representing them upon the stage) had used a harmony surpassing that of ordinary speech but falling so far below the melody of song as to take an intermediate form. And this is why we find their poems admitting the iambic verse, a form less elevated than the hexameter but said to be advanced beyond the confines of familiar conversation. For this reason, discarding every other manner of singing hitherto heard [today], I devoted myself wholly to seeking out the kind of imitation that the ancients assigned to singing and that they called 'diastematica'[11] (that is, sustained or suspended) could in part be hastened and made to take an intermediate course, lying between the slow and suspended movements of song and the swift and rapid movements of speech, and that it could be adapted to my purpose (as they adapted it in reading poems and heroic verses).[12]

Peri is undoubtedly taking credit here for a consensus arrived at over long discussions by the entire group. Unfortunately he does not explain in more detail the actual technique of the actor/singer, but he does add a comment on the resultant melodic style.

> I knew likewise that in our speech some words are so intoned that harmony can be based upon them and that in the course of speaking it passes through many others that are not so intoned until it returns to another that will bear a progression to a fresh consonance.

He is speaking here, in more familiar terms, of long and short notes. He says it was the long notes which were harmonized and we add that it was the long notes which were subject to personal improvisation. It was the improvisation which turned an apparent simple, dull, speech-like series of tones into melody. Nothing could make less sense than to program these first generation operas today and to sing only what is on paper.

Continuing backward in time, the next hint is found in the most important book on music by a 'pagan' (non-Church) philosopher, the allegorical description of 'The Marriage of Philology and Mercury,' by Martianus Capella, written in the fifth century. This work is a defense of the importance of the seven liberal arts, which were by this time established in the Roman schools. These were the *Trivium*, consisting of grammar, dialectic, and rhetoric, and the *Quadrivium*, consisting of geometry, arithmetic, astronomy, and music [here called Harmony]. The book was written at a time when Christianity had not yet won its final battle against the 'pagans' and might well be thought of as an attempt to fight back against the efforts of the new Church to shut down traditional education and knowledge. While this book did not have the far-reaching influence of the writings of men like Boethius or Cassiodorus, nevertheless it represents one of the efforts which helped keep the liberal arts alive during the 'Dark Ages.'

---

[11] From the ancient Greek *Diastematikos* ('alternated') and thought to have something to do with notation. Peri's translation cannot be otherwise documented today. The word also appears as the title of a song in the oldest English songbook, copied ca. 1200 AD.

[12] Oliver Strunk, *Source Readings in Music History* (New York: Norton, 1950), 374.

Capella seems to imply that all sung poetry was in a vocal form between speech and music.

> Let us now deal with the voice as the parent of all sound, so to speak. All voice production is divided into two categories: continuous and discrete. The continuous is found in flowing conversation; the discrete is used in music. There is an intermediate form, having elements of both; for it neither adheres strictly to the continuous variation of the one nor is discretely varied in modulation like the other. It is the form which is used in the recitation of all poetry.[13]

The remaining clue we find interesting is found in a letter by Pliny the Younger (62–115 AD). In this letter he objects to some formal speakers, lawyers, who to engage the audience use a 'sing-song' style of speaking, to which Pliny adds you might as well add cymbals and drums![14] When we first read this we not only thought of the rhapsodist, but also of Chinese opera. Perhaps Chinese opera, which officially dates from the twelfth century, with its recitation forms using wide vocal tessitura is our last chance to hear something similar to these men who 'sang' the works of Homer from memory.

The most extensive document we have of the performance of the rhapsodist is the conversation between one of its famous representatives, Ion of Epidaurus and Socrates in Plato's book *Ion*. Plato first identifies Ion as the winner of all available prizes in his profession. Next, Plato quotes Socrates making one of the greatest points about the value of classical music, the fact that it allows one to come into personal contact with great minds. Socrates, observes,

> I often envy the profession of a rhapsodist, Ion; for you have always to wear fine clothes, and to look as beautiful as you can is a part of your art. Then, again, you are obliged to be continually in the company of many good poets; and especially of Homer, who is the best and most divine of them; and to understand him, and not merely learn his words by rote, is a thing greatly to be envied.

Related to this idea, it is in this book where one finds the brilliant analogy of a magnet to explain how the listener comes into contact with the great mind. Socrates says the mind of the poet/composer is like a magnet to which pieces of iron are attached. Socrates also maintains this is the source of the 'divine connection' in sung poetry and so the chain goes: God –> singer/poet –> listener. Because of this divine connection he finds,

> The lyric poets are not in their right mind when they are composing their beautiful strains: but when falling under the power of music and meter they are inspired and possessed.

To make sure the reader does not minimize this point, Plato now has Socrates make the point even stronger.

---

[13] *Martianus Capella and the Seven Liberal Arts*, trans. William Harris Stahl and Richard Johnson (New York: Columbia University Press, 1977), II, 363.

[14] Pliny the Younger, letter XXII, *Letters of Plinius*, trans. William Melmoth (Collier Press, 1909).

> For not by art does the poet sing, but by power divine … Therefore God takes away the minds of poets, and uses them as his ministers, as he also uses diviners and holy prophets, in order that we who hear them may know them to be speaking not of themselves who utter these priceless words in a state of unconsciousness, but that God himself is the speaker, and that through them he is conversing with us … These beautiful poems are not human, or the works of man, but divine and the work of God.

This state of 'not being in their right mind' is inseparable from the artist, or poet/singer in this case, being filled with the emotions which are at the heart of what he hopes to communicate to the listener. It is this emotional state of performer and listener which Socrates now emphasizes.

> I wish you would frankly tell me, Ion, what I am going to ask you: When you produce the greatest effect upon the audience in the recitation of some striking passage, such as the apparition of Odysseus leaping forth on the floor, recognized by the suitors and shaking out his arrows at his feet, or the description of Achilles springing upon Hector, or the sorrows of Andromache, Hecuba, or Priam,—are you in your right mind? Are you not carried out of yourself, and does not your soul in an ecstasy seem to be among the persons or places of which you are speaking …?
> Ion. That proof strikes home to me, Socrates. For I must frankly confess that at the tale of pity my eyes are filled with tears, and when I speak of horrors, my hair stands on end and my heart throbs.
> Socrates. Well, Ion, and what are we to say of a man who at a sacrifice or festival, when he is dressed in an embroidered robe, and has golden crowns upon his head, of which nobody has robbed him, appears weeping and panic-stricken in the presence of more than twenty thousand friendly faces, when there is no one despoiling or wronging him;—is he in his right mind or is he not?
> Ion. No indeed, Socrates, I must say that, strictly speaking, he is not in his right mind.
> Socrates. And are you aware that you produce similar effects on most of the spectators?
> Ion. Only too well; for I look down upon them from the stage, and behold the various emotions of pity, wonder, sternness, stamped upon their faces when I am performing: and I am obliged to give my very best attention to them; for if I make them cry I myself shall laugh, and if I make them laugh I myself shall cry, when the time of payment arrives.[15]

The festivals which Socrates mentioned above, and in which the rhapsodist participated, receive more discussion by Plato in another book. Some of these festivals included contests in music education and in this discussion the rhapsodists are also mentioned. It is interesting here that Plato says those who judge gymnastic events can also judge horses, but the judges of music are specialized and do only that.

> It will be proper to appoint directors of music and gymnastic, two kinds of each—of the one kind the business will be education, of the other, the superintendence of contests.... In speaking of contests, the law refers to the judges of gymnastics and of music; these again are divided into two classes, the one having to do with music, the other with gymnastics; and the same who judge of the gymnastic contests of men, shall judge of horses; but in music there shall be one set of judges of solo singing, and of imitation—I mean of rhapsodists, players on the harp, the flute and the like, and another who shall judge of choral songs.[16]

---

[15] *Ion*, 534, c - 535e.

[16] *Laws*, 764d.

Some festivals were religious festivals and in his discussion of these Plato again signifies the presence of the rhapsodists.

> As to rhapsodists and the like, and the contests of choruses which are to perform at feasts, all this shall be arranged when the months and days and years have been appointed for gods and demigods, whether every third year, or again every fifth year, or in whatever way or manner the gods may put into men's minds the distribution and order of them.[17]

These festivals also included competition in music and in other fields. In another place in this book, *Laws*, Plato raises the question of how one determines the winner, especially in those cases where performers from various fields compete. In this discussion the rhapsodist once again makes his appearance.

> AN ATHENIAN STRANGER. Is it altogether unmeaning to say, as the common people do about festivals, that he should be adjudged the wisest of men, and the winner of the palm, who gives us the greatest amount of pleasure and mirth? For on such occasions, and when mirth is the order of the day, ought not he to be honored most, and, as I was saying, bear the palm, who gives most mirth to the greatest number? Now is this a true way of speaking or of acting?
> CLEINIAS. Possibly.
> AN ATHENIAN STRANGER. But, my dear friend, let us distinguish between different cases, and not be hasty in forming a judgment: One way of considering the question will be to imagine a festival at which there are entertainments of all sorts, including gymnastic, musical, and equestrian contests: the citizens assembled; prizes are offered, and proclamation is made that anyone who likes may enter the lists, and that he is to bear the palm who gives the most pleasure to the spectators—there is to be no regulation about the manner how; but he who is most successful in giving pleasure is to be crowned victor, and deemed to be the pleasantest of the candidates. What is likely to be the result of such a proclamation?
> CLEINIAS. In what respect?
> AN ATHENIAN STRANGER. There would be various exhibitions: one man, like Homer, will exhibit a rhapsody, another a performance on the lute; one will have a tragedy, and another a comedy. Nor would there be anything astonishing in someone imagining that he could gain the prize by exhibiting a puppet-show. Suppose these competitors to meet, and not these only, but innumerable others as well—can you tell me who ought to be the victor?
> CLEINIAS. I do not see how anyone can answer you, or pretend to know, unless he has heard with his own ears the several competitors; the question is absurd.
> AN ATHENIAN STRANGER. Well, then, if neither of you can answer, shall I answer this question which you deem so absurd?
> CLEINIAS. By all means.
> AN ATHENIAN STRANGER. If very small children are to determine the question, they will decide for the puppet-show.
> CLEINIAS. Of course.
> AN ATHENIAN STRANGER. The older children will be advocates of comedy; educated women, and young men, and people in general, will favor tragedy.
> CLEINIAS. Very likely.

---

[17] Ibid., 835.

> AN ATHENIAN STRANGER. And I believe that we old men would have the greatest pleasure in hearing a rhapsodist recite well the Iliad and Odyssey, or one of the Hesiodic poems, and would award an overwhelming victory to him.

In this discussion Plato goes on to define what kind of music represents the highest aesthetic character.

> AN ATHENIAN STRANGER. The fairest music is that which delights the best and best educated, and especially that which delights the one man who is preeminent in virtue and education.[18]

Music, Plato therefore contends, should be aimed at the highest level of society. He goes on to say that he who would maintain this quality must have 'courage … and not be unnerved by the clamor of the many … and he ought to be the enemy of all pandering to the pleasure of the spectators.'

Today we ignore this wisdom and do the reverse. The resultant negative impact on our society would not surprise Plato in the least.

---

[18] *Laws*, 657d.

On Women Performers of the Ancient World

> *Our sister, with her flowing hair arrayed*
> *In ivy wreaths. She tried the plaintive chords,*
> *Running her thumb across the strings, then, sweeping*
> *The music soft and low, she sang this song,*
> *The praise of Ceres.*
>
> Ovid, on the mythical Greek goddess, Calliope,
> mother of the famous musician, Orpheus.[1]

THE POET-SINGER WHO ACCOMPANIED HERSELF on a string instrument, above, matches similar descriptions of male poet-singers throughout the entire ancient world. The fact that she is also mythical probably suggests a tradition older than literature. On the basis of extant literature of the ancient world, all that is unusual is that it is a woman, for time has preserved relatively few surviving descriptions of female artists in the performance of art music. But one has the feeling that that is a criticism of the writing of history and that in truth such female art singers were common in ancient Greece. A few later poems in honor of Greek musicians include women as well, with no indication that they were considered rare. A poem by Agathias Scholasticus, for example, honors a deceased woman singer and lyre player.

> Alas! alas! this earth covers the tenth Muse, the lyric chanter of Rome and Alexandria. They have perished, the notes of the lyre; song hath perished as if dying together with Joanna. Perchance the nine Muses have imposed on themselves a law worthy of them—to dwell in Joanna's tomb instead of on Helicon.[2]

Additional aesthetic insights by this poet are found in a poem which speaks of a harp-playing tragic actress named Ariadne. The poet voices his fear that this artist of art music might be taken over for use in the Bacchus ceremonies.

> Whenever she strikes her harp with the plectrum, it seems to be the echo of Terpsichore's strings, and if she tunes her voice to the high tragic strain, it is the hum of Melpomene that she reproduces. Were there a new contest for beauty too, Cypris herself were more likely to lose the prize than she, and Paris would revise his judgment. But hush! let us keep it to our own selves, lest Bacchus overhear and long for the embraces of this Ariadne too.[3]

---

[1] Ovid, *Metamorphoses*, V, 307ff.

[2] *The Greek Anthology*, trans. W. R. Paton (Cambridge: Harvard University Press, 1939), II, vii, 612.

[3] Ibid., I, v, 222.

We do not know what kind of music, exactly, was performed during the ancient Greek ceremonies in honor of Bacchus, as mentioned above, but in a stage note found in a play by the same name, *Bacchae,* by Euripides, there is a procession of women performers who seem honorable enough.

> There comes stealing in from the left a band of fifteen Eastern Women, the light of the sunrise streaming upon their long white robes and ivy-bound hair. They wear fawn-skins over the robes, and carry some of them timbrels, some pipes and other instruments. Many bear the thyrsus, or sacred Wand, made of reed ringed with ivy.

Most ancient accounts, however, picture women musicians as slaves, and usually singers. A Sumerian stone slab (ca. 800 BC) lists titles and first lines for the kinds of songs a slave might have sung in the court of her powerful patron, including religious songs, royal songs, festival songs, songs that recount heroic deeds, folk songs for shepherds and craftsmen, and love songs.[4] The women slave/musicians employed by the early kings no doubt enjoyed many privileges, but also certain drawbacks. The excavations of Ur have uncovered mass graves demonstrating that the king was buried with his entire court, in one case seventy-four people! In one of these mass graves the musical instruments were found together with female skeletons. Drinking cups found by each skeleton suggest an obligatory mass suicide.[5]

Women performers are also mentioned as employees of the temple. One document lists sixty-four female temple slaves for the temple at Lagash.[6] The titles of some of these musicians perhaps indicates early conductors for one was in charge of supervising the choir and another responsible for the rehearsal of the choir.

The women musicians mentioned in the Old Testament also fall into these two categories, slaves and temple employees. The Old Testament fails to give much information about the period of captivity in Babylonia, after the destruction of Solomon's Temple in 537 BC, but, it appears the Jews were not 'captives' in the modern sense of the word. When the 42,000 of them were allowed to return they brought back with them 7,337 slaves of their own, in addition to 245 male and female [slave] singers![7] One of the apocryphal books also mentions that they returned with all their musical instruments.[8] With regard to women musicians in the service, Psalm 68 gives us the order of the procession: singers in front, then 'maidens playing timbrels,' and finally the instrumentalists.

One also finds a reference in the Old Testament to the prostitute/singer who is frequently described in both Greek and Roman literature as a fixture at banquets.

---

4   Alfred Sendrey, in *Music in the Social and Religious Life of Antiquity* (Rutherford: Fairleigh Dickinson University Press, 1974), 32.

5   Ibid., 35.

6   Ibid., 32.

7   Nehemiah 7:67 and 1 Esdras 5:42. Ezra 2:65 gives two hundred singers.

8   1 Esdras 5:2. The apocryphal books appear in the early Septuagint and Vulgate versions of the Old Testament, but are considered spurious by the modern Jewish and Protestant faiths.

> Take a harp, go about the city, O forgotten harlot!
> Make sweet melody, sing many songs, that you may be remembered.[9]

It is this type of female singer that is meant when we read in another ancient religious text,

> Use not much the company of a woman that is a singer, lest thou be taken with her attempts.[10]

The earliest female musician we know from ancient Greece was Sappho (ca. 640–550 BC), one of the remarkable group of poet-singers known as lyric poets. She is said by Plutarch[11] to be the first to introduce the mixolydian, which the ancients heard as melancholic. An early writer said she was a harp player from Mytilene in Lesbos and another claims she was the first to use a plectrum.[12] She has always been the most discussed of the ancient poets, and is even the central subject of an opera by Charles Gounod, even though very little more than a few fragments of her poetry have survived. Among them one finds these lines:

> while no voices sang
> choruses without ours,
> no woodlot bloomed in spring without song …

There were also Olympic music contests which began with the 96th Olympiad of 396 BC. These seem to have been more physical contests, rather than musical, and perhaps the modern Olympic motto, *citius, altius, fortius* (faster, higher, stronger) describes them well. We know the names of a few of the famous performers and the information about them reads like a description of sumo wrestlers. For example, a women trumpeter who participated in these contests was Aglais, the daughter of Megacles. She wore a wig with a plume on her head and was reported to have eaten in a typical meal twelve pounds of meat, four pints of wheat bread and a pitcher of wine![13]

Of much more interest to early (male) historians and philosophers were the 'single-pipe girls,' entertainers who performed on a double reed single pipe[14] and who were prostitutes. It is important that we also tell their story for it is rich in detail regarding the use of music. A story from the fifth century BC describes a banquet at which Socrates (470–399 BC) was a guest. In his subsequent comments one can see that the famous philosopher was somewhat condescending in the midst of the fun. This was a private banquet by Xenophon (430–355 BC) which included music of a purely entertainment nature performed by the single-pipe girl who was frequently associated with these kinds of affairs.

---

9   Isaiah 23:15ff.

10 Ecclesiasticus 9:4.

11 Quoted in Plutarch, 'Concerning Music.'

12 Menaechmus of Sicyon, quoted in Athenaeus, *Deipnosophistae*, XIV, 635.

13 Ibid., X, 414.

14 Many English translations incorrectly translate this instrument as 'flute,' which it was not. It should be thought of as an aulos, but with one pipe instead of two.

> When the tables had been removed and the guests had poured a libation and sung a hymn, there entered a man from Syracuse, to give them an evening's merriment. He had with him a fine single-pipe girl, a dancing girl—one of those skilled in acrobatic tricks,—and a very handsome boy, who was expert at playing the lyre and at dancing; the Syracusan made money by exhibiting their performances as a spectacle. They now played for the assemblage, the single-pipe girl on the single-pipe, the boy on the lyre; and it was agreed that both furnished capital amusement. Thereupon Socrates remarked: 'On my word, Callias, you are giving us a perfect dinner; for not only have you set before us a feast that is above criticism, but you are also offering us very delightful sights and sounds.'

Next the dancing girl performed while juggling twelve hoops, followed by turning somersaults around upright swords, all to the accompaniment of the single-pipe girl. Then one of the guests joined in dancing, asking the single-pipe girl to 'hit up the time faster.' Finally the boy sang while playing his lyre, again accompanied by the single-pipe.

After these performances, which one guest praised, Socrates makes one of those remarks which reveals that, talented or not, the performers were looked down upon.

> CHARMIDES. It seems to me, gentlemen, that, as Socrates said of the wine, so this blending of the young people's beauty and of the notes of the music lulls one's griefs to sleep and awakens the goddess of Love.
> SOCRATES. These people, gentlemen, show their competence to give us pleasure; and yet we, I am sure, think ourselves considerably superior to them.[15]

Plato (427–347 BC) must also have kept himself somewhat distanced from such entertainment. He makes passing references to the lowest forms of the use of music in entertainment, drinking songs[16] and the prostitute 'flute-girl,' who played for male banquets. Regarding the latter, he could not understand why a group of cultivated men would not find greater pleasure merely in intelligent discussion among themselves.[17]

> To talk about poetry would make our gathering like the symposia of common and vulgar men. For being unable, through lack of cultivation, to amuse one another in company at a symposium, by their own resources or through their own voices and conversation, they raise high the market-price of flute-girls, hiring for a large sum an alien voice—that of the flutes—and for this they come together. But wherever men of gentle breeding and culture are gathered at a symposium, you will see neither flute-girls nor dancing-girls nor harp-girls; on the contrary, they are quite capable of entertaining themselves without such nonsense and child's play, but with their own voices, talking and listening in their turn, and always decently, even when they have drunk much wine.[18]

---

[15] 'The Anabasis of Cyrus,' trans. Carleton L. Brownson (Cambridge: Harvard University Press, 1947), II.
[16] *Gorgias*, 451e.
[17] Also in *Symposium*, 176e. Socrates said, 'Send her away so we can have a good conversation!'
[18] 'Protagoras,' 347c, here as quoted by Athenaeus, *Deipnosophistae*, III, 97.

We have a rather extraordinary description by Athenaeus of a banquet which Caranus of Macedonia (d. 329 BC) gave for twenty of his friends to celebrate his marriage.[19] We are told that as the guests arrived they received as gifts gold tiaras and silver cups. The first course included duck, ringdove, chicken, and a goose; the second course featured rabbit, more geese, young goats, pigeons, turtle-doves, partridge, and other fowl. The custom was for the guest to merely sample this and then pass the rest back to their servants behind a curtain. More gifts followed and then drinks.

Now the single-pipe girls entered, together with other entertainers. 'To me,' goes the account, 'these girls looked quite naked, but some said that they had on tunics. After a prelude they withdrew.' Another round of gifts followed: jars of gold and silver, perfume, and a great silver platter with a roast pig, filled with a variety of small fowl. Again gifts were distributed: more perfume, more gold and silver, and breadbaskets made of ivory.

Next more entertainers appeared, including naked female jugglers who performed tumbling acts among swords and blew fire from their mouths. This was followed by more gifts: a large gold cup for each guest, a large silver platter filled with baked fish, a double jar of perfume and gold tiaras twice the size of the first ones.

After a round of drinking a chorus of one hundred men entered, 'singing tunefully a wedding hymn; then came in dancing girls, some attired as Nereids, others as Nymphs.' Now a curtain was drawn back revealing statues of Cupids, Dianas, Pans, and Hermae holding torches in silver brackets. While they were admiring this, 'veritable Erymanthian boars' were served to each guest, on square platters rimmed with gold and skewered with silver spears.

The sounding of a trumpet announced the end of the banquet and the enriched guests all went out to look for real estate agents!

An account from the third century BC by Persaeus goes into more detail about how the girls were auctioned off at the end of the banquet.

> There was a philosopher drinking with us, and when a single-pipe girl entered and desired to sit beside him, although there was plenty of room for the girl at his side, he refused to permit it, and assumed an attitude of insensibility. But later, when the single-pipe girl was put up for the highest bidder, as is the custom in drinking-bouts, he became very vehement during the bargaining, and when the auctioneer too quickly assigned the girl to someone else, he expostulated with him, denying that he had completed the sale, and finally that insensible philosopher came to blows, although at the beginning he would not permit the single-pipe girl even to sit beside him.[20]

---

[19] Ibid., IV, 128ff.

[20] Persaeus of Citium, *Convivial Notes*, quoted in Athenaeus, *Deipnosophistae*, XIII, 607. Plutarch gives, in 'Concerning the Cure of Anger,' a particularly sordid reference to the single-pipe girl.

> Wherefore, when we go to the houses of drunkards, we may hear a wench playing the flute betimes in the morning, and behold there, as one said, the muddy dregs of wine, and scattered fragments of garlands, and servants drunk at the door ...

With the general decay of the Greek culture during the third century, the single-pipe girls prospered and some now became wealthy. Athenaeus gives a lengthy account of such a girl, named Lamia who even gave a dinner for the king of Macedonia![21]

Theocritus (315–264 BC), a member of the Alexandrian school of poets of ancient Greece, mentions in his 'Idyll II,' 'the mother of her who performs on the flute at parties.' A more interesting reference, again by Theocritus, tells of a farm worker, a reaper, who has been unable to work because he can not take his mind off one of these girls.

> MILON. Which of the local young ladies distresses you so?
> BUCAEUS. Polybotas, she who was playing the flute at Hippokion's yesterday for us.
> MILON. Heaven discovers the sinner! You've got what you prayed for this long while:
>   Namely a girl like a grasshopper willing to cuddle you all night.
> BUCAEUS. Now you're beginning to tease me, but money is not the unique blind God; there's indifferent
>   Love. So you'd better not talk highfalutin.
> MILON. I do not talk highfalutin! However, abandon your reaping
>   Now, and take up an affectionate tune for your girl.
>   You will work more happily then.
>   And you used in the past to be quite a musician.[22]

One continues to find references to the single-pipe girl during the final period of ancient Greece, the so-called Roman Period of Ancient Greece (146 BC–529 AD). These women performers were no doubt what Plutarch was thinking of when he mentions 'light music and wanton songs and discourses which suggest to men obscene fancies debauch their manners, and incline them to an unmanly way of living in luxury and wantonness.'[23] Such was the case with the Lydians at this time, according to Athenaeus.

> So dissolute did they become in unseasonable carousing that some of them never saw the sun either rising or setting. And so they passed a law, which was still in force in our day, that the flute-girls and harp-girls and all such entertainers should receive wages from early in the morning until midday, and from then until lamplight; and from this time on they were immersed in drinking for the rest of the night.[24]

Some flute-girls are mentioned as being part of the highest society, one being named after a religious festival and others having houses named for them.[25] The level of their popularity was such among the wealthy that one such girl, named Bromias, we are told,

---

[21] Athenaeus, in *Deipnosophistae*, III, 101 and XIII, 577ff.

[22] Theocritus, 'Idyll X.'

[23] 'How a Young Man Ought to hear Poems.'

[24] Athenaeus, *Deipnosophistae*, XII, 526. In XIII, 571, Athenaeus suggests that some of these girls were quite young, 'just beginning to ripe.'

[25] Ibid., XIII, 587 and 576.

would even have played the flute-accompaniment to the Pythian Games had she not been prevented from doing so by the populace.[26]

In the extant literature of ancient Rome there is again little surviving description of women art performers. In spite of this, we know that aristocratic women were active in taking lessons, singing and attending recitals of their favorites. We do have one nice poem by Ovid which discusses a virtuoso singer.

> She's a fine singer, quite a virtuoso;
> I'm longing, as she sings, to snatch a kiss.
> She sweeps the plaintive strings with clever fingers;
> Who could not fall in love with hands like this?[27]

In another place he says that the woman's education is not complete without the study of music.

> The Sirens were sea fairies, who by force
> Of song could stay the swiftest vessel's course.
> Ulysses nigh broke loose upon the sound,
> His comrades' ears, we're told, in wax were bound.
> Learn singing, fair ones. Song's a thing of grace;
> Voice oft's a better procuress than face.
> Airs from the marble theater repeat,
> Or tunes danced with light Egyptian beat.
> No woman trained according to my will
> Should lack the art to handle lyre and quill.[28]

During the Republic Period of Rome (240–27 BC), one finds a number of authors who make reference to the single-pipe girls. In fact, Livy gives a specific date for the importation of this custom to Rome, a celebration to honor the victory of Gnaeus Manlius Volso over the Gauls, in 187 BC.

> It was at this time that female lutenists and harpists and other purveyors of convivial entertainment became adjuncts to dinner parties; the banquets themselves also began to be laid on with greater elaboration and at greater expense.[29]

Plautus, one of the great Roman playwrights, mentions this female entertainer several times in his plays. In *The Haunted House* there are both flute and lute girl entertainers.[30]

---

[26] Ibid., XIII, 605.

[27] Ovid, *The Love Poems*, II, 4.

[28] Ibid., III, lines 311ff.

[29] Livy, *History of Rome*, XXXIX, 6.

[30] Terence's *The Brothers* has a character, Ctesipho, who is a lute girl.

PHANISCUS. There haven't been three days here without a party—eating and drinking, bringing in strumpets and flute girls and lute girls, and fast living.[31]

In another play Plautus mentions that these girls were purchased at a market along with the other supplies for a banquet.

STROBILUS. After my master had laid in his stores,
    And hired his cooks and flute players at the market ...[32]

Terence's play, *The Eunuch*, also refers to selling these girls, in this case by auction.

THAIS. Her brother, who tends, where money's concerned,
    To greed, took one look at the girl and saw
    Her beauty and musical talent as potential profit.
    He listed her right on the spot and sold her at auction.[33]

In *Epidicus* we learn that some of these girls were owned as slaves by individuals. One such girl who had been given her freedom actually has a brief speaking part in this play.

PERIPHANES *(To the Music Girl)*. Did Apoecides buy you from the pimp today?
MUSIC GIRL. I've never heard the man mentioned before today, and besides, no one could buy me at any price. I've been a free woman for more than five years.
PERIPHANES. What business do you have in my house, then?
MUSIC GIRL. I'll tell you. I was hired to come and sing to the lute for an old man while he offered sacrifice.
PERIPHANES *(aside)*. I'm the most worthless old idiot in all Attic Athens, I realize it. *(To the Music Girl)* Look here, you, do you know the music girl Acropolistis?
MUSIC GIRL. As well as I know myself.
PERIPHANES. Where does she live?
MUSIC GIRL. I can't really say where she does live, now that she's free.
PERIPHANES. What's that? She's free? Who freed her, I want to know, in case you know.
MUSIC GIRL. I'll tell you what I've heard. They say that Stratippocles, the son of Periphanes, arranged to have her freed during his absence.
PERIPHANES *(aside)*. Jupiter! I'm royally ruined, if this is true. Epidicus has eviscerated that purse of mine, no doubt about it.
MUSIC GIRL. That's what I've heard. *(Sweetly)* There isn't anything else you wish, is there?
PERIPHANES *(shouting)*. Yes, that you die a horrible death and get out of here at once.
MUSIC GIRL. Won't you give me back my lute?
PERIPHANES. Neither lutes nor flutes! Hurry up and get out of here, if the gods love you!

---

[31] Lines 960ff.

[32] *The Pot of Gold*, Act II, Scene iv. In *Epidicus*, Act I, Scene i, Plautus indicates that these girls were sometimes acquired from the army.

[33] Line 130.

In the works of Horace (65–8 BC) we discover that the single-pipe girls had now organized themselves into guilds like the other musicians in Rome.[34] These, the first 'unions' in music history were called, 'colleges.' In another of his poems we see this female performer now using the lyre, which had been the instrument associated with solo art singers.

> Won't someone go fetch Lyde, the easy wench
> From down the path? And tell her to hurry up,
> And bring her ivory lyre, and wear her
> Hair in a bun like a Spartan woman.[35]

The most extraordinary body of love songs of this period are the poems written by Propertius (50–16 BC) for Cynthia, a musical prostitute. These love poems, which are filled with references to music, cover the entire course of their relationship. In one of these poems he states he would not write of great historical events, neither is he inspired by the Muses. Rather, it is Cynthia who inspires his lyric poetry. In this same poem he tells us that she also plays the lyre.

> Or if her ivory fingers
>   strike a song through the lyre
> I display suitable wonder
>   at her artful touch on the strings …[36]

He sings of the depth of his love for her, of his inability to get her out of his mind, of the impossibility to go about his usual studies. It is not her beauty, nor her dress, but her singing and lyre playing which has so firmly drawn him to her.

> But with the cups thrown down
>   she dances like lovely Ariadne
>   leading the bacchanalian chorus,
>   and when she strikes up a tune
>   with Aeolian plectrum,
>   her lyre equals a goddess's, a muse by her fountain;
>
> Her graven verses rival those
>   of antique Corinna,
>   & if she reckons her songs as fine
>   as Erinna's were,
>   can she be far wrong?[37]

---

34 Horace, *Satires*, I, 2.
35 Horace, *Odes*, II, 11, 21.
36 Propertius, *The Poems*, II, 1.
37 Ibid., II, 3.

During the Empire Period of Rome (14–476 AD), the emperor Theodosius in 385 AD banned the sale of harp girls, as well as their use in performing for banquets.[38] One famous Greek harp girl of this time, named Leaena, which also means lioness, was a prostitute employed by the tyrants Harmodius and Aristogeiton. She was tortured to death, but refused to betray a plot to assassinate these tyrants. Consequently the Athenians honored her by commissioning Amphicrates to sculpt a statue of a lioness without a tongue.[39]

There is far less information in the ancient Roman literature about aristocratic ladies who were performers, ladies who were not prostitutes. One reference we particularly like is found in one of the letters of Pliny the Younger, at the end of the first century AD. He writes of the daughter of Calpurnia Hispulla,

> She has even set my verses to music and sings them, to the accompaniment of her lyre, with no musician to teach her but the best of masters, love.[40]

Once the Church won its battle with Rome, we begin the 'Dark Ages,' so called because the Church destroyed as many of the old Greek and Roman books they could find, shut down the schools, established a hostile attitude toward women, tried to forbid the Christian from attending theaters or 'loving' art and took control over the publishing of books. Obviously, it was an atmosphere which permitted very few references to women performers.

We do know, however, that there were a few women jongleurs and minstrels during the Middle Ages. For example, in the famous *Domesday Book* of 1086 in England, a census taken at the request of William the Conqueror, we find the name of a female jongleur named Adelinda, who was in the service of Earl Roger.[41] There are a few drawings of these ladies in medieval books and there was a painting of one on a wall in Bohemia which did not survive WWII.

As the Middle Ages came to a close we have the period we call the pre-Renaissance when once again art begins to flower. From this time we have a reference in the works of Gottfried von Strassburg (fl. 1200–1210) where he speaks of a rare lady minnesinger, who specializes in the songs of Vogelweide, while accompanying herself on a small organ.[42]

And, of course, we cannot pass by Hildegard of Bingen, a twelfth-century composer and singer. Several times in her writings she emphasizes that it is the outer form of music, the performance, which teaches us about our inner person. She should be required reading for all music educators!

---

[38] Sendrey, *Music in the Social and Religious Life of Antiquity*, 388. Pliny the Elder, in *Natural History*, X, xxvi, mentions Glauce, harp girl to King Ptolemy of Egypt, whom he says both a goose and a ram fell in love with.

[39] Pliny the Elder, *Natural History*, XXXIV, xix, 72. In the course of his discussion of art, he also mentions a famous statue of the time called 'Tipsy Girl playing the Aulos,' by Lysippus [XXXIV, xix, 63], a 'Trumpet player' by Epigonus [XXXIV, xix, 88.] and 'Murmuring Athene,' by Ctesilaus, designed so that the dragons on her Gorgon's head reverberated to the sound of a harp [XXXIX, xix, 76]. Tacitus, *Annals*, XIV, 60, also tells of slave girls being tortured in an attempt to gain information about a slave flute player implicated in a love affair.

[40] *The Letters of the Younger Pliny* (New York: Penguin, 1985), 126.

[41] E. K. Chambers, *The Mediaeval Stage* (Oxford, 1903), I, 43–44.

[42] Gottfried von Strassburg, *Tristan*, trans. Arthus Hatto (Harmondsworth: Penguin Books, 1960), 106ff.

> In these words outer realities [performance] teach us about inner ones—namely how, in accordance with the material composition and quality of instruments, we can best transform and shape the performance of our inner being towards praises of the Creator.[43]

She mentions this again as part of a very concise history of Church music. She begins by citing the use of music in the Old Testament and then gives the following explanation for the invention of musical instruments,[44] which again focuses on the inner impact of music on the listener.

> They invented musical instruments of diverse kinds ... by which the songs could be expressed in multitudinous sounds, so that listeners, aroused and made adept outwardly, might be nurtured within by the forms and qualities of the instruments, as by the meaning of the words performed with them.[45]

And throughout her writings there is a warmth, a feeling of joy in music which one will not find in any other Church philosopher after Augustine. She understood that music was all about emotion and that that is what affected the listener.

> ... at times, when hearing some melody, a human being often sighs and moans ...[46]

With the coming of the Renaissance we get women like Beatrice and Isabella d'Este, among many more, who were performers at the very top of society. But, ironically, it was a seventeenth-century tavern singer and prostitute named Nell, in England, who, as the king's favorite, was the first woman to be allowed to appear on the professional stage. Almost immediately thereafter appear the prima donnas, the centerpiece of Italian opera. These women were the most famous performers in Europe.

---

43 Letter to the Mainz prelates, in *Hildegard of Bingen*, ed. Fiona Bowie and Oliver Davies (New York: Crossroad, 1993), 150.

44 In the Divine Words, 'Vision Seven: 10,' Hildegard suggests a slight preference for string instruments, which she says have 'look up to God ... with the simplicity of a dove.' Players of wind instruments, on the other hand, 'serve humbly upon the Earth.'

45 Ibid., 150.

46 *Hildegard of Bingen*, 151.

On Ancient Conductors

When one reads the surviving descriptions of conductors and how they worked several thousand years ago, one is first surprised that these descriptions seem so little different from conductors today. It is also surprising how many actual names have come down to us. The oldest descriptions of conductors are associated with religious activities. From the Eastern Mediterranean areas of Sumeria, ca. 3,000 BC, there is an extant document lists sixty-four female temple slaves for the temple at Lagash.[1] The titles of some of these musicians indicate conductors, one was in charge of supervising the choir and another responsible for the rehearsal of the choir. Farmer mentions a similar document from the same period, from Akkad, in which some temple musicians are described as those who 'know the melodies' and are 'masters of the musical movements.'[2]

One who 'knows the melodies,' or 'knows the music,' is a pretty good description of the first requirement of a conductor and it is also very similar to some text of the Old Testament. Here, in a passage describing the organization of the music of the temple, we are told 'Chenaniah, leader of the Levites in music, should direct the music, for he understood it.'[3] We are also told, in Psalm 105, that God was a choral conductor.

In the tomb paintings of ancient Egypt we find considerable information about conductors and have our earliest opportunity to see one actually conducting.

Beginning with the Old Kingdom (2686–2181 BC) we can see a testimonial to the importance of individual musicians simply from the fact that they were allowed to have their tombs in the vicinity of the royal ones. Also, the hieroglyphic texts which accompany the tomb paintings speak of the importance of these musicians in their very titles, such as in the case of the conductors, 'royal music director' and 'leader of ritual music.'

These paintings include a wide variety of musical instruments and performers, including a remarkable painting of a female musician playing the trumpet for the god Osiris, who is pictured shedding tears.[4] Where there are ensembles there is often pictured facing the players, a man with his hands in the air and who seems to be listening and whom is called by some scholars today, a 'chironomist.' The hieroglyph used to describe what this figure is doing means 'singing,' but it is always qualified by another hieroglyph in the form of a human arm, as it were 'singing with the arm.'[5] What a wonderful description for a conductor!

---

[1] Alfred Sendrey, in *Music in the Social and Religious Life of Antiquity* (Rutherford: Fairleigh Dickinson University Press, 1974), 32.

[2] Henry G. Farmer, 'The Music of Ancient Mesopotamia,' in *The New Oxford History of Music* (London: Oxford University Press, 1966), 235.

[3] 1 Chronicles 15:16ff.

[4] Quoted in Lise Manniche, *Music and Musicians in Ancient Egypt* (London: British Museum Press, 1991), 58.

[5] Ibid., 30.

Given the fact that ancient Egyptian music apparently had no notated form, we are inclined to the theory that this chironomist/conductor supplied to the players some kind of visual notation. This view is strengthened by a painting from the Eighteenth Dynasty (1580–1320 BC) in which we see one of these 'conductors' supplying the rhythm as well, with the heel of his foot while snapping a thumb and finger of each hand. Manniche adds an important observation,[6] however, that this figure appears regularly in the paintings of the Old Kingdom, rarely in those of the Middle Kingdom and disappears during the New Kingdom. Therefore the question remains: if there were no notation, how did the musicians gradually learn to do without him?

With all the musical activities we see in the tomb paintings, we can also assume the existence of formal music education. Indeed, the hieroglyphs actually tell us the names of some of these educators and two of them are the most ancient music educators known by name, Nikaure, 'instructor of the singers of the pyramid of King Userkaf,' and Rewer, 'teacher of the royal singers,' who lived during the Fifth Dynasty (2563–2423 BC). The recent discovery of the tombs of Nufer and Kaha at Saqqara introduce us to two conductors who were 'director of singers,' as well as teachers. The information given here confirms what Herodotus suggests, that some professions such as music were maintained by family birthright.

> Their heralds and aulos players, and cooks inherit the craft from their fathers ... no others usurp their places...they ply their craft by right of birth.[7]

Regarding the tomb of Nufer and Kaha, Manniche points to Nufer as being the head of such a family.

> Kaha was both 'director' and 'instructor' of singers. He also held a title as priest of the 'southern Merit,' the music goddess, and the inscriptions mention that he was 'unique' among the singers and had a beautiful voice. Nufer, as well as being director of singers, was also instructor in the royal artisans' workshops. Three of his sons were 'instructors of singers,' and a fourth was 'director of singers in the palace.' Four other male relatives were 'instructors of singers,' and two of them were also priests of Merit.[8]

When female musicians appear in the New Kingdom (1567–1085 BC), some of them also have apparent conducting positions in the temple, with titles such as 'Chief of the Singers.'

From ancient Greece we find among the famous lyric poets one who was also a conductor. Alkman (ca. 640–600 BC) was a slave and choral conductor. He was admired by Goethe and Aristotle said he suffered terribly from lice. Chamaeleon says Alkman 'led the way as a composer of erotic songs, and was the first to publish a licentious song, being prone in his habits of life to the pursuit of women and to poetry of that kind.'[9]

---

6   Ibid. She also points to one painting which shows five musicians and six chironomists!
7   Herodotus, *Histories*, II, 59.
8   Manniche, *Music and Musicians in Ancient Egypt*, 122.
9   Chamaeleon, quoted by Archytas of Mytilene, in Athenaeus, *Deipnosophistae*, XIII, 600.

Plutarch provides us with a nice story about Damonidas, a member of one of the choruses which are so frequently mentioned in the literature of ancient Greece. When the chorus conductor placed him in the lowest place for the choral dance, Damonidas is said to have responded, 'Well, sir, you have found a way to make this place, which was infamous before, noble and honorable!'[10]

These choruses should be thought of as representatives of their cities. Indeed, the Spartans actually called the interior civic space the *Khoros*. Nagy explains this civic association and provides us with the name for the ancient Greek choral conductor.

> As a representative of the polis, the chorus is concerned partly with local interests, and it can therefore serve as a formal vehicle of ritual ... which constitute part of the ritual chain of athletics. The range, however, of choral self-expression in matters of ritual is certainly not limited to the Games. Besides epinician odes, a given chorus in a given polis may perform a wide variety of other kinds of compositions related to various local or civic rituals.
>
> ......
>
> As a microcosm of society, it is equally important to note the khoros is also a microcosm of social hierarchy. Within the hierarchy that is the chorus ... a majority of younger members act out a patter of subordination to a minority of older leaders; this acting out conforms to the role of the chorus as an educational collectivization of experience ... the concept of older leaders, within the hierarchy of the chorus, is in most instances embodied in the central persona of the *khoregos* 'chorus leader.'[11]

The ancient Greek historians frequently mention these choruses in their participation of festivals and choral competitions. Xenophon also tells us that long periods of training and large sums of money were necessary to prepare a chorus for competition and he seems almost perplexed that they do this when the goal is only a 'paltry' prize. He apparently failed to realize that it is the honor of winning which propels the competition, not the value of the trophy the winner receives. In a conversation with a political leader, Hiero, Xenophon speaks through the character of Simonides, one of the lyric poets, and refers to the choral rehearsals.

> In case you fear, Hiero, that the cost of offering prizes for many subjects may prove heavy, you should reflect that no commodities are cheaper than those that are bought for a prize. Think of the large sums that men are induced to spend on horse races, gymnastic and choral competitions, and the long course of training and practice they undergo for the sake of a paltry prize.[12]

The chief end of this 'long course of training,' which he sees in terms of artistic value, is discipline. The reader will also notice here the reference to the enigmatic, though well-known, practice by the Greek choirs of including movement with their singing.

---

[10] Quoted in Plutarch, 'Laconic Apophthegms.'
[11] Gregory Nagy, *Pindar's Homer* (Baltimore: Johns Hopkins University Press, 1982), 399, 345.
[12] Xenophon, 'Hiero,' IX, in *Scripta Minora*, trans. E. C. Marchant (Cambridge: Harvard University Press, 1956).

> There is nothing so convenient nor so good for human beings as order. Thus, a chorus is a combination of human beings; but when the members of it do as they choose, it becomes mere confusion, and there is no pleasure in watching it; but when they act and sing in an orderly fashion, then those same men at once seem worth seeing and worth hearing.[13]

Xenophon, now in the voice of Socrates, also tells us that the most successful choruses are those which have as their conductors, 'the best experts.'[14]

Of particular interest is a speech, known as 'On the Chorus Boy,' which Antiphon wrote for an unknown defendant who was in charge of the chorus at Thargelia in 412 BC. According to Athenaeus,[15] the term, 'choregus,' meant 'conductor' at this time, and not an administrator. Many modern school conductors would find the administrative duties given by this conductor to be familiar today.

> When I was appointed in charge of the chorus at Thargelia ..., I performed the office as well and conscientiously as I could. In the first place, I provided a room for training in the most convenient part of my house, where I used to train when I was *choregus* at the Dionysia. Secondly, I enrolled a chorus in the best way I could, not penalizing anyone nor forcibly exacting security nor making an enemy of anyone; but, as was most agreeable and convenient to both parties, I made my requests and demands, while the parents sent their sons with good grace and willingly ...
>
> I appointed Phanostratus to look after the chorus in case they needed anything. Phanostratus is a fellow demesman of the prosecutors and a kinsman of mine, in fact, my son-in-law, and I expected him to look after them well. A appointed two other men too, Ameinias of the tribe Erechtheis, whom the tribesmen themselves regularly elected to enroll and look after the tribe, a man with a good reputation; and the second man from the Cecropid tribe, who regularly convened that tribe. Then I appointed a fourth, Philippus, who was commissioned to buy and spend any money necessary on the authority of the poet or of an other of the officials, so that the boys should enjoy the best possible *choregia* and should go in want of nothing because of my inability to give them my attention.

There is an extraordinary passage in the works of Plato in which we are given his recommendations on the election of conductors. It should be noted that a clear separation was maintained between music education and contests; it is a line which has been blurred by twenty centuries.

> It will be proper to appoint directors of music and gymnastic, two kinds of each—of the one kind the business will be education, of the other, the superintendence of contests ... First of all, we must choose directors for the choruses of boys, and men, and maidens, whom they shall follow in the amusement of the dance, and for our other musical arrangements;—one director will be enough for the choruses, and he should be not less than forty years of age. One director will also be enough to introduce the solo singers, and to give judgment on the competitors, and he ought to be less than thirty years of age. The director and manager of the choruses shall be elected after the following manner:—Let any persons who commonly take an interest in such matters go to the meeting, and

---

[13] Xenophon, 'Oeconomicus,' VIII, *Memorabilia and Oeconomicus*, trans. E. C. Marchant (Cambridge: Harvard University Press, 1953).

[14] 'Memorabilia,' III, in *Ibid*.

[15] Athenaeus, *Deipnosophistae*, XIV, 633.

be fined if they do not go, but those who have no interest shall not be compelled. Any elector may propose as director someone who understands music, and he in the scrutiny may be challenged on the one part by those who say he has no skill, and defended on the other hand by those who say that he has. Ten are to be elected by vote, and he of the ten who is chosen by lot shall undergo a scrutiny, and lead the choruses for a year according to law. And in like manner the competitor who wins the lot shall be leader of the solo and concert music for that year; and he who is thus elected shall deliver the award to the judges.[16]

As in the Psalms, Aristotle also identifies God as being a choral conductor.[17] In various places, Aristotle mentions the institution of the chorus, how it is supported,[18] and that the conductors should be elected.[19]

It is with the generation after Aristotle that we come to the one person who should have answered all our questions about Greek music of the fourth and fifth centuries BC. His name was Aristoxenus (b. ca. 379 BC), he was a student of Aristotle's and he specialized in writing books on music. Unfortunately, most of his books are lost, among them *On Aulos Players, On The Aulos and Musical Instruments*,[20] *On Aulos Boring*,[21] *On Music*, and *Brief Notes*, whose titles are mentioned by Athenaeus. All that has come down to us is one chapter of his book, *Elements of Rhythm*, and three chapters of another, *Elements of Harmony*. In the case of the latter, it is especially interesting that in discussing the division of Time, in two places he seems to suggest the existence of something like the modern conductor, once saying 'signals' are necessary to make the division of the Time and in another place, 'Rhythm cannot exist without … someone to divide the Time.'

We also have a nice tribute to a choral conductor who worked in the third century BC, in the form of an epigram by Theocritus (ca. 315–264 BC). We can see that this conductor was musical!

> Damomenes the choirmaster put us this tripod,
> Dionysus, and your image, blest and blythest god.
> Measured in all things, he won the victory
> With his male choir, observing beauty and degree.[22]

The Roman poet, Ovid (43 BC–17 AD) has left one poem which includes a choral conductor participating in a religious rite for the god, Ibis.

---

16 *Memorabilia and Oeconomicus*, 764d.
17 Ibid., 399a.15.
18 *Atheniensium Republica*, 56.2.
19 *Politica*, 1299a.17.
20 Athenaeus, *Deipnosophistae*, IV, 174.
21 Ibid., XIV, 634.
22 Theocritus, 'Epigram XII.'

> I pray
>   that whatever spirits attend me may hear and approve and will fly,
>   as only spirits can, to wait on Ibis,
>   return to Rome in the wink of an eye and mark how the tears
>   pour down his face. Greet him in evil omen
>   with the left foot forward and clad in funereal black.
>   The procession is ready? Good! Let it begin.
>   The priest does not delay but turns to face the assembled
>   congregation, bows three times to the altar,
>   signals the chorus master for the pious hymn to commence,
>   takes a breath, and intones: 'Offer thy throat,
>   O terrified victim, freely to me.' He raises
>   the shining knife and holds it high, as the rite,
>   awesome, dreadful, but beautiful too, is re-enacted.[23]

Before leaving the subject of the ancient choirs and their conductors, there is an interesting passage in a work by the early Church father, St. Gregory Nazianzus (b. ca. 329 AD), which throws light on the role of the conductor and the placement of the singers.

> I thought, in my vain imaginings, that once I had control of this throne (outward show carries great weight) I could act like a chorus leader between two choruses. Putting the two groups chorus-fashion, one on this side of me, the other on that, I could blend them with myself and thus weld into a unity what had been so badly divided.[24]

Although our object in this chapter has been to throw some light on the very earliest of conductors, there are a few more later references which we think are very special and we include them now for those who may not have read them in the traditional history texts.

We have mentioned above the 'chironomist' found in the paintings on the walls of the ancient Egyptian tombs. It is our belief that the hand 'signals' of the conductor we see in the Egyptian tomb paintings may well have inspired the small gestures symbolized in the early Western European nueme notation. In this regard we wish to point to a comment made by the remarkable Hildegard of Bingen, a twelfth-century nun and composer, 'and they adapted their singing to the bending of the finger-joints.'[25]

Although there are older pictures of conductors with batons, the earliest text description is found in Hercole Bottrigari (1531–1612). He writes of the famous twenty-three member nun orchestra, the Nuns of S. Vito in Ferrara,[26] whom he introduces as representing 'the highest degree of perfection.'

---

[23] Ovid, *Tristia*, 94ff.

[24] Saint Gregory of Nazianzus, 'Concerning his own Life,' trans. Denis Meehan (Washington, D.C.: The Catholic University of America Press), 119.

[25] *The Book of Divine Works*, ed. Matthew Fox (Santa Fe: Bear & Company, 1987), 151.

[26] He also mentions in passing the three noble ladies in the court of the duchess of Ferrara who performed as part of her private music.

> How you would melt away when you see them convene and play together with so much beauty and grace, and such quietness! ...
>
> They are indubitably women; and when you watch them come ... to the place where a long table has been prepared, at one end of which is found a large clavicembalo, you would see them enter one by one, quietly bringing their instruments, either stringed or wind. They all enter quietly and approach the table without making the least noise and place themselves in their proper place, and some sit, who must do so in order to use their instruments, and others remain standing. Finally the Maestra of the concert sits down at one end of the table and with a long, slender and well-polished baton, and when all the other sisters clearly are ready, gives them without noise several signs to begin, and then continues by beating the measure of the time which they must obey in singing and playing ... And you would certainly hear such harmony that it would seem to you either that you were carried off to Helicona or that Helicona together with all the chorus of the Muses singing and playing had been transported to that place ...
>
> Neither Fiorino nor Luzzasco, though both are held in great honor by them, nor any other musician or living man, has had any part in their work or in advising them; and so it is all the more marvelous, even stupendous, to everyone who delights in music.[27]

Another of our favorite references to conducting was made by Monteverdi, in his *Madrigali guerrieri et amorosi* (Venice, 1638). He speaks of the voice following 'her lament, which is sung to the time of the heart's feeling [*affetto del animo*], and not to that of the hand.' In other words, the tempo should follow the feeling and not the strict beat. One immediately recalls the comment by Beethoven about the newly invented metronome, 'It is only good for the first measures; after that feeling has its own tempo.' This is something which is frequently mentioned in contemporary Baroque discussions and therefore how this natural and musical style ever developed into today's 'sewing machine' concept of Baroque performance is a mystery to us.

And speaking of the Baroque, there is one wonderful eye-witness description, by a contemporary, Johann Gesner, of J. S. Bach conducting in 1738.

> If you could see him ... singing with one voice and playing his own parts, but watching over everything and bringing back to the rhythm and the beat, out of thirty or even forty musicians, the one with a nod, another by tapping with his foot, the third with a warning finger, giving the right note to one from the top of his voice, to another from the bottom, and to a third from the middle of it—all alone, in the midst of the greatest din made by all the participants, and, although he is executing the most difficult parts himself, noticing at once whenever and wherever a mistake occurs, holding everyone together, taking precautions everywhere, and repairing any unsteadiness, full of rhythm in every part of his body ...[28]

---

[27] Hercole Bottrigari, *Il Desiderio*, trans. Carol MacClintock (American Institute of Musicology, 1962), 58ff.

[28] Quoted in Hans T. David and Arthur Mendel, *The Bach Reader* (New York: Norton, 1966), 231. His son reported that Bach conducted an orchestra with a violin as he played. See Ibid., 277.

We should also like to introduce the reader to Johann Mattheson, who left, in 1739, the earliest extended discussion of the qualities and education needed by a conductor. In his *Der vollkommene Capellmeister*,[29] he begins by placing the greatest emphasis on the integrity and character of the conductor and points to examples he has known of conductors who had cheated their singers out of money due them. But in general,

> He should in no way be offensive or scandalous in his living and conduct, for commonly the greatest contempt arises from that. A good reputation and esteem are such delicate things that with a single false step everything one has gained for oneself in many years through great assiduousness can be destroyed.

A central challenge for the conductor, in Mattheson's view, is the need to balance being friendly as a person with the necessary authority in rehearsal.

> A director of the choir must not be lazy with unconstrained words of praise, but must copiously employ them, even if he finds only scant cause for them among his students. But if he is to and must admonish and contradict someone, then he should do it quite seriously, yet as gently and politely as is possible. Affability is considered a most favored and rewarding virtue by people in all ranks: a director then should of course also strive for it, and should be very gregarious, sociable and obliging: especially when he is not performing his official tasks. In his official duties, becoming seriousness and precise observation of them probably does more service than too great familiarity.[30]

As for conducting itself, while some 'pound with sticks, keys and feet,' he has found 'that a little sign, not only with the hand but merely with the eyes and gestures, could accomplish most of this; if only the performers would assiduously keep their eyes on the director.'

The personal accomplishments which Mattheson believed were important for a conductor included ability to sing, to play the clavier, knowledge of tuning, knowledge of principles of seating plans and 'the greatest difficulty' of all: having the discernment required to succeed in divining the sense and meaning of another composer's thoughts. One cannot emphasize enough how important these abilities are. Few wind ensemble conductors understand the acoustic consequences of seating designs, and the ability to 'divine the sense and meaning of another composer's thoughts' is taught in American universities only through analysis of what is on paper—where the 'sense and meaning of another composer's thoughts' cannot be found.

---

[29] Johann Mattheson, *Der vollkommene Capellmeister* (1739), trans. Ernest Harriss (Ann Arbor: UMI Research Press, 1981), III, xxvi.

[30] Ibid., III, xxvi, 7. He points to the ideal example of J. S. Cousser, formerly Kapellmeister at Wolffenbüttel, who so charmed and helped his singers cordially in his home that they all loved him. However, in rehearsal, the musicians,

> almost all had fear and trembling before him, not only in the orchestra but also on the stage: for he knew how to reproach a person for his errors in such a sharp manner that often the eyes of the latter filled with tears. On the other hand, he calmed down again immediately, and diligently sought an opportunity to bind the thus-produced wounds through extraordinary politeness.

Mattheson stresses the importance of rehearsals and points out that the conductor often needs the rehearsal as much as the players.[31] Most Baroque performances were also premieres, thus he adds that one important purpose of the rehearsal is make the necessary corrections.

> It is no disgrace but rather an honor to improve that which has not turned out well. How then can one know or perceive it without rehearsal?

With regard to the rehearsal, he cannot help but add that some responsibility lies with the attitudes of the individual musicians as well.

> The director as well as the performers should set their heart and soul on nothing other than the service of God ... [they] must certainly put away all other, dissolute thoughts, and must direct their mind, from reverence, only on the holy work at hand. If this occurs, then the execution will proceed well: for all mistakes which are made derive from inattentiveness and from such a disposition wherewith one is at another place with his thoughts.[32]

A final requirement for the successful conductor or composer contains some timeless advice.

> A composer and director of music must be of a vigorous, high-spirited, indefatigable, diligent, and energetic nature; yet also orderly: yet most often the most active are deficient in this last. Idleness must be hated as a devil, because it is his place of repose ...
>
> Neither impatience nor a sudden flush of emotion serves any purpose here. If one does not have enough desire or deep-felt love for the thing so that he can suppress many a displeasure over it and so that adversity cannot alienate him from his noble plan; then he is not well suited for the exercise of this discipline and its sphere of duties.
>
> Indeed, with music and its pursuit very few roses are strewn in the path; moreover persons of authority and in high esteem seek, though it is unfair, to suppress and disparage everything about it as much as possible ... A master must have the heart in such circumstances to set a cheerful example for others, and must know how to create in himself so many pleasures from this noble pursuit that he would always be in the position, all obstacles notwithstanding, of finding his greatest peace in harmony and of reviving his spirit.[33]

---

[31] Ibid., III, xxvi, 23.

[32] Ibid., III, xxvi, 25.

[33] Ibid., II, ii, 55ff.

Matheson, in passing, gives a rather impressive list of topics which must be taught if the 'essence of music' is to be understood.[34] The list includes all the elements of what we would call theory and composition today, plus organ building. Included as well are acoustics, music history,[35] a study of how music functions in society and the training of the voice as well as various instruments.[36] Interesting specific topics include,

> The special qualities of a conductor.
> Expression in singing.
> The difference between vocal and instrumental melodies.
> How to direct, produce and execute music.

In another place,[37] Mattheson focuses specifically on the education and skills needed by the Kapellmeister and composer. Without education, he says, a musician can exercise his trade, but he cannot be an artist. This education need not be found at a university, but can be gained at home under 'clever leadership.'

The specific requirements of this education begin with languages: Greek, Latin, French and Italian, the language of the theater. Without these languages, how can the Kapellmeister ever be a *galant homme*? He must also have considerable knowledge in poetry and, in an emergency, be able to write good verse himself.

Mattheson considered music to be a 'substantial part of erudition and one of the disciplines which is closest to theology.' Perhaps this explains his following statement that 'whoever advances in music and goes backwards in morals walks like a crab and misses the proper goal.'

Finally, we should point out that every conductor during the periods we have mentioned to this point conducted without a score. Even in the Classical Period conductors conducted from a violin part or a fragmentary keyboard part, the score being considered mainly as a document from which to extract parts. Even so, we were astonished once in Milano to see an autograph score in which Mozart had reduced his *Marriage of Figaro* to two staves. On the cover he wrote, 'Conductor's score.' It was the custom in opera for a large manuscript book was not well suited to the frail music stand on the top of a harpsichord. Furthermore it was a problem turning all those pages so fast while still cueing the stage and playing on the keyboard just below the big score. But if one had a condensed score, when open to some point one could see a large

---

34 Ibid., I, i, 9ff.

35 Ibid., I, iv, 6ff, divides the field of music history into Chronology, Biography and the study of instruments. He divides the history of music into three eras: the beginning of time until the sixth century AD (a total of 4,000 years!), the sixth century until 1600 and 1600 until the present (1739). This last period, he says, contains so much material that the first two periods seem only trifling by comparison.

36 Ibid., III, xxiv, discusses the need for someone to write an up-to-date treatise on instruments. He mentions the fine work by Praetorius [of 1619], but points out that 'all musical instruments have changed a great deal since then.' The topics which he recommends for such a book range from a technical description and how to actually play each instrument to discussion of their use in churches, theaters and chambers.

37 Ibid., II, iiff.

number of measures without having to turn pages. Still, it is somewhat startling to think of Mozart taking the time to make a kind of piano version of the entire opera even though he owned the autograph score itself.

Conductors only began to conduct from full scores during the second quarter of the nineteenth century and that, together with the ingenious idea of adding rehearsal numbers, changed the nature of rehearsals and consequently conducting. However one must wonder if maybe the players, in the long period before rehearsal numbers, of necessity were better listeners in rehearsal. As a matter of fact, in the Classical Period, one finds scores where the composer did not even bother to change the key signature for the dominant section of the first movement sonata form, it being assumed the players knew this and would know by ear where to add the change.

But there was a price to pay for the custom of publishing full scores with rehearsal numbers, for then conductor's began to think of the score as something you looked at, rather than heard. And so until this very day, as the reader has no doubt noticed, most educational conductors conduct the score instead of the music.

On the Ancient Aulos

Music of aulos, soothing and sweet …[1]

......

Soon shall the glorious voice of the aulos go up for you again …
with such music as the lyre maketh to the gods![2]

THE MOST IMPORTANT WOODWIND INSTRUMENT OF ANTIQUITY was of course the aulos, the double-pipe instrument which is so often pictured in vases of this period. It is usually mistranslated as a 'flute' in English literature, an error the origin of which is lost in time. But it was clearly a double-reed instrument and one of several similar instruments which were all ancestors of the modern oboe. Because a single body version was also popular, in our view there is no reason not to suppose there was an unbroken link between the ancient aulos and the medieval shawm which returned to Western Europe from the crusades.[3] The aulos was unquestionably a double-reed instrument as we know, for example, from Theophrastus, a pupil of both Plato and Aristotle, who described the cane plant used in making the aulos reeds which grew at Lake Copais in Boeotia. When referring to the vibrating part of the reed he uses the term *zeugos* which implies a pair of matched objects, i.e. the two blades.[4]

The ancient iconography nearly always pictures the player wearing a leather band to support his cheeks, implying some exertion in blowing was required. This explains the myth of the goddess Minerva, who invented the aulos, but threw it away as she observed, when looking in a river, how the exertion in playing it deformed her face!

Athenaeus (ca. 200 AD), quoting from a now lost book by Aristoxenus (fourth century BC), writes that the latter knew five kinds of aulos, which he named: the virginal, child-pipes, harp-pipes, complete, and super-complete.[5] A fifth century BC fresco in the tomb of Leopardi, near Tarquinia, shows a bell on each body similar to that of the modern oboe.

---

[1] Sophocles, *Ajax*, 1204.

[2] Sophocles, *The Trachiniae*, 637.

[3] Herodotus, the fifth century BC historian, in his *Histories*, VI, 58, maintains that as in ancient Egypt, town-criers, aulos players and cooks are all sons of fathers who practiced the same profession.

[4] *Historia Plantarum*.

[5] Athenaeus, *Deipnosophistae*, XIV, 634.

We find some additional information about the reeds in Pliny the Elder's (23–79 AD) *Natural History*. He offers the following miscellaneous information: that 'melodious auloi' are made from the lotus tree[6], that some auloi were made from a type of bamboo[7] and that some auloi were made from reeds grown on the shores of Lake Orchomenus, a type of reed which required an unusual amount of curing.

> These supplied the instruments for glorious music, though mention must also not be omitted of the further remarkable trouble required to grow them, so that excuse may be made for the present-day preference for musical instruments of silver. Down to the time of the aulos player Antigenides, when a simple style of music was still practiced, the reeds used to be regarded as ready for cutting after the rising of Arcturus. When thus prepared the reeds began to be fit for use a few years later, though even then the actual auloi needed maturing with a great deal of practice, and educating to sing of themselves, with the tongues pressing themselves down, which was more serviceable for the theatrical fashions then prevailing. But after variety came into fashion, and luxury even in music, the reeds began to be cut before midsummer and made ready for use in three years, their tongues being wider open to modulate the sounds, and these continue to the present day. But at that time it was firmly believed that only a tongue cut from the same reed as the pipe in each case would do, and that one taken from just above the root was suitable for a left-hand aulos and one from just below the top for a right-hand aulos; the reeds that had been washed by the waters of Cephisus itself were rated as immeasurably superior.[8]

We even have a fragment of contemporary advice on the technique of playing the aulos. The rhetorician and biographer, Flavius Philostratus[9], recounts a visit by a traveler named Apollonius to the most famous aulos player of the first century AD, a man named Canus. The instrument as he understood it had evolved from an instrument made from a plant to one made from a variety of materials, 'of gold or brass and the skin of a stag, or perhaps the shin of a donkey.'[10] Canus provided this very rare glimpse into the basic technique of playing the aulos.

> … namely reserves of breath … and facility with the lips consisting in their taking in the reed of the pipe and playing without blowing out the cheeks; and manual skill I consider very important, for the wrist must not weary from being bent, nor must the fingers be slow in fluttering over the notes.

---

6   Pliny the Elder, *Natural History*, III, xxxii, 106.

7   Ibid., III, xvi.

8   Ibid., XVI, lxvi, 170ff.

9   Philostratus, *The Life of Apollonius of Tyana*, V, xxi.

10 Isidore, bishop of Seville, in his *Etymologiarum* gives the Latin name for the aulos as *tibiae*, which derives from the belief that they 'were first made from the leg bones of deer and fawns.' Marcus Varro, in *On the Latin Language*, VI, 75 and VIII, 61, gives *tibiae* for the aulos and *tibicines* for the players.

Canus also made the interesting statement that if the audiences only knew how much pleasure he received from playing, instead of paying him, he would be required to pay them.[11] In describing the kinds of music he played, Canus provides a list of types of music which would seem familiar today: music for those who are sad, music for celebration, music for lovers and music for religious usage.

> [The purpose of my music is] that the mourner may have his sorrow lulled to sleep by the pipe, and that they that rejoice may have their cheerfulness enhanced, and the lover may wax warmer in his passion, and that the lover of sacrifice may become more inspired and full of sacred song.

Upon further questioning, Canus admits it is the music itself which accomplishes these ends, not the aulos.

We know some additional names of ancient aulos players. Athenaeus mentions a player named Asopodorus of Phlius who, participating in a contest, was shocked to see the old noble art declining to the level of mere entertainment.

> In olden times the feeling for nobility was always maintained in the art of music, and all its elements skilfully retained the orderly beauty appropriate to them. Hence there were auloi peculiarly adapted to every mode, and every player had auloi suited to every mode used in the public contests. But Pronomus of Thebes began the practice of playing all the modes on the same auloi. Today, however, people take up music in a haphazard and irrational manner. In early times popularity with the masses was a sign of bad art; hence, when a certain aulos player once received loud applause, Asopodorus of Phlius, who was himself still wating in the wings, said, 'What's this? Something awful must have happened!' The player evidently could not have won approval with the crowd otherwise. And yet the musicians of our day set as the goal of their art success with their audiences.[12]

Athenaeus mentions a strong-willed aulos player of the Alexandrian Period, named Dorion, who is discussed by several early writers.[13] Once when dining in the house of a nobleman in Cyprus he praised a cup. When the nobleman offered to have another made for him by the same craftsman, Dorion answered, 'No, he can make one for you; I'll take this one!' Athenaeus explained this improper response to a nobleman by a musician in an old saying, 'In an aulos player the gods implanted no sense; no, for with his blowing his sense takes wing and flies from him.'[14] Athenaeus quotes another, more touching, story about this musician by the writer, Aristodemus.

> Dorion the music master, who was club-footed, once lost the shoe of his lame foot at a dinner party. He said: 'I shall utter no heavier curse upon the thief than the wish that that sandal may fit him.'

---

[11] Alfred Sendrey, in *Music in the Social and Religious Life of Antiquity* (Rutherford: Fairleigh Dickinson University Press, 1974), 411.

[12] Athenaeus, *Deipnosophistae*, XIV 631.

[13] Ibid., VIII, 337ff.

[14] One wonders if this is the origin of the old tale that oboists go crazy from the vibrations of their instrument.

Zeno (300–260 BC) compliments an aulos player,

> The wise man does all things well, just as we say that Ismenias plays all melodies on the aulos well,[15]

whom is mentioned rather disrespectfully by another aulos player, Dionysodorus, who comments that no one will ever hear him play, like Ismenias, on ships or at the fountain in the town square![16]

We know that by the fourth century BC the aulos players were regular contract members of drama companies and that they wore costumes. We have considerable documentation for at least one famous player who was associated with the theater, Kraton of Chalkedon.[17]

Finally, we have a tragic poem of the second century AD which refers to the suicide of an aulos player:

> Clytosthenes, his feet that raced in fury now enfeebled by age, dedicates to thee, Rhea of the lion-car, his tambourines beaten by the hand, his shrill hollow-rimmed cymbals, his double-flute that calls through its horn, on which he once made shrieking music, twisting his neck about, and the two-edged knife with which he opened his veins.[18]

The reference to the aulos 'with horn' describes a bell of animal horn which had begun to be used in Rome after the first century AD.

Athenaeus mentions a number of famous teachers and their (now lost) treatises as well as famous aulos schools at Olypiodorus and Orthagoras.[19] Additional lost treatises that we know of are the three by Aristoxenus (b. ca. 379 BC), a student of Aristotle, *On Aulos Players*, *On The Aulos and Musical Instruments*,[20] *On Aulos Boring*.[21]

Aside from the comment by Canus, above, we have a few more clues to the nature of the repertoire of the aulos players. First, Strabo provides a description of an actual repertoire work played at a contest at Delphi, and we even know the name of the composer, one Timosthenes (fl. ca. 270 BC). This work, performed by a rhapsodist with either aulos or lyre accompanying, told the story of a contest between Apollo and a dragon. It consisted of a prelude, the battle, the triumph following the victory, and the expiration of the dragon—with the aulos player

---

[15] Quoted in Diogenes Laertius, *Lives of the Eminent Philosophers*, trans. R. D. Hicks (Cambridge: Harvard University Press, 1950), II, 229.

[16] Ibid., I, 399.

[17] Sir Arthur Pickard-Cambridge, *The Dramatic Festivals of Athens* (Oxford: Clarendon Press, 1953), 164, 218, 300ff.

[18] Philippus of Thessalonica, in *Greek Anthology*, VI, 94.

[19] Athenaeus, *Deipnosophistae*, IV, 184 and XIV, 634.

[20] Ibid., IV, 174.

[21] Ibid., XIV, 634.

imitating the last hissings of the dragon.[22] By the way, Plutarch tells us that Alexander the Great organized aulos contests because he had little interest in the usual boxing and wrestling contests.[23]

Athenaeus gives a list of terms 'applied to aulos playing,' but which to us looks like the titles of repertoire pieces: comus, pastoral, gingras, tetracomus, epiphallus, choir-dance, triumph-song, battle-song, gentle comus, Satyr's whirl, door-knock, tickle-tune, and Helot-lad.[24]

The earliest functional employment of the aulos was to accompany the lyric poets of the seventh century BC. Apparently the performance skills of the aulos players gradually began to usurp the attention of the public, as we notice several writers, Plato among them, vigorously complaining over liberties being taken by the aulos player. Pratinas, in 500 BC, for example, reminded his listeners that the Muse had ordained that the song should be the mistress and the aulos the servant, and not the other way around!ial[25]

By the fifth century BC the great dramatists held center stage and while the lyre is still mentioned in these plays, it does seem that the aulos begins to be the preferred instrument for accompaniment in the fifth century. Sir Arthur Pickard-Cambridge provides the reasoning of the time:

> The instrument by which both the singing and recitative were normally accompanied in tragedy and comedy was the aulos. In the *Problems* of Aristotle, xix, 43, it is argued that the aulos gives a better accompaniment to the human voice than the lyre, because both aulos and voice are wind instruments and so blend better ... It appears probable that the lyre was used in the drama mainly for special effects, as when the young Sophocles played it in his *Thamyris*.[26]

The importance which the ancient Greeks assigned to the role of music in education is well-known. Aristotle, who supported the general importance of music in education, drew a line when it came to the aulos. First, he felt the aulos was simply too difficult for student to master. But he had three additional concerns which made this instrument unsuitable for public education.

> The aulos is not an instrument which is expressive of moral character; it is too exciting. The proper time for using it is when the performance aims not at instruction, but at the relief of the passions.[27]

......

---

[22] *The Geography of Strabo*, trans. Horace L. Jones (Cambridge: Harvard University Press, 1960), IX.3.10.

[23] Plutarch, *Lives*, 'Alexander,' 4.

[24] Athenaeus, *Deipnosophistae*, XIV, 618.

[25] Richard C. Jebb, *Bacchylides* (Hildesheim, Georg Olms Verlagsbuchhandlung, 1967), 46.

[26] Pickard-Cambridge, *The Dramatic Festivals of Athens*, 163. Sir Arthur goes into considerable detail regarding his belief that the aulos was used in specific relationships with the metrics of the text. An example (p. 162):

> It has been made plain that the anapaests of the parabasis were accompanied by the aulos, as also, in all probability, were any tetrameter speeches delivered by an actor while the chorus or a semi-chorus was dancing, and in particular the epirrhema and antepirrhema of the parabasis, which were commonly in trochaic or iambic tetrameters.

[27] *Politica*, 1341a.21.

> Another objection is that when you play aulos you cannot at the same time sing—thus detracting from its educational value. The ancients therefore were right in forbidding the aulos to youths …[28]
>
> ……
>
> Also it distorts the face, as the old myth goes.

Finally, because the professional player, in Aristotle's experience, cannot resist being influenced by the popular taste of the audience, the subsequent influence of this dimension on the character of the player represents yet another reason why an emphasis on a high level of performance is not appropriate to public education.

> Thus then we reject the professional instruments and also the professional mode of education in music (and by professional we mean that which is adopted in contests), for in this the performer practices the art, not for the sake of his own improvement, but in order to give pleasure, and that of a vulgar sort, to his hearers … The result is that the performers are vulgarized, for the end at which they aim is bad. The vulgarity of the spectator tends to lower the character of the music and therefore of the performers.[29]

Nevertheless, it appears the aulos did play an important part in education and continued to do so for more than a century after Aristotle. We can see evidence of this in a writer of the following period, Strabo, who mentions the use of the aulos in the course of his attack on the philosophy of the Alexandrian writer Eratosthenes (276–194 BC).

> Eratosthenes contends that the aim of every poet is to entertain, not to instruct. The ancients assert, on the contrary, that poetry is a kind of elementary philosophy, which, taking us in our very boyhood, introduces us to the art of life and instructs us, with pleasure to ourselves, in character, emotions, and actions … Why, even the musicians, when they give instruction in singing, in lyre playing, or in aulos playing … maintain that these studies tend to discipline and correct the character.[30]

Strabo goes on to say that Aristoxenus was one of those who 'declares the same thing.' Plutarch, who knew the now lost books on music by Aristoxenus, also mentions that the latter spoke on the value of music in forming character. Indeed, Plutarch quotes from one of these lost books a story by which Aristoxenus meant to demonstrate that proper lessons once learned become part of the character and cannot be easily changed.

> Now that the right molding or ruin of ingenuous manners and civil conduct lies in a well-grounded musical education, Aristoxenus has made apparent. For, of those that were contemporary with him, he gives an account of Telesias the Theban, who in his youth was bred up in the noblest excellences of music, and moreover studied the works of the most famous lyric poets, Pindar, Dionysius the Theban, Lamprus, Pratinas, and all the rest who were accounted most eminent; who played also to perfection upon the aulos, and was not a little industrious to furnish himself with all those other accomplishments of learning; but being past the prime of his age, he was so bewitched with the

---

[28] Ibid., 1341a.25.

[29] Ibid., 1341b.9.

[30] Strabo, *The Geography of Strabo*, I.2.3.

theater's new fangles and the innovations of multiplied notes, that despising those noble precepts and that solid practice to which he had been educated, he betook himself to Philoxenus and Timotheus, and among those delighted chiefly in such as were most depraved with diversity of notes and baneful innovation. And yet, when he made it his business to make verses and labor both ways, as well in that of Pindar as that of Philoxenus, he could have no success in the latter. And the reason proceeded from the truth and exactness of his first education.[31]

No early writer addresses this topic with more heartfelt passion than the historian Polybius. He departs from his description of the internal wars of the period 220–216 BC to give a fervent testimonial to the role music plays in shaping the character of entire peoples and a plea that the Cynaetheans return to this use of music to save themselves. In the course of his argument he gives us one of the most extraordinary pictures of the educational use of music ('I mean *real* music,' he says) in ancient Greece.

> It is worth while to give a moment's consideration to the question of the savagery of the Cynaetheans, and ask ourselves why, though unquestionably of Arcadian stock, they so far surpassed all other Greeks at this period in cruelty and wickedness. I think the reason was they they were the first and indeed the only people in Arcadia to abandon an admirable institution, introduced by their forefathers with a nice regard for the natural conditions under which all the inhabitants of that country live. For the practice of music, I mean real music, is beneficial to all men, but to Arcadians it is a necessity. For we must not suppose, as Ephorus, in his Preface to his History, making a hasty assertion quite unworthy of him, says, that music was introduced by men for the purpose of deception and delusion; we should not think that the ancient Cretans and Lacedaemonians acted at haphazard in substituting the aulos and rhythmic movement for the bugle in war, or that the early Arcadians had no good reason for incorporating music in their whole public life to such an extent that not only boys, but young men up to the age of thirty were compelled to study it constantly, although in other matters their lives were most austere.
>
> For it is a well-known fact, familiar to all, that it is hardly known except in Arcadia, that in the first place the boys from their earliest childhood are trained to sing in measure the hymns and paeans in which by traditional usage they celebrate the heroes and gods of each particular place; later they learn the measures of Philoxenus and Timotheus, and every year in the theater they compete keenly in choral singing to the accompaniment of professional aulos players, the boys in the contest proper to them and the young men in what is called the men's contest. And not only this, but through their whole life they entertain themselves at banquets not by listening to hired musicians but by their own efforts, calling for a song from each in turn. Whereas they are not ashamed of denying acquaintance with other studies, in the case of singing it is neither possible for them to deny a knowledge of it because they all are compelled to learn it, nor, if they confess to such knowledge can they excuse themselves, so great a disgrace is this considered in that country. Besides this the young men practice military parades to the music of the aulos and perfect themselves in dances and give annual performances in the theaters, all under state supervision and at public expense.[32]

---

[31] Quoted by Plutarch in 'Concerning Music.'

[32] Polybius, *The Histories*, IV.20.5ff, trans. W. R. Paton (Cambridge: Harvard University Press, 1954).

Polybius mentions as well, above, another of the jobs of the aulos player, to accompany the chorus in its performances. One of the most noble of the old traditions were the choral odes of the sixth century BC. By the following century, however, there were some who were very concerned with the evolution of this tradition.

> Pratinas of Phlius, when hired aulos players and dancers usurped the dancing places, became indignant at the way in which the aulos players failed to accompany the choruses in the traditional fashion, and choruses now sang a mere accompaniment to the aulos players; ... 'What uproar is this? What dances are these? What outrage hath assailed the alter of Dionysus with its loud clatter? ... 'Tis the song that is queen, established by the Pierian Muse; but the aulos must be second in the dance, for he is even a servant; let him be content to be leader in the revel only, in the fist-fights of tipsy youngsters raging at the front door. Beat back him who has the breath of a mottled toad, burn up in flames that spit-wasting, babbling raucous reed, spoiling melody and rhythm in its march, that hireling whose body is fashioned by an auger!'[33]

The Etruscans, who formed an intermediate civilization chronologically between ancient Greece and Rome, also seem to have experimented with the Greek aulos, adding a bell to it, which, again, we find later in Rome. They may have also renamed it, for Varro (first century BC) finds in a fragment of poetry by Ennius (236–169 BC) that the Etruscan aulos players were called *Subulo*.[34]

> Once a subulo was standing by the stretches of the sea ...[35]

The Roman poet, Ovid (43 BC–17 AD), mentions Etruscan aulos players and their 'homely' music, which suggests perhaps that he associated them with folk music, rather than as artists.[36]

There is an extraordinary tale involving hunting and Etruscan aulos players which seems to us quite unbelievable!

> There is an Etruscan story current which says that the wild boars and the stags in that country are caught by using nets and hounds, as is the usual manner of hunting, but that music plays a part, and even the larger part, in the struggle. And how this happens I will now relate. They set the nets and other hunting gear that ensnare the animals in a circle, and a man proficient on the aulos stands there and tries his utmost to play a rather soft tune, avoiding any shriller note, but playing the sweetest melodies possible. The quiet and stillness easily carry [the sound] abroad; and the music streams up to the heights and into ravines and thickets—in a word into every lair and resting place of these animals. Now at first when the sound penetrates to their ears it strikes them with terror and fills them with dread, and then an unalloyed and irresistible delight in the music takes hold of them, and they are so beguiled as to forget about their offspring and their homes. And yet wild beasts do not care to wander

---

33 Athenaeus, *Deipnosophistae*, XIV, 617. .

34 *On the Latin Language*, VII, 35.

35 Ibid.

36 Ovid, *The Art of Love*, I, 111.

away from their native haunts. But little by little these creatures in Etruria are attracted as though by some persuasive spell, and beneath the wizardry of the music they come and fall into the snares, overpowered by the melody.[37]

Strange as this tale is, Aelianus (175–235 AD) provides an even more extraordinary testimonial for the aulos. In Libya, he claims, the performance of aulos music 'throws mares into an amorous frenzy and makes horses mad with desire to couple. This in fact is how the mating of horses is brought about.'[38]

While we read little of the use of the aulos in Greek religious ceremonies, among the ancient Romans it is much discussed. The origin of the use of music in the religious-cult celebrations in Rome is assigned, by tradition, to the time of Numa Pompilius (seventh to eighth centuries BC) when singers and dancers performed rites in honor of the god Mars. During the earliest years it appears to have been the brass instruments from the Etruscans and the aulos which participated in these kinds of ceremonies. Something of the spirit of these primitive celebrations can be seen in a description of the worship of the Idaean Mother by Lucretius (99–55 BC).

> Their open palms slap the taut drums
> To Terrible thunder, the hollow cymbals clash,
> The horns blare raucous, and the auloi shrill
> With sharp insistence.[39]

On one famous occasion in the fourth century BC, the aulos players who performed for the religious festivals went on strike when the city could not pay their full wages for participating in the Feast of Jupiter. The aulos players actually left town and took up residence in Tibur, leaving Rome without the whole range of services usually rendered by these players, as noted by Ovid.

> The aulos was missed in the theater, missed at the alters; no dirge accompanied the bier on the last march.[40]

After negotiations failed to secure the return of these players, citizens of Tibur proposed to trick them into returning. They threw a great party for them and when they were 'reeling with heady wine' they arranged to take them to their lodgings by wagon. The wagons instead took the sleeping aulos players to Rome, where, in order to help them save face, they were disguised in masks and long gowns. For some time this was commemorated in an annual festival, during which musicians would parade in long gowns and masks.

---

37 Claudius Aelianus (second century AD), *Of the Characteristics of Animals*, XII, 46.
38 Ibid., XII, 44.
39 *The Way Things Are*, Book II, 619ff.
40 Ovid, *Fasti*, VI, 666ff.

There are two early accounts of this incident which provide interesting detail. The earliest is by Livy, who not only characterizes these aulos players in an unfavorable light, but reveals his general disinterest in music itself by noting that this story 'would scarcely be worth mentioning, were it not connected to religion.'

> The aulos players were angry at having been forbidden by the last censors to hold their feast in the temple of Jupiter, according to ancient custom, and marched off to Tibur in a body, with the result that there was no one in the City to play the auloi at sacrifices. The Senate was seized with pious misgivings about the incident, and sent delegates to Tibur to request the citizens to do their best to return the men to Rome. The Tiburtines courteously promised to do so, and first summoned the aulos players to their senate house and urged them to go back to Rome. Then, when they found that persuasion achieved nothing, they dealt with the men by a ruse nicely in tune with their nature. On a public holiday various citizens invited parties of aulos players to their homes on the pretext of celebrating the feast with music, and sent them to sleep by plying them with wine, for which men of their kind are generally greedy. In that condition they dumped them, heavily asleep, in carts and carried them off to Rome. The carts were left in the Forum and the aulos players knew nothing until daylight surprised them there, still very drunk. The people quickly gathered round them and prevailed on them to stay. They were given permission on three days a year to roam the City in fancy dress, making music and enjoying the license which is now customary, and those of them who played auloi at sacrifices had their right to hold a feast in the temple restored.[41]

We must assume that the music of the aulos continued to play an important role in the celebration of the religious-cult ceremonies. In another extant icon, we see an aulos playing during a sacrifice (an axe is poised over a cow) in a sarcophagus carving from the second century AD in the Museo del Palazzo Ducale, Mantua.

With the Roman theater, as was the case in Greece, we find the employment of the aulos from a very early date. Livy provides a remarkable and logical summary of the birth of art song and theater, which he dates from the middle of the fourth century BC, as part of ceremonies meant to reconcile the people to the gods following a plague.

> Amongst their other ceremonies intended to placate divine wrath, they are said to have introduced scenic entertainments, something quite novel for a warlike people whose only previous public spectacle had been that of the circus. These began only in a modest way, as most things do, and were in fact imported from abroad. Players were brought from Etruria to dance to the strains of the aulos without any singing or miming of song, and made quite graceful movements in the Etruscan style. Then the young Romans began to copy them, exchanging jokes at the same time in crude improvised verse, with gestures to fit the words. Thus the entertainment was adopted and became established by frequent repetition. The native actors were called *histriones*, because the Etruscan word for an actor is *ister*; they stopped bandying ribald improvised lines, like Fescennine verses, and began to perform *saturae* or medleys amplified with music, the singing properly arranged to fit the aulos and movement in harmony with it.

---

[41] Livy, *A History of Rome*, IX, 30. The aulos guild, called *Collegium tibicinum*, was one of the oldest professional organizations in Rome [*The New Grove Dictionary of Music and Musicians*, XVI, 147] and was fed at public expense in the temple of Jupiter.

> Some years later, Livius first ventured to give up the *satura* and compose a play with a plot. Like everyone else at the time, he also acted in his own dramas; and the tale is told that when he lost his voice after repeated recalls, he was given permission to place a boy in front of the aulos player to sing the songs while he acted them himself, and did so with a good deal more vigor when not hampered by having to use his voice. From then on began the actors' practice of employing singers while they confined themselves to gesture and used their voices only for dialog. This style of performance began to detach the play from impromptu joking to raise a laugh, and drama gradually developed into an art.[42]

Extant iconography certainly supports Livy's general date for the introduction of the aulos in the theater. There is a vase from this period (fourth century BC), now in the Hermitage which pictures an aulos player playing in the theater and a relief (Inv. Nr. 6687, Museo, Nazionale, Naples) from the second century BC also shows an aulos player in the theater.

In the plays of Terence there is extant information which actually gives us the name of the composer of the music for the play. In *The Girl from Andros*, for example, we read, 'Scored for equal auloi by Flaccus, freedman of Claudius.' This same composer composed the music for *The Brothers*, but here specified Etruscian ('Tyrian') auloi.

Sometimes things did not go as planned in theatrical performances and the audiences were rather entertained than moved. An extraordinary case in point is related by the historian, Polybius (second century BC). He tells of a special performance in the arena [Circus] organized by the Roman General, Lucius Anicius, to celebrate his defeat and capture of King Genthius of the Illyrians.

> Having summoned the most distinguished artists of Greece and constructed a very large stage in the Circus, he first brought on the aulos players; there were Theodorus of Boeotia, Theopompus, Hermippus, Lysimachus, all of them the most distinguished. Posting them, then, at the front of the stage with the chorus, he directed them to play all together. As they started to perform their music to accompany the dance motions which corresponded to it, he sent word to them that they were not playing in the right way, and ordered them to whoop up the contest against one another. Since they were puzzled at this, one of the officials indicated that they should turn and advance upon one another and act as if they were fighting. Quickly the players caught the idea, and taking on motions in keeping with their own licentious characters they caused great confusion. For the aulos players by a concerted movement turned the middle choruses against those at the ends, while they blew on their auloi unintelligible notes, and all differing, and then they drew away in turn upon each other; and at the same time the members of the choruses clashed noisily against the players as they shook their gear at them and rushed upon their antagonists, to turn again and retreat. And so in one case a member of the chorus girded himself, and stepping out of the ranks he turned and raised his fists as if to box against the aulos player who plunged against him; and then, if not before, the applause and shouts that arose from the spectators knew no bounds. Furthermore, while these were contending in a pitched battle, two dancers entered with castanets, and four boxers mounted upon the stage accompanied by trumpeters and horn players. All these contests went on together, and the result was indescribable.[43]

---

[42] Ibid., VII, 2.

[43] *Histories*, XXX.

During the Augustian Age (27 BC–14 AD) the great Roman philosopher, Horace, reports even more decay in the formerly distinguished theater tradition.

> The aulos—not, as now, bound with brass and a rival of the trumpet, but slight and simple, with few stops—was once of use to lead and aid the chorus and to fill with its breath benches not yet too crowded, where, to be sure, folk gathered, easy to count, because few—sober folk, too, and chaste and modest. But when a conquering race began to widen its domain, and an ampler wall embraced its cities, and when, on festal days, appeasing the Genius by daylight drinking brought no penalty, then both time and tune won greater license. For what taste could you expect of an unlettered throng just freed from toil, rustic mixed up with city folk, vulgar with nobly born? So to the early art the aulos player added movement and display, and, strutting over the stage, trailed a robe in train. So, too, to the sober lyre new tones were given, and an impetuous style brought in an unwonted diction; and the thought, full of wise saws and prophetic of the future, was attuned to the oracles of Delphi.[44]

Funeral processions continued to depend on music as a symbol of the status of the deceased. We obtain some idea of the importance of this status symbol when Ovid mentions that a government regulation at this time limited the number of aulos players for such occasions at 10.[45] The principal funeral song was the *Nenia*, which praised the deceased in song with aulos accompaniment.

Propertius mentions a very rare use of the trumpet with the aulos in funeral ceremonies, a practice not found elsewhere in this early Roman literature.

> What dreams would my aulos sing to you then,
> aulos sadder than funeral tuba [trumpet]?[46]

Once the Christian church takes over, with their general opposition to music and the emotions, we read little of the aulos. Even the late medieval romantic, Peter Abelard, in one of his famous letters to Heloise warns her that the aulos,

> emits a sound for the delectation of the sense, not for the understanding of the mind.[47]

---

44 Horace, *The Art of Poetry*, trans. H. Rushton Fairclough (Cambridge: Harvard University Press, 1955), 467.

45 *Fasti*, VI, 663–664.

46 Propertius, *The Poems*, II, 7.

47 Letter to Heloise, in *The Letters of Abelard and Heloise*, trans. C. K. Scott Moncrieff (New York: Knopf, 1933), 254.

On the Ancient Trumpet

THE TRUMPET-TYPE INSTRUMENT is rarely pictured in the iconography of Mesopotamia but it seems present in several references to military music, such as when in Sumeria (3,000 BC) the sound of an instrument is compared 'to the howling of the storm and the roaring of the bull.'[1] Perhaps it is the trumpet again which is described as being used among the ancient Persians in their schools:

> And these teachers wake the boys up before dawn by the sound of brazen instruments, and assemble them in one place.[2]

Perhaps the most familiar references to ancient trumpets are those associated with the early Hebrews in the Old Testament. Most of the books of the Old Testament were written five hundred to one thousand years after the events they describe and in cases such as this one must allow for some exaggeration during the long period in which these stories were retold. An obvious illustration is the story of the dedication of Solomon's Temple in the account by Josephus.[3] He reports that this ceremony included a performance by 200,000 trumpets, a figure which would not only have exceeded all the extant ram-horn trumpets [shofar] in the area at this time, but also would have probably exceeded the number of goats as well.

The Old Testament documents the use of the trumpet in the religious service and even provides the names of some of the trumpet players, as well as the names of performers of harps, lyres and cymbals.[4] In one place we read,

> with 120 priests who were trumpeters; and it was the duty of the trumpeters and singers to make themselves heard in unison in praise and thanksgiving.[5]

Another passage speaks of cymbals, harps, lyres, trumpets and singing altogether in the service.[6] And then there are those passages such as Psalm 150 which cry, 'Praise him with the trumpet sound.'

---

1 Alfred Sendrey, in *Music in the Social and Religious Life of Antiquity* (Rutherford: Fairleigh Dickinson University Press, 1974).
2 Strabo, *On Geography*, XV, 18.
3 Josephus, *Jewish Antiquities*, VIII, 95.
4 1 Chronicles 15:16ff; 16:5ff, 42; Nehemiah 12:34ff.
5 2 Chronicles 5:12ff.
6 2 Chronicles 29:25ff.

Other than their use in the service, the Old Testament mentions the use of the trumpet in a wide variety of other situations, including dancing,[7] processionals[8], for appointed feasts,[9] to mark the beginnings of months, for burnt offerings and for sacrifices for peace offerings[10] for welcoming music,[11] for coronations,[12] for the taking of oaths,[13] by civic watchmen[14] and the trumpet is to be played on that occasion when the scattered people will be called back from the various nations.[15]

Of course the trumpet is central to the well-known military stories of Jericho[16] and Gideon's famous surprise attack with his three hundred trumpeters.[17] Another military reference in Zechariah 9:14ff reveals that God, himself, was a trumpet player and would protect the soldiers in battle as they devour their enemies and drink their blood.

The most important discussion of the trumpet in the Old Testament is found in the tenth book of Numbers. Here we are first told how silver trumpets are made ('of hammered work you shall make them') and we may assume that this reference applies to the long period the Hebrews lived in Egypt. Modern scholars find no evidence of the ability to make new silver instruments in the desert and, in fact, it was for this reason that the ram's horn was used as a replacement when the instruments they may have carried with them from Egypt eventually wore out.

This discussion in the Book of Numbers discusses at length the use of the trumpet for signal purposes and is a vivid document of the instrument's importance for this use. In fact the implication is that because of the use for signaling the movements of the tribes only the high priest was permitted to play the trumpet. A very rare exception is found in 2 Samuel 20:1 where we read,

> Now there happened to be there a worthless fellow, whose name was Sheba, the son of Bichri, a Benjaminite; and he blew the trumpet.

Two questions occur to us from this discussion. First, when the instruction is given,

---

[7] 1 Chronicles 13:8.

[8] 1 Chronicles 15:28, 2 Samuel 6:13.

[9] Numbers 29:1, 2 chronicles 29:25 and Leviticus 23:24 and 25:9.

[10] Numbers 10.

[11] 1 Kings 1:34ff.

[12] 2 Kings 9:13 and 2 Chronicles 23:12.

[13] 2 Chronicles 15:14.

[14] Ezekiel 33:2ff.

[15] Isaiah 27:12.

[16] Joshua 6:4ff.

[17] Judges 6:34ff. Other references to the use of military trumpets can be found in Numbers 31:6, 2 Samuel 2:28, 2 Chronicles 13:12, Jeremiah 4:19ff, Jeremiah 6, Jeremiah 42:14, Hosea 8, Joel 2:1 and 15, Amos 3:6 and Zephaniah 1:16.

when both [trumpets] are blown, all the congregation shall gather themselves to you at the entrance of the tent of meeting. But if they blow only one, then the leaders, the heads of the tribes of Israel, shall gather themselves to you,

we wonder if the distant tribes, spread across the desert, could distinguish between one versus two trumpets playing, unless they played a signal in two separate voices. We also wonder about the acoustics, could these presumably narrow bore trumpets be heard distinctly over great distances? Of course, it was a more quiet world, but the question remains, particularly in view of another curious passage where we read of a 'long blast,' followed by 'a very loud blast' and followed again by 'the sound of the trumpet grew louder and louder.'[18] Perhaps there is here, once again, the case of exaggeration sneaking into an often retold story.

We have no extant literature to describe the use of trumpets in ancient Egypt, but we can see them in the paintings of the ancient tombs. In Tomb 90 of the Theban necropolis (ca. 1425–1405 BC) we see a trumpet player in his helmet and in Tomb 74 two trumpeters marching with their instruments over the shoulder. The only actual surviving ancient Egyptian trumpets, by the way, were found in the famous tomb of Tutankhamen. When one of these was blown in a trial, it was the only instance that people of our own time have heard the sounds the ancient Egyptians heard.

An instrument known to the ancient Greeks was the long, straight trumpet, called *salpinx*.[19] An early reference is found in a fragment of thirteen lines by the lyric poet, Bacchylides (fifth century BC). Here we have part of a prayer to the gods for peace. It speaks of 'flowers of honeyed song,' and the music of aulos. Quite a different adjective is used for the war trumpet.

> No blast of bronze trumpet is heard; sleep of gentle spirit, that comforts the heart at dawn, is not stolen from the eyelids.[20]

Also from the fifth century BC the trumpet is frequently mentioned in its military connection. The various trumpet signals which are described were apparently sufficiently recognized that on occasion we read of some general fooling the enemy by the deliberate use of false signals. In addition to its use for signals, the trumpet was also a symbol for the noise and anxiety of the battle, as we see in an example by Aeschylus:

> Wild brazen bells make music of affright.[21]

In this same passage, by the way, we find a reference similar to those found in ancient Hebrew and Roman literature, of the change in the character of the horse when he hears the battle trumpet.

---

[18] Exodus 19:13ff.

[19] The trumpet is rarely mentioned in early Greek poetry. Homer, for example, never mentions it in his otherwise vivid battle descriptions.

[20] Fragment Nr. 3 in Richard C. Jebb, *Bacchylides* (Hildesheim, Georg Olms Verlagsbuchhandlung, 1967).

[21] *The Seven Against Thebes*, in *The Complete Plays of Aeschylus*, trans. Gilbert Murray (London: George Allen, 1952), 386.

> As some wild war-horse when the trumpets sound
> Stiffens and champs the curb and paws the ground.

In the ancient Greek plays we also find a new instrument, a trumpet which they associated with the Etruscans. The Etruscans [Latin: *tusci*; Greek: *Tyrrhenoi*] inhabited the western region of Italy, known today as Tuscany. These people, of Eastern Mediterranean origin, migrated to the Italian Peninsula in the ninth or tenth century BC and formed a strong cultural entity until their eventual absorption into the Roman Empire in 27 BC. Because the Etruscans traded with the Greeks, their musical culture was based on Grecian models and it was the Etruscans who seem to have played an important role in passing these traditions on to the Roman Empire. Our knowledge of the Etruscans' role in the transfer of culture from Greece to Rome is limited primarily to observations we can make from iconography, especially paintings in tombs.[22] We also gain insight from a few Greek and Roman references, which are all the more valuable since the language of the Etruscans themselves cannot yet be deciphered.

Although the Greek trumpet [*salpinx*] was the familiar instrument, beginning with the sixth century BC the Greek playwrights occasionally mention a different instrument which they associated with the Etruscans.

> Sophocles: I hear thy call and seize it in my soul, as when a Tyrrhenian bell speaks from mouth of bronze![23]
>
> ......
>
> Euripides: Then the Tyrrhenian trumpet blast burst forth, like fire.[24]
>
> ......
>
> Aeschylus: Let the piercing Tyrrene trumpet, filled with human breath, send forth its shrill blare to the folk![25]

This new instrument with which the Greeks were familiar was probably the *cornu*, a great hoop-shaped instrument of bronze or iron, with transverse grip, looking somewhat like a capital letter 'G,' which becomes a basic instrument of the Roman army. We can see this instrument already in the seventh century BC in an Etruscan wall painting of the tomb of Castel Rubello, Orvieto.

Another new kind of trumpet, which the Etruscans passed on to the Romans, was the *lituus*, recognizable by its bell bent backward, looking somewhat like an horizontal letter 'J.' Two early lituus actually survive: one Etruscan instrument (Rome, Villa Giulia Museum, Nr. 51216) and one Roman instrument (Rome, Museo Etrusco-Gregoriano, Room III).

---

[22] Like the Egyptians, the Etruscans believed that in the life after death the deceased would continue his same activities.

[23] *Ajax*, 16–17.

[24] *The Phoenician Woman*, 1377–1378.

[25] *Eumenides*, 567.

Before leaving the ancient Greeks we must mention an interesting appearance of the trumpet which music literature rarely mentions and that is the trumpet contests which began with the 96th Olympiad of 396 BC. These seem to have been more physical contests, rather than musical, and perhaps the modern Olympic motto, *citius, altius, fortius* (faster, higher, stronger) describes them well. We know the names of a few of the famous and the information about them reads like a description of sumo wrestlers. We are told, for example, that Heradorus of Megara consumed, in a typical meal, six pints of wheat bread, twenty pounds of meat and six quarts of wine! We also know of a women trumpeter who participated in these contests, Aglais, the daughter of Megacles. She wore a wig with a plume on her head and had an appetite similar to the male trumpeter, eating in a typical meal twelve pounds of meat, four pints of wheat bread and a pitcher of wine![26]

The earliest historical period of ancient Rome is known as the Republic (240–27 BC). Already in this early period we find accounts of the trumpet used throughout society. Varro (116–27 BC) quotes from a document which describes the trumpet being used for civic signal duty.

> Likewise in what pertains to those who have received from the censors the contract for the trumpeter who gives the summons to the centuriate assembly, they shall see to it that on that day, on which the assembly shall take place, the trumpeter shall sound the trumpet on the Citadel and around the walls.[27]

Similarly, Livy (59 BC–17 AD), mentions an instance of the trumpet being used together with the civic announcer, exactly as would become the custom in medieval Europe.

> The people took their seats for the show; and the herald advanced, in the customary fashion, with his trumpeter. He came into the middle of the arena where, according to usage, the festival is opened with a traditional formula. The trumpet call imposed silence; and then the herald made this pronouncement ...[28]

Another reference is to the night watchman, who, with his instrument, served as a surrogate clock. This is a common feature in descriptions of medieval civic life, but only in this single reference can we see that the tradition is much older. In this instance it is the instrumental signal given to announce impending dawn, which in the Middle Ages became the form of music known as the *aubade*.

> Now the fourth horn sings coming light,
> & the stars glide down seaward,

---

[26] Athenaeus, *Deipnosophistae*, X, 414.

[27] Marcus Varro, *On the Latin Language*, VI, 92. Varro, in Ibid., VI, 75 and VIII, 61, gives *tuba* for trumpet and *tubicines* for the players (*liticines* and *bucinator* for the other types of trumpet); *cornicines* for 'horn blowers'; *tibiae* for auloi and *tibicines* for the players; and *cithara* for lute.

[28] Livy, *History of Rome*, XXXIII, 32.

> I will search for sleep,
> search for you in dreams....[29]

This use of the trumpet as a kind of aural clock can perhaps also be seen in a reference by Tacitus to 'the dismissal of the guests by the sound of a trumpet.'[30] Trumpets also served to designate the beginning of activities ranging from the signal to begin construction work[31] and to lead processions into Rome.[32]

Another well-known medieval tradition which appears to be older than generally thought is the use of the trumpet player as a form of passport to accompany diplomats, as is implied in Horace's (65–8 BC) brief mention of 'trumpeting envoys.'[33]

Propertius (50–16 BC) mentions a use of the trumpet which is not found elsewhere in this early Roman literature, the use of the trumpet in the funeral ceremony.

> What dreams would my aulos sing to you then,
> aulos sadder than funeral trumpet [*tuba*]?[34]

Regarding the military trumpet, Horace mentions this type only twice, in the first instance acknowledging a certain popularity for the entire environment of this sort of music.

> Many people enjoy camps and the din of curved
> Trumpets in signal calls, warfare itself, indeed,
> By all mothers abhorred.[35]

For him, however, this kind of music was clearly too noisy. Let's not forget, he says, the softer arts.

> At times you deafen ears with the din and threat
> Of trumpet blasts, the bugles at times shrill forth ...
> And yet, pert Muse, you must not abandon jest
> And love song for the grief of a Cean dirge:
> Together in Dione's grotto
> Let us seek music of lighter poems.[36]

---

[29] Ibid., IV, 4. The third century BC inventor, Stesibius, made for Ptolemy's queen, Arsinoe, a water powered clock, with sounding trumpets.

[30] Tacitus, *The Annals* (New York: Modern Library, 1942), 373.

[31] Suetonius, *The Twelve Caesars* (New York: Penguin, 1989), 222 [the period of Nero].

[32] Ibid., 272 [period of Vitellius].

[33] Horace, *Odes*, IV, 4, 69.

[34] Propertius, *The Poems*, II, 7. The funeral trumpet is mentioned again in Poem, II, 13a.

[35] Horace, *Odes*, I, 1, 23.

[36] Ibid., II, 1.

Virgil mentions the military trumpet three times in his *Aeneid*, one of which is a curious reference to a 'hollow' trumpet.[37] More interesting is his attempt to describe the most ancient form of such trumpet signals. We feel, in this passage, a sense of the terror that primitive people must have felt in hearing the 'war horn,' as it is sometimes described.

> But the terrible goddess
> Had spied out the moment for further harm from her lofty
> Look-out and flew to the top of the stable and from that
> Summit she sang out the shepherd's signal: she blew
> A blast out of Tartarus on her curved horn. The deep woodlands
> And groves re-echoed and trembled. The lake of Diana
> Heard from afar; and Nar River, its stream white with sulfur,
> Heard it, and the springs of Velinus; and shuddering
> Mothers pressed children close to their breasts. Then swiftly
> Men ran when they heard the sound of the frightening horn.[38]

A poem by Propertius conveys a similar image as the 'frightening horn,' above, when we read, 'trumpeter, put away that wild music.'[39] One can understand how some of these poets expressed their opposition to war in general. Tibullus (55–19 BC), for example, wrote,

> What man, what devil, first conceived the sword?
>   shaper of iron, himself an iron heart,
>   begetter of battles on a innocent world,
>   marking new routes to death on mankind's chart! …
>   If I could choose an age, I would live in that one,
>   with no trumpet-call, no war's alarms and shocks.[40]

Finally, there is also a touching elegy by Propertius in honor of one, Marcellus, who drowned at Baiae, a resort on the Bay of Naples. As part of an interesting description of this town, Propertius writes,

> Where Misenus, Trojan trumpet player, lies sand-buried,
>   & Hercules' causeway booms in the ocean,
>   & where the cymbals rang for the Theban god
>   When he went auspiciously searching
>   through mortal cities.[41]

---

37 Virgil, *Aeneid*, III, 272. Also see VI, 246 and VII, 658, 664.

38 Ibid., VII, 511.

39 Propertius, *The Poems*, IV, 4.

40 Tibullus, *The Poems*, I, x.

41 Propertius, *The Poems*, III, 18. This may be a reference to a statue. Pliny the Elder (23–79 AD), in his *Natural History*, in the course of his discussion of art (XXXIV, xix, 88), also mentions a famous statue of the time called a 'Trumpet player' by Epigonus.

During the period of ancient Rome known as the Empire (14–476 AD), there are accounts of at least two leaders who played the trumpet. The Consul Lucius Flaccus (first century AD) was a diligent trumpet player, practicing daily it would appear.[42] The Emperor Elagabalus (205–222 AD) is recorded as having been a performer of the aulos and panpipes in religious-cult services honoring Baal and again during the ceremonies relative to his coronation. He also performed on the trumpet, lute, water organ and sang.

Calpurnius Siculus, a first-century Roman poet, has left us a lengthy poem, rich in musical detail, which is an example of an ode in honor of, and intended to please, the emperor Nero. This poem expresses a dislike for the more hostile trumpet,

> *Amyntas*
>
> There's peace by his permission on my hills, and thanks
> To him, look, no one stops me if I like to sing
> Or foot the slow grass thrice, and I can play for dances
> And I can keep my songs in writing on green bark
> And snarling trumpets no more deafen our reed-pipes.[43]

References continue to be found for the use of the trumpet for a variety of purposes. In 284 AD Carinus presented a series of plays in which he used, among other things, one hundred trumpeters and one hundred horn players.[44] Pliny the Younger (first century AD), while making the point that many soldiers were ordinary men who had never seen battle, adds that many of them had never heard a trumpet except in the theater.[45]

Juvenal mentions trumpets in a civic procession[46] and there was also music used for entertainment in the games in the arena. A first-century mosaic in the amphitheater at Zliten shows a trumpet player and two cornu players performing while two gladiators engage in combat.

We must assume that music continued to play an important role in the celebration of the religious-cult ceremonies. An excellent example of three trumpets participating in an offering procession can be seen in the first-century altarpiece in the Museo del Vaticano, Belvedere, Rome. And we conclude with another reference to the trumpeter in these cult offering ceremonies. Once, while sacrificing,

> Tiberius took an erotic fancy to the acolyte who carried the incense casket, and could hardly wait for the ceremony to end before hurrying him and his brother, the sacred trumpeter, out of the temple and indecently assaulting them both. When they jointly protested at this disgusting behavior he had their legs broken.[47]

No one ever said the life of a trumpet player was easy!

---

[42] Sendrey, *Music in the Social and Religious Life of Antiquity*, 391.

[43] Calpurnius Siculus, *Eclogue* IV.

[44] Sendrey, *Music in the Social and Religious Life of Antiquity*, 412.

[45] *The Letters of the Younger Pliny* (New York: Penguin, 1985, 64.

[46] *Satire* X, 44.

[47] Suetonius, *The Twelve Caesars*, 136.

PART 2
IN MEDIEVAL EUROPE

On the Medieval Trumpet

EVERY READER WILL RECALL those Old Testament passages which cry, 'Praise the Lord with the Trumpet,' not to mention one passage which says God himself was a trumpet player.[1] Why then does this instrument disappear in the New Testament? Perhaps, in view of the hostile comments toward instrumental music in general which we find expressed in the views of the early Church fathers, we should not be surprised. We must also remember, of course, that during much of the first two centuries the Christians were an underground organization holding secret church services. Obviously, if one wishes to hold a secret service, it is not in one's interest to have trumpets playing and cymbals crashing.[2]

Nevertheless, it seems odd that an instrument like the trumpet, an instrument so much a part of every ancient culture, should be entirely absent in this book. Actually, the word appears, but there is no description of an actual person playing the trumpet. It is played by angels (once a septet of angels!),[3] once by God,[4] once as the 'last trumpet' of Judgment Day,[5] once it is heard from City of God,[6] once as a symbol of God's loud voice,[7] and when God will destroy Babylon—then we will finally be rid of all these trumpeters, harp players, flute players, and 'minstrels.'[8]

Christianity was well established by the eighth century in Britain and several extant poems are on its themes. The most popular image was the Day of Judgment, when, as one poem tells us 'A horn is never sounded so loudly or a trumpet blown, but that the word of the Lord, that clear voice, is not louder to men all over the world.'[9] Musically it is going to be quite a day, according to these poets, for one tells us that on this day angels shall sound their trumpets from the four corners of the earth.

> Then from the world's four corners,
> from the uttermost regions of the realm of earth,
> resplendent angels shall loudly, with one accord,
> sound their trumpets, and mid-earth shall quake,
> and the region under men. Boldly and gloriously

---

[1] Zechariah 9:14.

[2] Nowhere is this more evident than in Salzburg where one can still visit a church carved out inside a mountain by early Christians as a means of achieving secrecy.

[3] Matthew 24:31 and Revelation 8:02.

[4] 1 Thessalonians 4:16.

[5] 1 Corinthians 15:52.

[6] Hebrews 12:19.

[7] Revelation 10:10.

[8] Revelation 18:22. 'Flute' players here, of course, mean auloi.

[9] 'The Day of Judgment,' in *The Exeter Book* (Oxford University Press, 1958), II, xxii, 109ff.

shall they blow together toward the stars' career,
and sing and chant from south and north,
from east and west, o'er all creation.[10]

Several poems describe musical instruments and among these is a charming riddle song which describes an instrument which the reader will surely guess.

I was an armed warrior. Now a gallant young bachelor
covers me with gold and silver,
with twisted wires. Sometimes men kiss me,
Sometimes, by means of my sound, I summon
good comrades to battle. Sometimes a horse
carries me over the march. Sometimes the steed of the sea
bears me, bright with ornaments, over the waves.
Sometimes a woman, ring-adorned,
fills my bosom. Sometimes I must lie stripped,
hard and headless, on the boards of a table.
Sometimes, decked with trappings, and beautiful,
I hang on the wall where men are drinking.
Sometimes warriors carry me on horseback,
a noble ornament in an army, when, treasure-adorned,
I must swallow the breath from some one's breast.
Sometimes, by means of my notes, I invite
gallant men to their wine. Sometimes, by my voice,
I must rescue from foes what has been stolen
and put enemies to flight. Discover what I am called.[11]

The remaining references to music in this poem deal with the use of the primitive trumpet. There must have been some form of music played by this instrument which represented a specific noble, as an aural representation in the way a coat of arms would be a visual symbol. In the following passage the noble is clearly recognized by the music of his personal trumpet.

But rescue came
with dawn of day for those desperate men
when they heard the horn of Hygelac sound,
tones of his trumpet.[12]

There is a similar reference to the use of the trumpets as an aural coat of arms in a song by the Minnesinger, Ulrich von Liechtenstein. It is clear here that the trumpets play an actual melody for this purpose.

---

[10] 'Christ,' Ibid, I, i, 878ff.
[11] Riddle 14, describing a primitive trumpet, Ibid., II.
[12] 'Beowulf,' trans. Francis Gummere in *Epic and Saga*, vol. 49, *The Harvard Classics* (New York: Collier), XL.

> My buglers played a melody,
> a pretty tune in a treble key,
> and thus they told all people near
> that I was shortly to appear.[13]

Towns and cities take on a stronger sense of identity during later centuries of the Middle Ages, as is found expressed in many new civic institutions. It was this period in which the watch towers were built on city walls everywhere and musicians hired to serve as both watchmen[14] and surrogate clocks during hours of darkness. These civic musicians were also available to perform a wide variety of official entertainment music and official civic duties, including playing for public punishment of the guilty. It is no surprise, therefore, to find trumpet players listed in some of the earliest civic lists of civic musicians, such as civic 'trombe e i corni' in Milan in 1121.[15]

One soon begins to find a wide variety of other appearances by these musicians. They are always to be found following the town crier around as he makes his announcements. Such a civic trumpet player is mentioned in a twelfth-century poem by the Goliard poet known as Archpoet of Cologne.

> Rumor, with its trumpet blowing
> Mid the heralds' voices glowing
> Tells the people far and wide
> That a virtuous man has nighed,
> Friend of peace and champion;
> In Vienne there is a throne
> Which for him the peers prepare.
> Crowds of players rend the air
> Making ready tune on tune,
> Many kinds of jongleurs soon
> Enter, waiting not a week.
> Largess they and presents seek.[16]

Departure ceremonies were equally important occasions for music. A typical example is given by Matthew Paris who describes the papal legate leaving England in 1241, 'in great pomp, amidst the sound of trumpets.'[17]

---

[13] Ulrich von Liechtenstein, *In Service of Ladies*, trans. J. W. Thomas (Chapel Hill: The University of North Carolina Press, 1969), lines 580ff.

[14] A famous anecdote tells of a tower musician blowing a warning on his trumpet on the approach of the Tartar hordes in 1241. In the middle of the fanfare a Tartar arrow pierced his throat and the fanfare was left unfinished. This fanfare is reproduced in S. Mizawa, *Nicholas Copernicus* (New York, 1943), 73.

[15] Bernardino Corio, *L'Historia di Milano volgarmente scritta* (Padoa, 1646), 57.

[16] 'Fama tuba dante sonum,' in Edwin H. Zeydel, *Vagabond Verse* (Detroit: Wayne State University Press, 1966), 251.

[17] Matthew Paris, *English History*, trans. J. A. Giles (London: Bohn, 1852), I, 319.

We have an interesting eyewitness account of the Doge leaving Venice to accompany the Fourth Crusade to the sound of two hundred trumpets. Pictured here are both the personal musicians of the Doge, together with those of the city itself.

> The Doge of Venice had with him fifteen galleys, all at his own cost. The galley wherein he himself was, was all vermilion-colored, and it had a pavilion stretched above it of vermilion samite, and there were four silver trumpets which sounded before him, and timbrels that made a most joyful noise …
> And when the fleet set forth from the haven of Venice … it was the goodliest thing to behold that ever hath been since the beginning of the world. For there were full an hundred pair of trumpets, both silver and brass, which all sounded for the departure, and so many timbrels and tabors and other instruments that it was a fair marvel to hear.[18]

The Emperor Frederick II returned from his Crusade with a number of Arabic slaves, including some young trumpet players who performed at meal times.

> He selected Negro boys between sixteen and twenty to form a musical corps; they were magnificently clad and taught to blow large and small silver trumpets.[19]

An eyewitness to the marriage of Henry III of England, in 1236, mentions the royal musicians in a performance which he regarded as musically unusual. It is one of many cases where we wish the early scribe had gone into more detail.

> … preceded by the king's trumpeters and with horns sounding, so that such a wonderful novelty struck all who beheld it with astonishment.[20]

There are, of course, many references to the use of trumpets in battle during this period, but usually little detail is given. A typical example portrays the citizens of Milan as they await an invasion by Frederick I, 'Barbarossa.'

> When the emperor went his rounds, tumult arose in the city in expectation of an assault. There was great trepidation; signals sounded, trumpets blew, the strong took up arms, women and feeble old men took to lamentation.[21]

A similar reference to the trumpet played in battle is found in the English classic, 'Beowulf.'

> These started away,
> swollen and savage that song to hear,
> that war-horn's blast.[22]

---

[18] 'Li estoires de chiaus qui conquisent Coustantinoble' [1216], quoted in 'La Chronique de Rains,' Edward Stone, trans., *Three Old French Chronicles of the Crusades* (Seattle: The University of Washington Press, 1939), 179.

[19] Ernst Kantorowicz, *Frederick the Second*, trans. E. O. Lorimer (New York, 1957), 312.

[20] Paris, *English History*, I, 8.

[21] Otto of Freising, *The Deeds of Frederick Barbarossa*, III, xlii, trans. Charles Mierow (New York: Columbia University Press, 1953), 216.

[22] 'Beowulf,' XXI.

Some of the most interesting eye-witness accounts of medieval trumpet playing are in association with the crusades. It might be appropriate here to remind the reader that Arabic historians identify the trumpet of the Saracens at this time as *anafir*, from which comes the word, 'fanfare.'

The Romances and poems of the twelfth and thirteenth centuries contain many dramatic accounts of trumpets. The famous poem, 'The Song of Roland,' is especially rich in the description of this kind of music. We find here trumpets whose sound is sometimes described as 'blare,'[23] but sometimes as 'clear-voiced.'[24] This certainly seems to suggest two different instruments, one perhaps a more primitive horn-type and the other the metallic instrument from the East.

We are told the trumpets were placed before and after the troops,[25] no doubt in order to insure the various signals would be heard by all. The descriptions of massed trumpets provide a few more clues to the sound of these instruments. When one thousand trumpets played a signal, to add 'more splendor,' it was nevertheless described as a deafening noise.[26] When seven thousand play 'sound the charge, the din is great throughout the countryside.'[27] When sixty thousand play, it created a 'blare so loud, the mountains ring, the valleys echo back.'[28] Is sixty thousand trumpets an exaggeration? Not by much, if one accepts the calculation here of more than three hundred thousand troops[29] and one remembers that it was crucial to the battle plan that every soldier be in range of hearing the signals being played by primitive instruments. Layamon's Romance, 'Brut' also mentions sixty thousand trumpets playing together, causing the ground to tremble.[30] Let us admit some literary exaggeration, but at a time when the loudest sound one might have heard was a small church organ, the aural phenomenon of battle field trumpets must have been impressive.

The central figure of this poem, Roland, a nephew to Charlemagne, plays an ivory trumpet called an oliphant. The descriptions of Roland playing this instrument are among the most remarkable in the early literature of the trumpet, reading like a personification of one of those trumpet players, their faces flushed with emotion, painted on the Sistine ceiling by Michelangelo.

> Count Roland brought the horn up to his mouth:
> he sets it firmly, blows with all his might.

---

23 'The Song of Roland,' trans. Robert Harrison (New York: Mentor, 1970), line 2116.

24 Ibid., 2150, 3194, 3309, and 3523.

25 Ibid., 1832.

26 Ibid., 1005.

27 Ibid., 1454.

28 Ibid., 2111.

29 Ibid., 3019ff.

30 Robert Wace, *Roman de Brut*, trans. Gwyn Jones (London: Dent, 1962), 253.

In producing this mighty blast, which we are told could be heard more than seventy miles away,[31] his temple burst!

> Count Roland, racked with agony and pain
> and great chagrin, now sounds his ivory horn:
> bright blood leaps in a torrent from his mouth:
> the temple has been ruptured in his brain.
> The horn he holds emits a piercing blast:
> Charles hears it as he crosses through the pass …
>
> Count Roland's mouth is filling up with blood;
> the temple has been ruptured in his brain.
> In grief and pain he sounds the oliphant;
> Charles hears it, and his Frenchmen listen, too.
> The king says then, 'That horn is long of wind.'[32]

Finally, there is an unusual reference to a real player we should have liked to have heard. He was described as a religious trumpeter who was responsible for a moment of religious fanaticism in 1233 known as the 'Great Hallelujah!' This man wore a black beard, a high Armenian cap, and a sack-like robe with a red cross on front and back. He played a copper trumpet from which he produced 'now sweet, now terrifying sounds.' When he played people followed him and when he arrived in a market place or public square it was said,

> all anmosities were suddenly forgotten, and a time of happiness and joy began; knights and people, citizens and peasants struck up hymns and songs in praise of God; people fell on each other's necks, and there was no wrath, no strife, no confusion: only Love and Peace.[33]

Some trumpet player!

---

[31] 'The Song of Roland,' 1756 ('30 leagues').
[32] Ibid., 1761ff.
[33] Kantorowicz, *Frederick the Second*, 397.

On the Jongleur

To tramp long miles in wind and rain, to stand wet to the skin and hungry and footsore, making the slow bourgeois laugh while the heart was bitter within ... And at the end to die like a dog in a ditch, under the ban of the Church and with the prospect of eternal damnation before the soul.[1]

THE ABOVE DESCRIPTION would have been familiar to a great many of the wandering musicians of Europe during the Middle Ages. History pays little attention to these poor nameless musicians who, in fact, accomplished a remarkable feat. As these wandering musicians traveled back and forth across Europe for one thousand years, trading repertoire and instruments as they went, they unified the musical culture. Had it not been for them, one traveling across Europe today might find the music changing with the borders as fundamentally as do the language and the food.

During the latter part of the fourth century AD, as the effective protection of the Roman Empire was evaporating and the 'barbarians,' the German tribes, the Huns and Goths began to flood into Central and Southern Europe, the first period of mass migration on the continent began. As the people of Europe began to pass from region to region, they were accompanied by a broad range of entertainers and fellow travelers, including jugglers, story-tellers, actors and performers of magic. Foremost among them were musicians, the earliest of whom we call the 'jongleur.'

While the early scribes were not too precise in their use of terms, the earliest form of Jongleur appears to be the medieval Latin, *Ioculator*, 'one who makes merry.' From this is derived *jouglere* and *jougleur* in French, *joglar* in Provencal and *jugelour*, *jugelere* and *jogeler* in English. In Germany, by about the eighth century, one finds a new term, *Spielmann*, which is also used first in a generic sense. Among the Nordic nations there were *scaldes*, an order associated with nobles as was the *Scops* of Germany. The Nordic *gliman* (*gleeman* in English) was specifically an actor or story-teller.

In general, although, as we have indicated, the scribes were careless, one should associate the term jongleur with the early Middle Ages and the term minstrel with the later Middle Ages. The later minstrel was specifically a musician and before 1550 almost exclusively a wind instrument player.[2] Other musicians were called 'voice-minstrel' (singer) or 'string-minstrel.'

The jongleur, on the other hand, was more of a general entertainer, not the specialist which appears later. Thus the 'resume' of an early jongleur reads,

---

[1] E.K. Chambers, *The Mediaeval Stage* (Oxford, 1903), I, 48, on the early wandering musician.

[2] In the inventories and pay-records of cities, courts and church very few string instruments appear before 1550.

> I can play the lute, vielle, pipe, bagpipe, panpipes, harp, fiddle, guittern, symphony, psaltery, organistrum, organ, tabor and the rote. I can sing a song well, and make tales to please young ladies, and can play the gallant for them if necessary. I can throw knives into the air and catch them without cutting my fingers. I can jump rope most extraordinary and amusing. I can balance chairs, and make tables dance. I can somersault and walk doing a handstand.[3]

Along with all these entertainment skills, the jongleur first had to master a number of musical instruments, as the reader has seen in the 'resume' above. Another 'resume,' this by a thirteenth-century French jongleur, again includes a number of instruments.

> I am a jongleur of the viele
> I know the muse, and the fretele
> And the harp, and the chifonie,
> And the gigue and the armonie:
> And I know how to sing well
> A melody on the salteire and rote.[4]

But, even by the late Middle Ages, the true wandering musician still had to depend on broad skills of entertainment to supplement his musicianship. A twelfth-century treatise, *Enseignamens*, warns the jongleur that he must be prepared to 'learn the arts of imitating birds, throwing knives, leaping through hoops, showing off performing asses and dogs, and dangling marionettes.'[5] One passage in 'The Romance of the Rose' is surely a testimonial to the broad talents some of these jongleurs possessed.

> Then with uplifted voice he sweetly sings,
> Expressing all his happy-heartedness,
> In place of masses, pretty chansonettes
> Of lovers' secrets; and the instruments,
> Of which he many owned, he makes resound
> Till one had thought the gods were back on earth.
> More skilled are his hands upon the strings
> Than Theban Amphion's fingers ever were;
> Zithers and harps, lutes and guitars he played.
> He had constructed clever chiming clocks,
> The artful wheels of which ran ceaselessly—
> Organs which could be carried in one hand,
> Which he himself not only blows and plays
> But sings to their accompaniment sweet
> Full-voiced motets in tenor or treble strains.
> Then each in turn he sounds, and plays with care
> Cymbals and pipes and fifes and tambourines,
> Timbrels and shalmes and flutes and psalteries,

---

[3] Anonymous, quoted in Howard D. McKinney and W. R. Anderson, *Music in History* (Boston, 1940), 170.

[4] 'Les Deux Bourdeurs Ribauds,' in E. Faral, ed., *Mimes Francais du XIII siecle* (Paris, 1910), 101.

[5] Quoted in Chambers, *The Mediaeval Stage*, I, 53.

> Bagpipes and trumpets, Cornish pipes and viols.
> See how he capers, dances, clogs, and trips,
> Cuts pigeonwings the whole length of the hall …[6]

Joinville, an important historian of the thirteenth century, observed an extraordinary example of musicians finding it necessary to extend their skills.

> When they began to play their trumpets you would have thought it was the voice of swans coming from the water, and they produced the sweetest and most gracious melodies, a marvel to hear. And these same minstrels did wonderful acrobatic feats. A towel was put under their feet and, holding themselves rigid, they turned a complete somersault, their feet returning to the towel. Two of them turned their heads to face behind them, and the eldest also, and when he turned it round again he crossed himself, for he was afraid of breaking his neck in the act of turning.[7]

How were these wandering musicians paid? On occasion, usually playing for a great aristocratic wedding where a noble wished to impress his guests with his liberal spending, they received actual coins. But, with their broad geographical experience, they seemed to know the real value of these coins.

> For in these Poitevin coins is little value:
> Greedy and parsimonious were they who had them struck.
> Never give them to a gentle minstrel.[8]

If they were lucky enough to attend these grand aristocratic celebrations they probably also had the rare experience of eating well.

> They get plenty of venison of deer and wild boar,
> And also cranes, wild geese, and peacocks seasoned with pepper;
> Wine and clary are gushing forth in abundance;
> The jongleurs are singing and playing the vielle and the rote.[9]

Most often the aristocrats thought it appropriate to pay them with cast-away clothes.

> We have seen princes who after having spent twenty or thirty marks on splendid garments wonderfully embroidered, have given them a week later to minstrels.[10]

But for the homeless, wandering musician, good clothes in the Winter were probably worth more than money. There must have been many who were in great need in this regard.

---

[6] Guillaume de Lorris and Jean de Meun, 'The Romance of the Rose,' trans. Harry Robbins (New York: Dutton, 1962), XCVII, 153ff. The work of de Meun begins with Chapter XX.

[7] Quoted in Fr. Funck-Brentano, *The Middle Ages* (New York, 1923), 184–185.

[8] Huon de Bordeaux, quoted in Ibid., 190.

[9] 'Pilgrimage of Charlemagne to Jerusalem,' [ca. 1115], in *The Journey of Charlemagne*, trans. Jean-Louis Picherit (Birmingham, AL: Summa, 1984), 36. A similar description is found in the 'Song of Rainoart,' lines 2249–2250.

[10] Quoted in Funck-Brentano, *The Middle Ages*, 186.

> But quite often in his shirt
> Was exposed to wind and blast.[11]

And having clothes perhaps caused some jealousy, as seems to be implied in a description of troubadours by Piere d'Alvernhe.

> And the sixth, Grimoart Gausmar,
> a knight who tries to pass for a jongleur,
> and whoever agrees to let him could not do worse,
> God damn whoever gives him clothing of motley and green,
> for once his costume has been seen,
> a hundred more will want to be jongleurs.[12]

And even if he had sufficient clothes, he sometimes had to leave them with an inn keeper for payment of food.

> When he has got together sous three, four, five,
> Into the tavern he soon goes
> And feasts with it while it lasts.
> And when he has tasted the good wine,
> And the landlord sees he has spent all:
> 'Brother,' says he, 'seek another inn,
> Give me pledge of what you owe.'
> And he leaves with him his hose and shoes.[13]

Toward the late Middle Ages the wandering musicians began to specialize, according to their skill, and the result was the appearance of various levels of social status. At the top were those singers who seem to have taken over the role of epic poetry, singing tales of the past heroes and their exploits. One clue to their social status can be seen in their robes of six colors, surpassed only by kings, who had seven. Lords were entitled to five, governors of fortresses four, officers and gentlemen three, soldiers two, and common people only one color.[14] This poet-musician, Gibbon says,

> Sung in the front of battle, excited their courage, and justified their depredations; and the songster claimed for his legitimate prize the fairest heifer of the spoil.[15]

---

[11] De Saint Pierre de du jongleur, quoted in Ibid., 190.

[12] 'Cantarai d'aquestz trobadors,' quoted in Frederick Goldin, *Lyrics of the Troubadours and Trouveres* (Garden City: Anchor Books, 1973), 171.

[13] Le Moniage Guillaume, quote in Ibid.

[14] Edmondstoune Duncan, *The Story of Minstrelsy* (Detroit: Singing Tree Press, 1968), 4.

[15] Edward Gibbon, *The History of the Decline and Fall of the Roman Empire* (Philadelphia: Coates), III, 359.

In the Romances of Marie de France, the source for the narrative itself is usually attributed to a jongleur. In one of these, the 'Lay of Gugemar,' which she recalled as, 'fair is that song and sweet the tune,' contains some interesting information about these singers. She describes these songs as being sung by the fireplace and she makes the aesthetic observation that 'the singer must be wary not to spoil good music with unseemly words.'[16] Then she digresses to speak of criticism, observing that the best singers are the most criticized.

> But this is the way of the world, that when a man or woman sings more tunably than his fellows, those about the fire fall upon him, pell-mell, for reason of their envy. They rehearse diligently the faults of his song, and steal away his praise with evil words. I will brand these folk as they deserve. They, and such as they, are like mad dogs—cowardly and felon—who traitorously bring to death men better than themselves.

One jongleur who similarly sings epic tales, we find in 'The Song of William,' one of the oldest of the *Chansons de geste*. This jongleur seems to have been valued as much for his sword as for his music.

> Howbeit, a jongleur hath William my lord;
> In all France no singer so good will ye find,
> Nor a hardier dealer of blows with the sword.
> All the songs of history hath he in mind:
> Of Clovis, first of the Frankish kings
> Who in God our Lord and Ruler believed,
> Of Flovent his son, the fighter, he sings,
> Who from him the rule of sweet France received,
> Of all the kings of warlike renown
> Clean to Pepin, the short but valiant, down;
> Of Charlemagne, Roland his nephew dear,
> Of Girart and of Oliver the peer:
> My lord's kinsmen these and his forbears.
> Right worthily my lord's love he shares.
> Since in him he'th a singer so prized by us
> And in combat a vassal victorious,
> He bringeth him back from the battle thus.[17]

A twelfth-century biography of the Englishman, Hereward the Wake, tells of a jongleur singing not praises, but verses of an abusive nature about this noble. Unfortunately for the jongleur, Hereward enters the hall unexpectedly and hears this performance.

---

[16] Marie de France, *French Mediaeval Romances from the Lays of Marie de France*, trans. Eugene Mason (London: Dent, 1924), 3.

[17] 'La Chancun de Guillelme,' in *The Song of William*, trans. Edward Stone (Seattle: University of Washington Press, 1951), CXXXII.

> Eventually unable to tolerate this any longer, Hereward leapt out and struck him through with a single blow of his sword, and then turned to attack the guests. Some were incapable of rising because they were drunk, and others unable to go to their help because they were unarmed. So he laid low fourteen of them ... and set their heads over the gate.[18]

A few individual jongleurs survive the negligence of history for their single accomplishments. One was a jongleur who guided Charlemagne over Mt. Cenis in 773 AD and was then given as a reward all the land over which his *tuba* [trumpet] could be heard when played from a hill.[19] For some we even know their names, such as one, Beldgabred, who 'surpassed all the musicians of ancient times, both in harmony and in playing every kind of musical instrument, so that he was called the god of minstrels.'[20]

When William the Conqueror made his historic voyage in 1066 to conqueror England, he was accompanied by a famous jongleur named Taillefer. It is recalled that Taillefer led the army in the Battle of Hastings, singing heroic tales of Roland, Charlemagne, and Roncesvalles.[21] In the famous *Domesday Book*, of 1086, a census taken at the request of William the Conqueror, we find the name of one of his jongleurs, Berdic, as well as a female jongleur named Adelinda, who was in the service of Earl Roger.[22]

A jongleur, named Rahere (d. 1144), in the employ of Henry I of England, retired and donated the money to build St. Bartholomew's Hospital in London. We also know the name of Cerveri de Girona, head of the musicians under Pedro III (1276–1285) of Aragon.[23]

A few jongleurs appear to have become literate, speaking well and capable of writing. Lull describes one of these:

> It happened one day that, while a certain Cardinal was dining, there came to his court a jongleur who was very well arrayed and adorned; he was a man of pleasing speech and personable, and he sang and played upon instruments very skillfully.[24]

---

[18] Richard of Ely, 'The Life of Hereward the Wake,' in *Three Lives of the Last Englishmen*, trans. Michael Swanton (New York: Garland Publishing, 1984), 63.

[19] Chambers, *The Mediaeval Stage*, I, 37, fn. 2.

[20] Geoffrey of Monmouth, *The History of the Kings of Britain*, trans. Lewis Thorpe (Baltimore: Penguin Books, 1966), 105.

[21] Wace (d. 1170), *Roman de Brut*.

> Taillefer, ki mult bien chantout,
> Sor un cheval ki tost alout,
> Devant le duc alout chantant
> De Karlegaigne et de Rolant
> Et d'Oliver de des vassals
> Qui morurent en Rencevals.

[22] Chambers, *The Mediaeval Stage*, I, 43–44.

[23] M. Balthasar Saldoni, *Diccionario biografio-bibliografico de Efemèrides de musicos españoles*, I, 334.

[24] *Libre d'Evast e d'Aloma e de Banquerna*, quoted in Christopher Page, *Voices and Instruments of the Middle Ages* (London: Dent, 1987), 181.

Another, one who could write, has left us a very important historical document involving the discovery of Richard I, of England, who was captured on his return from the Third Crusade and was being held captive by Austria for debts owed. He was discovered by Blondel, a fellow member of an aristocratic singing society in England, who heard Richard singing an art song known only to members of this society. In the following version of this tale, written by a jongleur of Reims in 1260, we are told Blondel found a castle which reportedly held a distinguished prisoner. He offered himself as a jongleur to work in the castle, as a means of discovering the identity of the prisoner. The knight in charge of the castle 'said he would keep him gladly.'

> Then was Blondel right glad, and he went and fetched his viol and his other instruments. And he continued to serve the castellan and pleased him well. And he was on good terms with them of the castle and with all the household. So Blondel abode there all that winter; yet never could he find out who the prisoner was, until one day in Eastertide he went all alone into a garden that adjoined the tower. And he looked about him and bethought himself if by any chance he might see the prisoner. And while he was yet thinking of this, the king looked out through a loophole and espied Blondel. And he took thought how he might make himself known to him. Then did he bethink himself of a song that the two of them had made betwixt them, which none other knew save they two. So began he to sing the first words thereof, loud and clear (for he sang passing well); and when Blondel heard him, then knew he of a surety that this was his lord. And he had in his heart the greatest joy that ever yet he had had in all his days. Straightway he left the garden and went into his own chamber, where he slept; and he took his viol and began to play a strain, and as he played he rejoiced over his lord whom he had found.[25]

By the late Middle Ages the better of the wandering jongleurs were being hired by town governments, thereby enjoying an improved social status by moving from beggar to civic official. Ramon Lull, in 1272, now lists the social status of musicians as being above painters, farm laborers, and artisans, but below the other professions, merchants, and seamen.[26]

Individual noblemen were also hiring the better jongleurs they could find and Lull complains that while the poor shiver in rags outside the palace door, the musicians are clothed in royal clothing.

The monks also needed entertainment and by the thirteenth century one begins to see frequent payment, or food and shelter, to jongleurs for performance in individual monasteries and priories, particularly in those of the Augustinian and Benedictine orders.[27] An attractive story says that in 1224 a Benedictine house in England received with joy two visitors assumed by their dress to be jongleurs. When it was discovered the two visitors were only visiting friars, they threw them out!

---

[25] 'La Chronique de Rains,' quoted in Edward Stone, trans., *Three Old French Chronicles of the Crusades* (Seattle: The University of Washington Press, 1939), 275.

[26] J. N. Hillgarth, *The Spanish Kingdoms* (Oxford, 1976), I, 46ff. Lull nevertheless grumbles that he finds no king who rules as he should, few judges not corrupted by gold, and few jongleurs who will not lie for money.

[27] Chambers, *The Mediaeval Stage*, I, 56.

The Church itself rarely welcomed the jongleur, whom they saw as a homeless, wandering vagrant. One twelfth-century reference reads,

> And of the organ alone the church has made use of in various kinds of singing ... other instruments being commonly rejected because of the abuses of the jongleurs.[28]

In the condemnation by some Churchmen, we learn some interesting details of these musicians and their activities. Lull, in a long anecdote, criticized a jongleur who, for a small fee, praises a knight.[29] It appears the jongleurs had a bad reputation for performing such services, for we also find this mentioned by John of Salisbury. He associates musicians in general ('Apollo') with 'empty praises like unto wind instruments' and says these players 'seldom or never are caught praising a man for that which is truly his own.'[30]

Such criticism during the late Middle Ages describes not the musician now employed by court or town, but the remaining true wandering musicians. It is this somewhat questionable musician that Ramon Lull describes in his following prayer:

> How one should be wary of the doings of jongleurs
>
> The art of the jongleurs, Lord, began in praising and in glorifying you, and it was for that purpose that instruments were invented, and dances and songs and new melodies with which men rejoice in you.
>
> But, as we may now see, Lord, in our time all the art of the jongleurs is changed, for those who apply themselves to playing upon instruments, to dancing and to composing neither sing, nor play their instruments, nor compose poems or songs save on the subject of lust and the vanity of this world.
>
> Such jongleurs, Lord, as play upon instruments and sing of wantonness, praising in their singing such things as are not worthy of praise; such are damned, for they pervert the art of the jongleurs away from the purpose for which it was founded in the beginning. But those jongleurs, Lord, who rejoice and take delight with their instruments, dances and songs in your praise, love and goodness are blessed, for they preserve the art of the jongleurs as it was first established ...
>
> If Mankind could only beware of, Lord, the evil which ensues from jongleurs and composers and how their songs and instruments are wretched and useless things, then these jongleurs and composers would not be so readily welcomed and accepted as they are.
>
> Through the instruments that the jongleurs play and the new poems which they compose and sing, through the new dances that they devise and the things which they say, your goodness is forgotten, Lord ...
>
> Might and virtue, holiness, greatness and blessedness and nobility may be known to be in you, Lord, for I greatly desire that you might see true jongleurs who praise those things which are to be praised and decry those things which are to be decried; and I further desire that no man should be able either to compose, sing, or play any instrument if he be not a servant and jongleur of true love and true worth, and a subject and lover of truth ...

---

28 Gilles de Zamore, 'Ars Musica,' in Martin Gerbert, *Scriptores ecclesiastici de musica sacra* (Saint Blaise, 1784), II, 388.

29 *Felix*, Book VIII, in *Selected Works of Ramon Lull*, trans. Anthony Bonner (Princeton University Press, 1985), II, 863.

30 *Policraticus*, in *The Statesman's Book of John of Salisbury*, 269–271.

> Lord, True God, who became incarnate in Our Lady Saint Mary so that you might renew the race of Mankind! We see, Lord, that jongleurs dance, sing and sound instruments before men, so that they move them to joy and pleasure with their singing and dancing and with the instruments which they play …
>
> Since jongleurs, Lord, through the art and skill which they possess, can harmonize the music, dances and songs which they perform on their instruments with the music which they imagine in their hearts, how does this wonder come about that they do not know how to open their hearts to praise you?

The troubadour, Giraut de Borneil (1165–1211), provides a description of one of the less desirable jongleurs:

> Cardaillac, they tell me that you are coming in search of a sirventes with which to earn yourself some money; but before the door-keeper lets you in I want you to thank me from a distance, for your breath is rather bad and you are apt to come too close. This is why a man is better off sending you a few pence rather than waiting for you to approach; for he suffers great torment if he does not turn away his face or cover his nose.[31]

Another autobiographical reference, in a song by the troubadour Raimbaut d'Orange (1150–1173), is typical of several which seem to use the ancient term for the wandering musician, 'jongleur,' as synonymous with 'troubadour.'

> Jongleur they call me, I go singing
> mad with love, in courtly ways.[32]

Our reading, however, suggests that one should consider the jongleur as basically still a wondering musician, whereas the troubadour tended to be employed in the courts of the aristocrats. The Goliards, on the other hand, were wandering clerics, called by one scholar the 'ecclesiastical equivalent of jongleurs,'[33] and indeed the song of one of them suggests the same impoverished existence.

> I, a cleric on the loose,
> Given to tribulation,
> Am for toil and travail born,
> Poverty's my ration.
>
> For the arts and literature
> I possess a yearning,
> Still, my indigence compels
> Me to cease from learning.
>
> All my clothing that I wear,
> Frail it is and torn;

---

31 'Cardaillac, per un sirventes,' in Ruth Sharman, *The Cansos and Sirventes of the Troubadour Giraut de Borneil* (Cambridge: Cambridge University Press, 1989), 401.

32 'Escotatz, mas no say,' in Goldin, *Lyrics of the Troubadores and Trouveres*, 181.

33 George Whicher, *The Goliard Poets* (George Whicher, 1949), 4.

> Oftentimes I suffer cold
> Since of warmth I'm shorn ...
>
> Take St. Martin's attitude,
> Never mean or shoddy,
> Give the pilgrim-scholar clothes,
> Cover up his body.[34]

By the fourteenth century there are few references to the jongleur, such as that found in an early miracle play, 'La Nonne qui Laissa son Abbaie,' where there is a brief discussion of the jongleurs performing in the castle.[35] Basically, their day had passed and it is sad that we see them referred to in Italy as *buffoni uomini del corte* ('buffoon men about the court').

---

34 'Exul ego clericus,' in *Vagabond Verse*, trans. Edwin H. Zeydel (Detroit: Wayne State University Press, 1966), 73.

35 'La Nonne qui laissa son abbaie,' ed. Nigel Wilkins in *Two Miracles* (Edinburgh: Scottish Academic Press, 1972), lines 727ff.

On the Minstrel

A STREET IN PARIS in the thirteenth century, *rue de Jugleeurs*, was renamed in the fourteenth century, *rue des Menetriers*.[1] This change reflected the fact that the name 'jongleur' had, during the late Middle Ages, been giving way to a new name, 'minstrel.'[2] The medieval minstrel was primarily a wind instrument player, as can be documented not only in extensive medieval iconography but also by the names formed from it, such as *menetrier de bouche* ('mouth minstrel,' or singer) and *menetrier de cordes* ('string minstrel'). Medieval literature also confirms this, as we see in an English scribe:

> For the most parte all maner minstrelsy
> By wynde they delyver thyr sound chefly.[3]

Whereas the medieval jongleur was a general entertainer, who also had musical skills, the minstrel was primarily a musician. By the later Middle Ages the better of the minstrels were finding regular employment by courts and cities. One can imagine how welcome a good musician was during the monotonous routine of castle life during the Middle Ages. We can see this in a description of a typical day by Gaston Phebus, a fourteenth-century nobleman who lived in a castle in the Pyrenees.

> Hunting; after the hunt, Mass; after Mass, the womenfold and the minstrels.[4]

And, of course, no one was happier than the minstrel, who could now give up his wandering life. One feels the heartfelt relief in this song by Walther von der Vogelweide,

> I've got my fief, everybody, I've got my fief!
> Now when it's cold I don't have to fear for my toes,
> I will beg a little less at stingy masters' doors—
> I have fresh air in the summer, in winter my fire roars,
> and the noble king, the sweet king, is the one I have to thank.
> My neighbors find me a much more presentable man—
> they don't look at me as though I were a scarecrow any more.
> I hated being poor, and I was poor too long—
> my mouth was so full of reproaches, my breath stank.
> Now the king has sweetened my breath—and my song.[5]

---

1   E. K. Chambers, *The Mediaeval Stage* (Oxford, 1903), II, 231ff.
2   From the ninth-century Latin, *ministerialis*, meaning an office-holder or functionary.
3   Quoted in John Stevens, *Music & Poetry in the Early Tudor Court* (London: Methuen), 302.
4   Quoted in Romain Goldron, *Minstrels and Masters* (H. S. Stuttman Co.), 25.
5   'Dankspruch,' in Frederick Goldin, trans., *German and Italian Lyrics of the Middle Ages* (Garden City: Anchor Books, 1973), 109.

Beginning about the twelfth century towns began to develop a sense of identity and this was followed by more numerous civic celebrations, all of which required music.[6] As minstrels began to be hired by towns they also began to wear distinguishing 'uniforms,' short coats or capes with hoods decorated by the city's coat of arms. With the arrival of the Renaissance consort principle, towns, churches and nobles began to purchase cases, or 'families' of instruments for their minstrels to use.

The most interesting part of the minstrel story was the 'minstrel schools,' *scolae ministrallorum*, which began in the twelfth century. These schools were held regularly during the week before Laetare Sunday in Lent, when minstrel performances were not allowed by the Church, and on a more informal basis whenever large numbers of minstrels gathered in the same town for a large fair, noble wedding or Church council. The numbers are surprising. An Italian town hosted 1,500 minstrels for one of these 'schools' in 1324.[7] And in England, in 1290, 426 minstrels arrived to celebrate the marriage of Margaret of England and John of Brabant.[8] As part of the knighthood ceremonies for the Prince of Wales in 1306, in London, a roll of payments lists nearly two hundred minstrels by name.[9] The main purpose of these 'schools' was to trade and learn the latest repertoire from different countries,[10] but also to buy and trade instruments.

Other than a number of references of various nobles sending their minstrels to these schools, and documentation of the various towns which hosted them, there is no literature which describes them—these were players, not writers. It is with this perspective, then, that our attention is drawn to a passage in Book III of Chaucer's *House of Fame*.[11] We believe this passage, which has been overlooked by musicologists, is a rare description by someone who had actually observed one of these minstrel schools. While this poem takes the form of a dream, it is our contention that he could *only* have imagined such a description of a large gathering of wind instrument minstrels if he had at some point witnessed one of these 'schools.'

The extraordinarily large number of instrumentalists in particular first attracts our attention for this reflects the large gatherings such as we have quoted above. Of the wind instrument players, Chaucer says he saw 'many thousand times twelve!' There were others, playing instruments whose names he did not know, and they were more numerous 'than there be stars in heaven.' These he says he won't bother to name because it would take too much time and 'time lost can in no way be recovered.' He concludes his description of players with the lowly jongleurs, some of whom were also famous and whose name he knew. But, again, to list them all, he says, 'would take from now until doomsday!'

---

[6] One of these, the civic bonfire, had it roots in ancient 'bones fires' when a more complete specimen was the guest of honor.

[7] Goldron, *Minstrels and Masters*, 38.

[8] Chambers, *The Mediaeval Stage*, I, 44, fn. 4.

[9] Ibid., I, Appendix C.

[10] The minstrels of Lille went to a school in Beauvais in 1436 'pour apprendre des nouvelles chansons.' Walter Salmen, *Der Fahrende Musiker im Europaischen Mittelalter* (Kassel, 1960), 181.

[11] *House of Fame*, 1197ff.

The contention that this description was inspired by his having observed a minstrel school is strengthened by his reference to the presence of famous players, as well as foreign visitors ('Pipers of the Duche tonge') and his specific mention that they all came 'to lerne.' It may be our only eye-witness description of one of these schools.

> Ful the castel alle aboute,
> Of alle maner of mynstralles
> And gestiours that tellen tales …
>
> Tho saugh I stonden hem behynde,
> Afer fro hem, al be hemselve,
> Many thousand tymes twelve,
> That maden lowde mynstralcyes
> In cornemuse and shalemyes,
> And many other maner pipe,
> That craftely begunne to pipe
> Bothe in doucet and in rede,
> That ben at festes with the brede,
> And many flowte and liltyng-horne,
> And pipes made of grfene corne …
>
> Ther saugh I famous, olde and yonge,
> Pipers of the Duche tonge,
> To lerne love-daunces, sprynges,
> Reyes, and these strange thynges …
>
> There saugh I sitte in other se's,
> Pleyinge upon sondry gle's,
> Whiche that I kan not nevene,
> Moo than sterres ben in hevene,
> Of whiche I nyl as now not ryme,
> For ese of yow, and los of tyme.
> For tyme ylost, this knowen ye,
> Be no way may recovered be.
> There saugh I pleye jugelours, …
>
> shuld I make lenger tale
> Of alle the pepil y ther say,
> Fro hennes into domes day!

Concurrent with the time minstrels were beginning to be employed on a relatively permanent basis by towns and nobles, there was also a growing awareness that some minstrels were better than others, as players and as persons. Therefore there was a gradual desire to create categories of definition under the general name 'minstrel.' In 1273 Alphonso X of Castile defined three levels of minstrel, which were basically composers, instrumentalists and reciters of 'delightful' stories and a lowest category of *bufos*, common entertainers.

The better minstrels themselves no doubt also wished to separate themselves from their unemployed, wandering colleagues. By the fourteenth century those employed by cities and nobles began to call themselves 'minstrel of honor.' This led to the impetus for attempting to legislate the rights of these minstrels, as we see in an English royal proclamation of 1316.

> Edward by the grace of God … to Sheriffes … greeting. Forasmuch as many idle persons, under colour of Minstrelsie, and going in messages [private homes] and other feigned business, have been and yet be received in other men's houses to meat and drink and be not therewith contented if they be not largely considered with gifts of the lords of the houses … We willing to restrain such outrageous enterprises and idleness, have ordained that to the houses of prelates, earls, and barons, none resort to meat and drink, unless he be a minstrel; and of these minstrels that there come none, except it be three or four minstrels of honour.[12]

Even though given better titles, minstrels employed by cities were still not considered as 'citizens' and lacked, among other things, legal protection. This situation led eventually to attempts by the minstrels to form civic guilds, the first of which was the *Nicolai-Bruderschaft* of Vienna, established in 1288. The first minstrel guild of Paris, the *Confrerie de St. Julien des menestriers*, was founded in 1321 by thirty-seven minstrels, of whom eight were women.

Meanwhile, the true wandering musician still existed appearing wherever extra musicians were needed to help with a celebration. But beginning with the fourteenth-century accounts of these musicians become more and more unflattering. In the *Tales* of Franco Sacchetti (1335–1400) we read of the sad desperation of a minstrel who fastened a cymbal to the saddle of his horse. By putting a thistle under the horse's tail, he caused the horse to continuously jump, causing the cymbal to sound for the purpose of attracting the public.[13]

An early fourteenth-century poem by Lovato de' Lovati describes *cantastorie*, wandering singers of romances.

> I was going by chance through the town of the springs
> Which takes its name from its three streets [Treviso],
> Passing the time by strolling along,
> When I see on a platform in the piazza
> A singer declaiming the story of Charlemagne
> And the *gestes* of the French. The rabble hang round,
> Listening intently, charmed by their Orpheus.
> In silence I hear it. With a crude pronunciation
> He deforms the song written in French,
> Mixing it all up at his whim, without heed
> To art or the story. Still, the mob liked it.[14]

---

[12] Quoted in Edmonstoune Duncan, *The Story of Minstrelsy* (Detroit, 1968), 78.

[13] *Tales from Sacchetti*, trans. Mary Steegmann (Westport: Hyperion Press, 1978)ccxxv, 292. On the other hand, Sacchetti mentions a minstrel named Dolcibene who was knighted by Charles IV when he visited Rome.

[14] Quoted in John Larner, *Culture and Society in Italy, 1290–1420* (New York: Scribner's, 1971), 176ff

The fourteenth-century English poet, William Langland, in his 'Piers Plowman,' gives some detailed portraits of the minstrel during the beginning of the decline of this practice. First, he finds some he does not condemn and then describes the true wandering musician.

> And some make mirth as minstrels can
> And get gold for their music, guiltless, I think.
> But jokers [*jongleurs*] and word jugglers, Judas' children,
> Invent fantasies to tell about and make fools of themselves,
> And have whatever wits they need to work if they wanted.
> What Paul preaches of them I don't dare repeat here:
> *Qui loguitur turpiloquium*[15] is Lucifer's henchman.
> Beadsmen and beggars bustled about
> Till both their bellies and their bags were crammed to the brim;
> Staged fights for their food, fought over beer.
> In gluttony, God knows, they go to bed.
> And rise up with ribaldry, those robber boys.
> Sleep and sloth pursue them always.[16]

At this time we also begin to find references to the wandering string player, who is almost always called a 'beer fiddler.' This is the musician Langland refers to when he writes,

> And not fare like a fiddler or friar seeking feasts,
> At home in other men's houses and hating his own.[17]

Langland provides a major sketch, almost an autobiography, of one of these less than admirable minstrels, a man named Hawkin. When we first meet him he calls himself 'Active Life,' a reference to the practical versus Scholastic theoretical definitions of music which were being formulated by the universities. In spite of his siding with the practical musicians, when Hawkin first describes himself, he presents a picture of a musician who simply doesn't have the skills to be successful. He hasn't even acquired the hand-down garments which even the wandering musicians often received.

> 'I am a minstrel,' said that man, 'my name is *Activa Vita*.
> I hate everything idle, for from 'active' is my name.
> A wafer-seller, if you want to know, and I work for many lords,
> But I've few robes as my fee from them, or fur-lined gowns.
> If I could lie to make men laugh, then I might look to get
> Either mantel or money among lords' minstrels.
> But because I can neither play a tabor nor a trumpet nor tell any stories
> Nor fart nor fiddle at feasts, nor play the harp,
> Joke nor juggle nor gently pipe,

---

[15] 'Who speaks filthy language.'

[16] William Langland, 'Piers Plowman,' trans. E. Talbot Donaldson (New York: Norton, 1990), Prologue, 33fff.

[17] Ibid., X, 95.

> Nor dance nor strum the psaltery, nor sing to the guitar,
> I have no good gifts from these great lords.[18]

To make up for his lack of musical skills, Hawkin appears to have earned his living by talk, primarily as an impostor of one kind or another. In fact, we next meet him in the habit of the clergy.

> I took close heed, by Christ, and Conscience did too,
> Of Hawkin the Active Man and how he was dressed.
> He had a coat of Christendom, as Holy Kirk believes,
> But it was soiled with many spots in sundry places,
> Here a spot of insolent speech, and there a spot of pride,
> Of scorning and of scoffing and unsuitable behavior;
> As in apparel and deportment proud among the people;
> Presenting himself as something more than he seems or is;
> Wishing all men would think him what he is not,
> And so he boasts and brags with many bold oaths;
> And impatient of reproof from any person living;
> And himself so singular as to seem to the people
> As if there were none such as himself, nor none so pope-holy;
> In the habit of a hermit, an order by himself,
> A religious *sans* rule or reasonable obedience;
> Belittling lettered men and unlettered both;
> Pretending to like lawful life and a liar in soul;
> With inwit and with outwit to imagine and study,
> As it would be best for his body, to be thought a bold man;
> And interfere everywhere where he has no business;
> Wishing every one to be assured his intellect was the best,
> Or that he was most clever at his craft, or a clerk of greatest wisdom,
> Or strongest on steed, or stiffest below the belt,
> And loveliest to look at and most lawful of deeds,
> And none so holy as he, nor any cleaner of life,
> Or fairest of features in form and in shape,
> And most splendid at song, or most skillful of hands,
> And glad to give generously, to get praise thereby,
> And if he gives to poor people, proclaims what he's giving;
> Poor of possession in purse and in coffer;
> And like a lion to look at, and lordly of speech;
> Boldest of beggars; a boaster who has nothing,
> In town and in taverns telling his tales,
> And speaking of something he never saw and swearing it true.[19]

---

[18] Ibid., XIII, 221ff.

[19] Ibid., XIII, 271ff.

And, finally, his most 'active life' was in pursuing the girls.

> For every maid that he met he made her a gesture
> Suggesting sin, and some he would savor
> About the mouth, or beneath begin to grope,
> Till their wills grow keen together and they get to work,
> As well on fasting days as Fridays and forbidden nights
> And as [well] in Lent as out of Lent, all times alike;
> Such works with them were never out of season.[20]

A character named Conscience tries to reform Hawkin, promising him success if he will follow the ethics of the Church.

> No herald nor harper will have a fairer garment
> Than Hawkin the Active Man, if you act according to my teaching,
> Nor any minstrel be held more worthy among poor and rich
> Than will Hawkin the waferer, who is *Active Vita*.[21]

Another character, Patience, now joins in and, taking bread from his bag, offers some to Hawkin in an impromptu Mass.

> 'Have some, Hawkin,' said Patience, 'and eat it when you're hungry,
> Or when your teeth chatter for chill, or you chew your cheek for thirst.
> Shall never handcuffs harm you, nor anger of great lords,
> Prison or pain, for *patientes vincunt*.'[22]

By the fifteenth century more of the better musicians had been hired by towns and nobles, leaving the remaining true wandering musicians as a somewhat dishonorable class of entertainers. François Villon, in his 'Great Testament,' mentions the musicians who waste their time playing in taverns.

> If you rhyme, jest, play cymbals or lute
> like a foolish and shameless impostor,
> or if you're a mummer, magician or flutist,
> or if in the towns and the cities
> you do farces, plays or moralities, or if
> you're a winner at dice, at cards or at ninepins,
> it soon is all gone (do you hear?)
> all to the girls and the taverns.[23]

---

[20] Ibid., XIII, 344ff.

[21] Ibid., XIV, 25ff.

[22] Ibid., XIV, 51ff. *Patientes vincunt*, means 'the patient overcome.'

[23] Francois Villon, 'The Testament,' in *The Complete Works of Francois Villon*, trans. Anthony Bonner (New York: David McKay, 1960), lines 1700ff.

Sometimes, no doubt, such behavior had ill results for these itinerant musicians, as we read in the text of a little ballade by Richard de Loqueville.

> When comrades sally forth to play
> In diverse countries here and there,
> They do not banquet every day
> On roasted capon or fat hare
> Save if with gold they are supplied.
> For just as sure it does betide
> That if a comrade lose his gains
> He ends with sorely wounded pride,
> His feet held fast by two stout chains.[24]

Christine de Pizan mentions one of these types, the goliards, remarking that the habits of 'such dubious characters are a sure road to damnation.'[25] On the other hand, in her *The Book of the Duke of True Lovers*, she describes the activities of minstrels in the entertainments surrounding a great court tournament performing roles not unlike the modern marching band.[26] Six minstrels, with trumpets and drums, greet the arrival of the nobles and 'blew so loudly that the hills and valleys resounded.'

> Menestrelz, trompes, naquaires
> y avoit plus de troys paires,
> qui si haultement cournoyent,
> que mons et vaulx resonnoyent.[27]

They performed for the banquet, 'lending luster to the festival.' After the meal was finished they performed again 'in gracious harmony.' During the course of the tournament itself, a piper played 'spreading cheer about' and 'minstrels trumpeted gaily.' The winners were greeted with music so loud 'that God thundering might not have been heard.'

> Lors menestrelz liement
> cournoient, hairaux crioent,
> Lances brisent, cops resonnent,
> et ces menestrelz haut sonnent
> si qu'on n'oist Dieu tonnant.

We have numerous extant accounts from sixteenth-century England which provide an extensive view of the final chapter in the decline of the ancient wandering minstrel. London was one of few cities at this time in which there was sufficient work, beyond that taken by the

---

[24] Translated by Gustave Reese, in *Music in the Renaissance* (New York: Norton, 1959)., 19.

[25] Christine de Pizan, *Mirror of Honor; the Treasury of the City of Ladies*, trans. Charity Willard (Tenafly, NJ: Bard Hall Press, 1989), III, ix.

[26] Christine de Pizan, *The Book of the Duke of True Lovers*, trans. Thelma Fenster (New York: Persea books, 1991), 60ff.

[27] Christine de Pizan, *Le livre du duc des vrais amants*, in *Oeuvres politiques* (Paris, 1896), 79ff and 89ff.

civic wind bands and the aristocratic ensembles, for independent minstrels to see the hope for sustaining themselves.[28] Their opportunity to make a living rested in their success in obtaining the remaining available work in place of the true wandering minstrels. To accomplish this they formed a Minstrels Guild, modeled after the numerous civic music guilds throughout Europe. They received a charter in London in 1500, took as their patron St. Anthony and swore to guard against improper language. In their request for this charter they mentioned,

> The continual recourse of foreign minstrels, daily resorting to this City out of all the countries of Europe and enjoying more freedom than the freemen, causes the Minstrels of the City to be brought to such poverty and decay that they are not able to pay 'lot and scot' and do their duty as other freemen do, since their living is taken from them by these foreigners.[29]

In particular, they accused the foreign, or wandering, musicians of outrageous behavior, appearing,

> uninvited, sometimes as many as five or six at a time crowding to the end of the tables, playing without skill and causing great pain and displeasure to the Citizens and to their honest friends and neighbors.[30]

By the time Henry VIII began his reign, the Minstrel Guild had become more organized, limiting the appearances of apprentices and establishing proficiency examinations. By mid-century, however, the pressure of competition sent the Guild back to court in an attempt to gain new restrictions against the wandering minstrels. The City Corporation complied, noting that competition was causing 'hinderaunce of the gaines and profitts of the poore minstrels being freemen of the Cytie.' The wandering minstrel was now forbidden to sing or play in public halls, taverns, etc., or to take apprentices and neither minstrels, freemen nor 'foreign musicion' could teach dancing.[31]

By mid-century other towns in England were passing local ordinances in an attempt to control the wandering minstrels. A civic code in Beverly, passed in 1555, forbids any part-time musician to play outside his parish.[32] In York an ordinance of 1561 specifies that 'no manner of foreigner' be allowed to practice any form of minstrelsy,

---

[28] At the beginning of the sixteenth century, seventy-five percent of the population was rural and only four cities in Western Europe had more than 100,000 inhabitants: Paris, Venice, Naples and Milan.

[29] H. A. F. Crewdson, *The Worshipful Company of Musicians* (London: Knight), 28.

[30] Ibid.

[31] Ibid., 36ff.

[32] Edmondstoune Duncan, *The Story of Minstrelsy*, 217.

singing or playing upon any instrument within any parish within this city or franchise thereof upon any church holidays or dedication days hallowed or kept within the same parish, or any brotherhood's or freeman's dinner or dinners.[33]

All these ordinances reflect an increasingly modern urban society concerned over beggars, peddlers, vagabond and rouges. A national law had been passed in 1547 which defined a vagabond as any able-bodied person without an income sufficient to support him who was found,

either like a serving man lacking a master or like a beggar, [wandering and] not applying himself to some honest and legal art, science, service or labor … for three days or more.[34]

A justice of the peace was empowered to decide, in the case of an independent minstrel, for example, if he were following an 'allowed art,' or was a vagabond. The penalties were rather serious: branding with a 'V,' enslaving for two years, whipping until bloody, or the loss of ears, to name a few! An ordinance of 1572 goes further, for now a person traveling without a patron or proper traveling papers could be 'grievously whipped, and burnt through the gristle of the right ear with a hot iron of the compass of an inch about' on first conviction and death on the third conviction![35]

At about this time the religious right, the early Puritans, also began to attack the wandering minstrels. Stephen Gosson, in his 'An Apologie of the Schoole of Abuse' attacks the wandering minstrels.

London is so full of unprofitable Pipers and Fidlers, that a man can no sooner enter a tavern, but two or three of them land at his heals, to give him a dance before he departs; therefore let men of gravity examine the case, and judge uprightly, whether the sufferance of such idle beggars be not a grievous abuse in a commonwealth.[36]

One of the books inspired by Gosson's attack on the arts was the *Anatomy of the Abuses in England* (1583) by Philip Stubbs. In this work, a dialogue between the speakers, Spudeus and Philoponus, Stubbs presents an unusually strong attack on the minstrel class, warning them to repent and stop playing, or go to Hell.

SPUDEUS. What say you, then, of musicians and minstrels, who live only upon music?
PHILOPONUS. I think that all good minstrels, sober and chaste musicians (speaking of such drunken sockets and bawdy parasites as range the country, rhyming and singing unclean, corrupt, and filthy songs in taverns, ale-houses, inns and other public assemblies) may dance the wild Morris through a needle's

---

[33] Walter Woodfill, *Musicians in English Society from Elizabeth to Charles I* (Princeton, 1953), 111ff. Another ordinance in York requires the freemen musicians to instruct their apprentices in the art of conversation, in addition to just music, so that 'he may be well thought of.'

[34] Ibid., 56.

[35] Ibid., 57.

[36] Stephen Gosson, 'An Apologie of the Schoole of Abuse,' in *The Schoole of Abuse*, ed. Edward Arber (London, 1868), 70.

eye. For how should they have chaste minds, seeing that their exercise is the pathway to all uncleanliness. There is no ship so balanced with massive matter, as their heads are fraught with all kinds of bawdy songs, filthy ballads and scurvy rhymes, serving for every purpose, and for every company.

......

But some of them will reply, and say, what, Sir! we have licenses from Justices of the Peace to pipe and use our minstrelsy to our best commodity. Cursed be those licenses which license any man to get his living with the destruction of many thousands!

But have you a license from the Arch-justice of Peace, Christ Jesus? If you have so, you may be glad; if you have not (for the Word of God is against your ungodly exercises, and condemeth them to Hell), then may you as rogues, extrauagantes, and stragglers from the Heavenly Country, be arrested of the high Justice of Peace, Christ Jesus, and be punished with eternal death, notwithstanding your pretended licenses of earthly men. Who shall stand between you and the Justice of God on the day of Judgment? Who shall excuse you for drawing so many thousands to Hell? shall the Justices of Peace? shall their licenses? Oh, no: For neither ought they to grant any licenses to any to do hurt withal; neither (if they would) ought any to take them.

Give over, therefore, your occupations, you pipers, you fiddlers, you minstrels, and you musicians, you drummers, you Tabretters, you flutists, and all other of that wicked brood; for the blood of all enticing allurements, shall be poured upon your heads at the day of judgment.[37]

In the sixteenth-century English poetry of John Skelton (1460–1529) we have a contemporary glimpse of the true wandering minstrel, who had become a rather rare sight in England. His descriptions reveal that Skelton himself was sophisticated in his knowledge of music. First, of particular interest is the suggestion that the minstrel's melodic improvisation is busy, but makes no sense.

> He solfas too haute, his treble is too high;
> He braggeth of his birth, that born was full base;
> His music without measure, too sharp in his *Mi*;
> He trimmeth in his tenor to counter pardee;
> His descant is busy, it is without mean;
> Too fat is his fancy, his wit is too lean.
> One minstrel he describes wishes he could read music,
> For on the book I cannot sing a note.
> Would to God, it would please you some day
> A ballad book before me for to lay,
> And learn me to sing *re me fa sol*![38]

And he mentions the string minstrel, the 'beer fiddler':

> And what blunderer is yonder that played fiddle diddle?
> He findeth false measures out of his fond fiddle.[39]

---

37 Philip Stubbs, *The Anatomy of the Abuses in England* [1583], ed. Frederick Furnivall (London: The New Shakespeare Society, n.d.), 171ff. In another place Stubbs says beggars, if they cannot work, should be hanged! [Ibid., II, 42].

38 John Skelton, 'The Bouge of Court,' in *The Complete Poems of John Skelton*, ed. Philip Henderson (London: Dent, 1959), 45.

39 John Skelton, 'The Garland of Laurel,' in Ibid., 371.

Finally, in a fitting close to this discussion, Skelton reports on his encounter with an older minstrel who had suffered from his years of travel.

> He bit the lip, he looked passing coy;
> His face was belimmed, as bees had him stung:
> It was no time with him to jape nor toy.
> Envy had wasted his liver and his lung,
> Hatred by the heart so had him wrung
> That he looked pale as ashes to my sight.[40]

---

[40] Ibid., 46.

On the Troubadours

THE THEMES OF THE RENEWAL OF SPRING, rural simplicity and love, of which the early Greek lyric poets sang were, and are, universal. The repertoire of lyric poetry became smaller as Rome's subjugation began, and smaller again under the influence of the Church. The Dark Ages have left us with an incomplete history of poetry, but it does seem apparent that the spirit of lyric poetry never completely died out.

In France, those who carried on this tradition during the glorious final two centuries of the Middle Ages are called troubadours. The troubadours sang in a new language, but they composed and sang poetry on the same themes as the Greek lyric poets. If their love songs seem more vivid and personal than the myths and allegories of the Greeks, it is because they celebrate their own experience rather than an allegorical ones.

With the East to West shift in political power, which began in the eleventh century, the south of France began to flourish. One might say that the patronage of these aristocratic families represents the real beginning of the Renaissance in the arts. It was here that the troubadours had their origin, one of the first being William of Aquitaine, Count of Poitiers (1071–1127 AD).

We are fortunate to possess some biographical information about many of these troubadours. It is generally assumed by scholars that these short biographies are somewhat exaggerated and romantically colored, but they nevertheless provide a valuable general view of this activity. We can see, for example, that the troubadours came from all levels of society. Some were nobles, some were poor bourgeois and even orphans, some were monks, and some were, or became, jongleurs—wandering musicians who traveled in many lands.

These early biographies also frankly tell us that some of the troubadours (Guillaume IX, Pons de Capdueill and Peire Vidal, for example) were outstanding composers and singers, while others are described as 'bad singers' (Gaucelm Faidit and Aimeric de Peguilhan). Within the latter category, presumably, were some who composed, but employed a jongleur to sing their songs for them. Such a one was Peire Cardenal, the son of aristocratic parents, who went through the courts of kings and noble barons, bringing a joglar with him who sang his *sirventes*.[1] And neither did being a noble guarantee lofty language. Jaufre Rudel, Prince of Blaia, was described as composing 'good verses, but with poor words, though the tunes were good.'[2]

The relatively brief period during which the troubadours, and their northern colleagues, the trouvères, existed, is presented in most literature clothed in the romance of courtly life. Some of them, indeed, had reputations as great lovers, such as Guillem de Montanhagol, a knight of Provence, who was called in an early biographical note, 'a good troubadour and a

---

[1] Quoted in Paul Blackburn, *Proensa* (Berkeley: University of California Press, 1978), 242. A sirventes was a song on a subject other than love.

[2] Ibid., 67.

great lover.'³ One finds here as well truly romantic tales of love, such as that of the troubadour Raimon Jordan who was inaccurately reported to have been killed in battle and returned to find his grieving wife had joined a convent.

On the other hand, one finds in these early biographies examples of behavior which depart dramatically from the traditional image of the troubadour. Marcabru, we are told, even 'spoke badly of women and of love.'⁴ This troubadour, who had a reputation for 'malicious songs,' was eventually murdered by one who was the object of his music. Peire Vidal, another who was known for speaking badly of others, had his tongue cut out by a noble!

Some troubadours, including Ventadorn, Mareuil and Cabestanh, violated the court's trust by making love with their patron's wife, although perhaps this was a frequent occurrence where marriages were often made only for political purposes. In the case of Cabestanh, the offended noble, Raimon, murdered him, carried the troubadour's heart home,

> and he had it roasted with pepper and served to his wife. And when the lady had eaten the heart of Cabestanh, Raimon told her what it was. When she heard that, she fainted away. And when she came to she said, 'My lord, you have given me such a good meal I shall never take another.' Hearing her speak thus, he came at her with his sword and would have split her head, but she ran to a balcony and threw herself down to her death.⁵

Some of the most revealing information about the troubadours is found in their own words, in their songs. In this regard, the most interesting song of all is one by Peire d'Alvernhe which describes the musical characteristics of twelve troubadours and himself. As this song is by far the most important eye-witness document we have of these lyric poets, we shall quote it in entirety.

> I shall sing about those troubadours
> who sing in many fashions, and all praise
> their own verses, even the most appalling;
> but they shall have to sing elsewhere,
> for a hundred competing shepherds I hear,
> and not one knows whether the melody's rising or falling.
>
> In this Peire Rogier is guilty,
> thus he shall be the first accused,
> for he carries tunes of love in public right now,
> and he would do better to carry
> a Psalter in church, or a candlestick
> with a great big burning candle.
>
> And the second: Giraut de Bornelh,
> who looks like a goatskin dried out in the sun,
> with that meager voice of his, and that whine,

---

3 Ibid., 238.

4 Ibid., 32.

5 Ibid., 189.

it is the song of an old lady bearing buckets of water;
if he saw himself in a mirror,
he would think himself less than an eglantine.

And the third: Bernart de Ventadorn,
a hand's breadth smaller than Bornelh;
a fellow who worked for a wage was his father,
he shot a laburnum handbow well,
and his mother heated the oven
and gathered the brushwood together.

And the fourth, from Brive, the Limousin,
a jongleur, and the most beggarly man
between Benevento and here;
and he looks like a sick
pilgrim when he sings, the wretch,
so that I nearly pity him myself.

En Guillem de Ribas is the fifth,
who is bad outside and in,
he recites all his verses with a raucous voice,
so his singing sounds like hell,
for a dog would sing as well,
and his eyes roll up like Christ in silver.

And the sixth, Grimoart Gausmar,
a knight who tries to pass for a jongleur,
and whoever agrees to let him could not do worse,
God damn whoever gives him clothing of motley and green,
for once his costume has been seen,
a hundred more will want to be jongleurs.

And Peire de Monz—makes seven,
since the Count of Toulouse sang him
a charming song, though he himself never sang;
and whoever stole it from him is to be respected,
except it was a pity he neglected
to amputate the little foot that hangs.

And the eighth, Bernart de Sayssac,
who never knew any other work
but going around begging little gifts;
and I have not thought him worth a piece of mud
since he begged En Bertran de Cardalhac
for an old cloak that stank of sweat.

And the ninth is En Raimbaut,
who thinks so highly of his poetry;
but I think nothing of his rhymes,
they have neither warmth nor cheer,
therefore I rank him with the bagpipers
who come up to you and beg for coins.

> En Ebles de Sagna is the tenth,
> who never had any luck in love,
> though he sweetly sings his little air;
> a vulgar puffed-up shyster
> who, they say, for two cents
> rents himself here, and sells himself there.
>
> And the eleventh, Gonzalgo Roitz,
> who vaunts his skill in song
> and thus presumes to call himself a knight;
> no strong blow was ever struck
> by him, he was never that well armed,
> unless, of course, he got off in flight.
>
> And twelfth is an old Lombard,
> who calls his friends all cowards,
> and he himself is terrified;
> and yet the songs he writes are valiant,
> with bastard phrases neither Occitan nor Italian,
> and he is known to all as Cossezen, 'Just Right.'
>
> Peire d'Alvernhe, now he has such a voice
> he sings the high notes, and the low (and the in-between).
> and before all people gives himself much praise;
> and so he is the master of all who here convene;
> if only he would make his words a little clearer,
> for hardly a man can tell what they mean.
>
> This verse was made to the noise of bagpipes
> at Puivert, with much laughter and play.⁶

Peire d'Alvernhe (fl. 1150–1180), as he freely admits here, was known for his propensity toward self-praise. In another song he suggests he has many jealous detractors, but knows he is the best because of the money he makes, 'of which there's plenty.'

> And no matter who seethes or grumbles about it, since my style
> of poetry is so fine …; for I am the root and say that I'm the
> first in perfect speech, defeating my stupid assailants who raise against me the outcry that I'm of no
> use in it.⁷

He adds that the careful listener will agree that his work is the best, even though it will always be subjected to criticism. The latter, he says, one must simply ignore.

> It's certainly not to be mocked at if one hears it, rather should
> it be most pleasing, even though the opinions of the overweening,
> with their stupid, feeble, feckless sniggers, drag down that

---

6   'Cantarai d'aquestz trobadors,' quoted in Frederick Goldin, *Lyrics of the Troubadours and Trouveres* (Garden City: Anchor Books, 1973), 171.

7   'Sobre.l vieill trobar,' in Alan Press, *Anthology of Troubadour Lyric Poetry* (Austin: University of Texas Press, 1971), 93.

> which is on high; we see that good makes its own way forward,
> while mockery stays galloping behind.
>
> Hence it is well to ignore it, for never does mockery or spite desist.[8]

No less confident than d'Alvernhe, was Bernart de Ventadorn (fl. 1150–1180) who began a song, 'It is no wonder that I sing better than any other singer.'[9] This singer, who personifies as much as any the traditional image we have today of the troubadour, has left a song which speaks of the place of love and music in the courtly life and reflects his alarm in seeing the beginning of the decline of chivalry.

> I am so saddened by what I see that I do not feel like singing. Men used to strive hard to win worth, honor, and praise, but now I do not see or hear anyone speak of love, and, as a result, reputation, nobility and joy become matters of indifference …
>
> Man can only achieve worthiness in the love and service of ladies, for sport and song, and all that pertains to nobility, begin there. No man is worth anything without love, and therefore I would not want to rule the whole world if I could not have joy.[10]

Another autobiographical reference, in a song by the troubadour Raimbaut d'Orange (1150–1173), is typical of several which seem to use the ancient term for the wandering musician, 'jongleur,' as synonymous with 'troubadour.'

> Jongleur they call me, I go singing
> mad with love, in courtly ways.[11]

Certainly the wandering musician of ill repute was still in existence, but he is always described differently from these troubadours. Consider, for example, Giraut de Borneil's (1165–1211) description of one of these men.

> Cardaillac, they tell me that you are coming in search of a *sirventes* with which to earn yourself some money; but before the door-keeper lets you in I want you to thank me from a distance, for your breath is rather bad and you are apt to come too close. This is why a man is better off sending you a few pence rather than waiting for you to approach; for he suffers great torment if he does not turn away his face or cover his nose! …
>
> Since men call you then the 'woolly minstrel …'[12]

---

[8] 'Cui bon vers,' in Ibid., 97.

[9] 'Non es meravelha,' in Stephen Nichols, *The Songs of Bernart de Ventadorn* (Chapel Hill: The University of North Carolina Press, 1965), 133.

[10] 'Ges de chantar,' in Ibid., 98.

[11] 'Escotatz, mas no say,' in Goldin, *Lyrics of the Troubadours and Trouveres*, 181.

[12] 'Cardaillac, per un sirventes,' in Ruth Sharman, *The Cansos and Sirventes of the Troubadour Giraut de Borneil* (Cambridge: Cambridge University Press, 1989), 401.

An entirely different kind of person was Arnaut Daniel (fl. 1180–1200). Born a noble, and praised by Dante as a craftsman of the modern tongue,[13] he nevertheless describes himself as a traveler, too poor to own a horse.

> I am Arnaut, who gathers the wind, and hunts the hare on oxback, and swims against the rising tide.[14]

And there were some troubadours, like Cerver' de Girona (fl. 1250–1280), who though attached to the royal court of Aragon, seems to have been, regardless of title, rather despondent over his place in the court.

> I go singing, thinking, fixing, rhyming, honing praising
> loving commands of affection without pleasure ...
>
> Praising, waiting, singing;
> my life is ignominious.[15]

Finally, the troubadour songs rarely mention other kinds of court music. References to string players are usually negative, as we can see in the example by a troubadour known as the Monk of Montaudon (fl. 1180–1215).

> And it irritates me, I swear by Saint Salvat,
> to hear a vile violinist in a good court.[16]

This, even though troubadours may have accompanied themselves with such instruments. A song by the trouvère Colin Muset, for example, includes the lines,

> I went to her in the little field
> with fiddle and bow
> and sang her my muset
> with great love.[17]

A song of Guilhem de Montanhagol (1233–1270) mentions the performance of melodies on bells, an instrument we see in iconography but rarely read about.[18]

---

[13] *Purgatorio*, XXVI, 115ff.

[14] Arnaut Daniel, 'En cest sonet,' in Press, *Anthology of Troubadour Lyric Poetry*, 185.

[15] Quoted in Anthony Bonner, *Songs of the Troubadours* (New York: Schocken Books, 1972), 217. The manuscript of this song is written with one syllable to a line.

[16] 'Fort m'enoia,' in Blackburn, *Proensa*, 179.

[17] 'Volex oir la muse Muset,' in Goldin, *Lyrics of the Troubadours and Trouveres*, 417.

[18] 'Bel m'es quan d'armatz,' in Press, *Anthology of Troubadour Lyric Poetry*, 263, 265.

On the Inspiration of the Composer

A large number of troubadour songs begin with a reference to the inspiration of the seasons, especially Spring which is associated with the renewal of life. A typical example can be seen in Ventadorn.

> When the flower appears by the green leaves, and I find the season clear and quiet, and soft songs of the birds in the grove sweeten my heart and refresh me, then the birds sing in their fashion; and I, who have more joy in my heart, must also sing well, for every day's work is mirth and melody; I think of nothing else.[19]

By far the greatest inspiration for the troubadour repertoire is, of course, the joy of love, for love is the general subject of almost every one of their songs. Raimbaut d'Orange provides a typical example, in which he begins by saying it is not the seasons that inspire him, but love.

> I sing not for bird or flower, not for snow or for ice and not even for cold or for warmth, nor for the meadow's growing green again; and for no other pleasure do I sing, nor have I ever sung, but for my mistress for whom I long, because she is the most lovely in the world.[20]

Some of the most poignant songs are inspired not by the joy of love, but by the grief and pain which often accompany love. A song of Borneil is one of many which mention this confluence of emotions.

> I grieve inwardly while outwardly I sing, so that this would seem like churlish inconstancy in me if I were not so firmly bound by Love, which teaches me that a sincere lover achieves perfection in his discouragement and that I should pretend to be cheerful and joyful and should suffer patiently; for the most precious riches are to be gained from noble suffering and fear.[21]

Another poet, the trouvere, Blondel de Nesle (second half, twelfth century), also sings without hope, but adds that he only continues to sing because, 'I die more pleasantly that way.'[22]

We see the other side of the coin in a similarly inspired song by a rare female troubadour, La Comtessa de Dia (fl. ca. 1160).

> It will be mine to sing of that which I would not desire,
> I am so aggrieved by the one to whom I am the friend,

---

[19] 'Can par la flors josta,' in Nichols, *The Songs of Bernart de Ventadorn*, 161. Additional troubadour repertoire which attributes inspiration to Spring are: Marcabru, 'Al departir'; Cercamon, 'Ab lo temps'; Ventadorn, 'Bel m'es qu'eu chan' and 'Can l'erba fresch'; Daniel, 'Doutz brais e critz' (specifically the birds of Spring); de Montanhagol, 'Ar ab lo coined'; de Borneil, 'Tostemps mi sol,' 'Can creis la fresca' and 'Era, quan vei Reverdezitz'; and from the trouvere repertoire: de Couci, 'Li nouviauz tanz'; and Brule, 'Les oiseillons.'

[20] 'Non chant per auzel,' in Press, *Anthology of Troubadour Lyric Poetry*, 113.

[21] 'Chans em broil,' in Sharman, *The Cansos and Sirventes of the Troubadour Giraut de Borneil*, 147. Troubadour poems of similar inspiration are: Ventadorn, 'Per melhs cobrir'; Vidal, 'Per miehs sofrir'; Borneil, 'Mas, com m'ave,' 'Quar non ai' and 'De chantar, Ab deport'; and trouvere poems by Bethune, 'Si voirement'; Couci, 'L'an que rose,' 19; and Brule, 'De bone amour,' 'Desconfortez, plains d'ire' and 'Ire d'amors.'

[22] 'Se savoient mon tourment,' in Goldin, *Lyrics of the Troubadours and Trouveres*, 367, line 8ff.

> for I love him more than anything that can be.
> Pity does not help me toward him, nor courtliness,
> nor my beauty, nor my good name, nor my wit;
> and so I am cheated and betrayed as much
> as I'd deserve to be if I were ugly.[23]

If, through this contest between joy and pain, the outcome should be a happy ending, then, of course, there is a burst of new inspiration. Such a song was composed by de Nesle:

> I must sing, for I have won joy again
> that always fled from me and stayed far away;
> I have paid with pain and sadness many a day—
> now it is my time to be free of pain;
> for the beautiful lady whom I have loved so long,
> who used to war against me for her love,
> has lately come to terms with me.[24]

But, on the other hand, if love is lost, then, as in this example by Ventadorn, there is no inspiration at all and the voice of the singer is stilled.

> I want all those who ask me to sing to know the truth, if I have occasion or leisure for it. Let him sing who wants to. I have not been able to do it since I lost my happiness through my dark destiny.[25]

There must have been many occasions when the troubadours were forced by necessity to write for monetary purposes. One song by Borneil begins by admitting that he must, 'put great effort into composing a song that I owe for my lodging.'[26] The trouvere, Colin Muset (fl. 1230), complains rather bitterly over the failure of his noble patron to provide the wages he feels entitled to.

> My Lord Count, I have fiddled
> for you in your court,
> and yet you have given me no gift
> nor delivered me my wages:
> that is ignoble!
> Faith I owe holy Mary,
> I won't follow you like this.
> There's poor provisions in my bag,
> There's nothing in my wallet.
>
> My Lord Count, command me
> to do what you want,
> only, Lord, if it please you,

---

[23] 'A chantar m'er,' in Ibid., 185.
[24] 'Chanter m'estuet,' in Ibid., 369.
[25] 'Tuih cil que'm,' in Nichols, *The Songs of Bernart de Ventadorn*, 174.
[26] 'En un Chantar,' in Sharman, *The Cansos and Sirventes of the Troubadour Giraut de Borneil*, 300.

> make me a nice gift,
> out of courtesy.²⁷

Successful composition in the court environment brought, of course, important recognition and esteem to the composer for his work. Borneil, observes that, 'fair renown, once acknowledged, lasts and never varies in hue.'²⁸ In another song, he advises a colleague,

> Why compose poetry if you do not wish everyone to know your poem immediately? For song brings no other reward.²⁹

For this proud troubadour, however, the esteem which comes to the composer is directly related to two aesthetic principles: the quality of the song itself and its reception by the listener. It is a perspective which corresponds perfectly with the Aristotelian definition of aesthetics.

> Then it is right that I sing in order to make entreaty as well as on command. But now they will say that it would be far better if I strove to sing in the light style. And yet this is not true, for poetry deep with meaning, rich and rare, brings and bestows fine reputation, just as unbridled nonsense detracts from it. But I firmly believe that a song is not worth as much to begin with, as later when a man understands it.³⁰

In another place, Borneil adds an additional aesthetic qualification. If his song is to have its true aesthetic effect, the listener must also be a listener of quality.

> Churlish men of base lineage consider many of my fine songs as idle nonsense, though no excellent man of noble birth, if he succeeded in catching their meaning, ever excused himself from listening to them or belittled the pleasure they afforded. And is a man who takes no pleasure in joy and song not thoroughly despicable?³¹

A specific source of inspiration which was related to the court was the death of the noble. Songs of this nature are invariably sincere, as in this example by the troubadour, Sordel (ca. 1200–1270).

> I want to mourn for En Blacatz in this simple song
> with a sad and desolate heart, and I have cause,
> for in him I have given up my dear friend and lord,
> and in his death every dignifying quality is lost.³²

---

27 'Sire Cuens,' in Goldin, *Lyrics of the Troubadours and Trouveres*, 427.

28 'S'es chantars,' in Sharman, *The Cansos and Sirventes of the Troubadour Giraut de Borneil*, 427.

29 'Era'm platz,' in Ibid., 396.

30 'La flors,' in Ibid., 172.

31 'De chantar, Ab deport,' in Ibid., 458. Similar references to the esteem which comes from the composer's work are found in Ventadorn, 'Tant ai mo cor'; Borneil, 'Alegrar mi volgr'en,' 'Quar non ai,' 'De chantar,' and 'Be m'era bels chanters'; and Adam de la Halle, 'Merveille est.'

32 'Planher vuelh en Blacatz,' in Goldin, *Lyrics of the Troubadours and Trouveres*, 313.

Finally, some songs address their inspiration to God. Although Nature is often praised in the love songs, God is rarely mentioned by name. Borneil, however, who often complains of a decay in aristocratic culture which he perceived in the thirteenth century, is one troubadour whose songs take a definite turn toward religion. We quote excerpts from two of his works because of their important reflections on the changing aesthetic environment.

> If it were not for [God] who tells me that I should sing and be cheerful, I could never be stirred by the gentle season when the grass grows, nor by meadow or bough or woodland or flower, or hard-hearted lord or vain love. But I comply with his request, for since joy fails and fades, renown and knighthood are in decline, and since the great rulers have forsaken joy, nothing that the worst among them does has been praised by me. For I have resolved not to seek the favor of any rich and powerful man who is an evil ruler.
>
> The world was good in the days when joy was welcomed by everyone, and when that man was well liked in whom joy most abounded, and when reputation and noble rank went hand in hand. For now the most vicious are called virtuous and the man sunk in deepest melancholy is held to be the best, and the man who takes the most he can from other people will be envied the most ...
>
> I have seen a time when a man valued songs and found pleasure in dance melodies and lays. Now that courtly pleasures and gracious deeds are forsaken, and true lovers, in all their concerns, have left the straight path for the crooked, I see that all sense of right has fled ...[33]
>
> ......
>
> To the honor of God I return to my song, from which I had taken my leave and departed, and not to the calls and cries of the birds, nor to the leaf on the bough do I return, nor do I find any joy in singing. On the contrary, I am angry and full of sorrow, for in many writings do I see and recognize that sin is strengthening its hold, so that trust and faith are failing and wickedness flourishes.
>
> And I wonder greatly when I think of how the world has fallen [spiritually] asleep.[34]

ON THE PURPOSE AND PROCESS OF COMPOSITION

The principal purpose of the entire repertoire of troubadour songs was, of course, to sing of love. Indeed, Bertran de Born (b. ca. 1140) observes that it is a sign that a lady has become old, if she doesn't like singers.[35] We might also note here a song by Borneil which suggests that, in the case of the troubadour in love with a noble lady, the strong emotions of love which could be communicated in song, might not be permitted in words.

> ... for in no other way dare I say how she fills me with joy and sad longing.[36]

---

33 'Si per mon Sobre-Totz,' in Sharman, *The Cansos and Sirventes of the Troubadour Giraut de Borneil*, 477.

34 'A l'honor Dieu,' in Ibid., 417.

35 'Bel m'es, quan vei chamjar,' line 14, in Goldin, *Lyrics of the Troubadours and Trouveres*, 241.

36 'Gen M'aten,' in Sharman, *The Cansos and Sirventes of the Troubadour Giraut de Borneil*, 112.

In their songs the troubadours cite a number of other specific purposes for their music. Several times we hear the poet say the purpose of his music is simply to bring pleasure. A song of Borneil says, 'I am composing just to give pleasure,'[37] and in another he says the troubadour 'is guilty of great stupidity if he objects to the delight and pleasure' his songs give to others.[38] This troubadour admits in several songs, however, that he found it difficult to sing of joy and pleasure if his audience was not in a conducive mood.

> For I never had to be pressed to sing as long as a fine song was appreciated, but since joy and wit receive such a poor welcome, I do not know how to be friendly and cheerful in the company of so many sad people, or how to throw myself eagerly into writing fine songs.[39]

One must suppose that these troubadours often had to discipline themselves to sing for the pleasure of the company when their own personal circumstances prevented them from feeling the emotions of their music. The trouvère, Le Chatelain de Couci (d. 1203), has left a song which gives evidence of being in such a position.

> Imploring mercy for the mad thing I have done,
> I shall sound the last note of my songs,
> for my loving heart has purposely betrayed
> and slain me, and I ought to hate it—
> it has made me suffer to give others pleasure.[40]

Another purpose familiar to music of all periods, is to give comfort. Sometimes the purpose of the song is to give comfort to the singer himself, rather than to others. A song of Audefroy le Bastard, for example, begins,

> True love has given me hope and a desire to sing in order to lighten the woes which I am forced to suffer by the lady who would certainly be able to reduce my pain; but I am much afraid she wants to punish me because of a vile slanderer.[41]

But there are times when even his music fails to bring the troubadour comfort, as in Ventadorn's plaint,

> I will no longer be a singer ... for neither my singing, my voice, nor my melodies do me any good.[42]

---

[37] 'A penas sai comenssar,' in Ibid., 197.
[38] 'De chantar,' in Ibid., 458.
[39] 'En un Chantar,' in Ibid., 300. A similar protest he makes in 'Be m'era bels chantars.'
[40] 'Merci clamans de mon,' in Goldin, *Lyrics of the Troubadours and Trouveres*, 359.
[41] 'Fine amours,' in Hendrik van der Werf, *The Chansons of the Troubadours and Trouveres*, 120.
[42] 'Lo tems vai e ven e vire,' in Nichols, *The Songs of Bernart de Ventadorn*, 131. He makes a similar complaint in 'Peirol, com a vetz.'

Direct didactic purpose is rare in this repertoire, although in one song by Borneil we find,

> For with melodies will I instruct and entreat those indifferent people who, wanting resolve rather than money, linger here rather than go in the service of God.[43]

Closely related, is the purpose to inspire the noble listener to take a specific action. Bertran de Born, for example, sings,

> Since the barons are vexed and offended by this peace which the two kings have made, I'll compose such a song that, when it is known of, each one of them will long to be at war.[44]

Finally, there are some songs which tell us that the poet's purpose was not achieved. Pons de Capdueill (1196–1236) finds his song does not gain his intended's love and mourns,

> I stand singing for myself alone,
> a damn fool in heart and sense.[45]

On Composition

This body of repertoire also contains songs which provide hints of the compositional process. As we shall see below, a well-crafted song was an important goal to these poets and one song by Borneil clearly suggests a period of drafting.

> I must set to work on a song with which I have only toyed till now, and make it good enough to rank with the best; for, with the time and the gentle season in my favor, I shall receive no honor or renown unless I compose it in such a way as to win more praise than any other.[46]

In composing another song he mentions, 'my progress is slow,' but that he has everything in his heart necessary for 'value and esteem' in a song.[47]

Some songs speak of a strong level of concentration in the creative process. Ventadorn, for example, states,

> Now I fear neither rain nor wind, so preoccupied am I with composing this song.[48]

---

43 'Jois sia commensamens,' in Sharman, *The Cansos and Sirventes of the Troubadour Giraut de Borneil*, 423.

44 'Puois als baros,' in Ibid., 163.

45 'Qui per nesci cuidar,' in Ibid., 217.

46 'Ben coven,' in Sharman, *The Cansos and Sirventes of the Troubadour Giraut de Borneil*, 128.

47 'Tostemps mi sol,' in Ibid., 138.

48 'Lonc tems,' in Nichols, *The Songs of Bernart de Ventadorn*, 119.

Borneil observes that all he needs to make an excellent song is 'a theme, an occasion, opportunity and a fitting moment for singing.'[49] These kinds of court parameters seemed to give flight to his creativity and if they were missing there was no focus to his work.

> I am composing a song … and I have no idea on what theme or about whom or how or why, nor can I remember anything that I know.[50]

Borneil maintained that he could compose easy and light songs 'almost without thinking about it,' and that he had the skill to make even difficult songs appear 'to have been simple and pleasant to compose.'[51] In another song, however, he makes it clear that composition was beyond him if his concentration were lacking.

> I would, if I could, compose a slight, clear song such as might match the wit of my godson and give delight to everyone; but this is beyond me, for my thoughts are on something else.[52]

The trouvère Blondel de Nesle found his 'writer's block' not in a lack of concentration, but in maintaining originality.

> It would be best to stop singing altogether,
> for when one sings nowadays, one doesn't know what to say.
> There's not a word or verse one can think up any more,
> no matter how much one picks and chooses,
> that hasn't been said and said again.[53]

It is interesting that sometimes we find a troubadour worrying about his own ability in composition. Ventadorn, for example, notes, 'I always need to make my song better than it is, although it is good.'[54] Borneil seems to find that as an older man he cannot compose as easily in some styles.

> If my heart does not serve me aright and if I do not incline it by force towards a subtle little song, it will not now, I think, bend willingly to the yoke of such broken words as these. There was a time when I sang in this subtle fashion more often than I do now, for my inspiration was greater, so that scarcely anyone recognized how subtly and minutely soldered were my light and cunning words.[55]

---

49 'Nuilla res,' in Sharman, *The Cansos and Sirventes of the Troubadour Giraut de Borneil*, 143.
50 'Un sonet fatz,' in Ibid., 371. Ventadorn, in 'Lo Rossinhols' and 'Peirol, com avetz estat,' mentions having to force himself to compose when the inspiration was absent.
51 'Ben deu en bona,' in Ibid., 291.
52 'Ajtal cansoneta,' in Ibid., 193.
53 'Mout se feist,' in Goldin, *Lyrics of the Troubadours and Trouveres*, 371. Raimbaut d'Orange, in 'Escotatz, mas no say,' satirizes poets who claim their works are original.
54 'Ja mos chantars,' in Nichols, *The Songs of Bernart de Ventadorn*, 102.
55 'Si'l cors no'm ministr'a dreig,' in Sharman, *The Cansos and Sirventes of the Troubadour Giraut de Borneil*, 213.

There is also evidence that these poets sometimes resorted to borrowing the music of others. Marcabru (1129–1150) begins a song, 'Singing on borrowed tune I'll see if I can make a poem.'[56] A song of Borneil, however, confirms that this was not an accepted policy.

> The poem that was heard and sung abroad as the work of a good troubadour later turned into a falsehood when the song was recognized, for … one man claimed as his own the words which another had stolen.[57]

Criticism robs even the finest artist of his confidence, as Peire d'Auvergne cries,

> Ah! Merit, how you are muted, deaf and squint, and Worthiness, how broken I see you and dragged to and fro! For whoever wants to so ill-treats you that a vile and wicked people, pulling and pushing and snapping, have confused and perverted you; and this robs you of sense and guidance.[58]

On the Characteristics of a Good Song

The first requirement of a good song is obvious, 'For it is the theme that makes the song.'[59] Beyond this, it is clear that the best troubadours took great pride in the careful use of language itself. The troubadour Gavaudan (1195–1230) simply concludes, 'the vers is good if it is well written.'[60] Arnaut Daniel gives more detail.

> And I then, whose heart is set on the most noble, should above all make a song finely wrought, so that there be in it no false word or rime unanswered.[61]

In another song,[62] he mentions fashioning words, 'I carve and plane them, so they'll be true and sure,' to a preexistent melody.

Beyond 'finely wrought,' one may assume there was a goal of eloquence and sophistication, appropriate to music associated with court life. One anonymous song begins, 'No country bumpkin made this song.'[63] The trouvère, Colin Muset, says in one song, that he 'made it handsome, fine, and elegant.'[64]

---

[56] 'Al son desviat chantaire,' in Press, *Anthology of Troubadour Lyric Poetry*, 55.

[57] 'S'es chantars ben entendutz,' in Sharman, *The Cansos and Sirventes of the Troubadour Giraut de Borneil*, 428.

[58] 'Belh m'es qu'ieu,' in Press, *Anthology of Troubadour Lyric Poetry*, 95.

[59] Borneil, 'De Bels Digz,' in Sharman, *The Cansos and Sirventes of the Troubadour Giraut de Borneil*, 432.

[60] 'Lo vers dech far,' in Blackburn, *Proensa*, 212.

[61] 'Doutz braise e critz,' in Press, *Anthology of Troubadour Lyric Poetry*, 177.

[62] 'En cest sonet.'

[63] 'Volez vos que,' in Goldin, *Lyrics of the Troubadours and Trouveres*, 409.

[64] 'Volez oir la muse Muset,' in Ibid., 417.

The most frequently mentioned characteristics of a good song all deal with meaning. First, a number of troubadours mention that an important feature of their music is Truth, that it come from the heart. A song of Ventadorn begins, 'There is no use in singing if the song does not spring from the heart.'[65] Some apparently did, however, for the trouvère Gace Brule seems to want to set himself apart from his colleagues.

> Most have sung of Love
> as an exercise and insincerely;
> so Love should give me thanks
> because I never sang like a hypocrite.[66]

Borneil seems to offer an apology for language that may not be appropriate to the court, for he is only being true to his heart.

> My tongue cannot keep itself from saying what my heart entrusts to it, for the heart acts in the manner of an overlord, each day giving orders to the limbs. And, therefore, if such speech is not akin to courtliness, it seems to me that the tongue can, without question, excuse itself on its lord's authority, since the tongue is the faithful servant of the heart.[67]

Finally, a song which the famous trouvère, Richard Coeur de Lion (1157–1199), wrote while a prisoner in an Austrian castle, suggests that he found he could express through music, feelings which his circumstances did not permit in words.

> No prisoner will ever speak his mind
> fittingly unless he speaks in grief.
> But he can, for consolation, make a song.[68]

Next, a song must have meaning expressed in subtle language, due to the troubadour's position in court. Borneil observes that if this, together with hard work, does not make a fine song, he doesn't know what does.

> If neither subtle meaning nor sheer effort help to improve the value of my light and easy song, raising it on high and refining it, I see no way in which it can be worth much.[69]

---

[65] 'Chantars no pot,' in Nichols, *The Songs of Bernart de Ventadorn*, 81.
[66] 'Li Pluseur,' in Goldin, *Lyrics of the Troubadours and Trouveres*, 385.
[67] 'No's pot sufrir,' in Sharman, *The Cansos and Sirventes of the Troubadour Giraut de Borneil*, 441.
[68] 'Ja nus hons pris,' in Goldin, *Lyrics of the Troubadours and Trouveres*, 377.
[69] 'Si soutils senz,' in Sharman, *The Cansos and Sirventes of the Troubadour Giraut de Borneil*, 296.

This poet admits that sometimes he gets a little too subtle!

> The better to construct my song, I keep looking for words which are gentle on the rein, all loaded to the full with meanings foreign to them and yet wholly theirs, though not everyone knows what those meanings are.[70]

Several poets emphasize the importance of genuine emotions to the success of a song. Borneil saw this as an indispensable prerequisite.

> No song, it seems to me, can have value or merit if expectation or fear, anxiety or pleasure do not teach a man how to sing.[71]

Because most of this repertoire consists of love songs, it is the emotions of love which are found most frequently. Several songs, such as this one by Ventadorn, argue on behalf of love that the joy is always stronger than the pain.

> Love will be worth more than any other good, even if it causes you so much grief; for if it causes pain, it compensates later on. A man can seldom have any real good without pain, but the joy always surpasses the weeping.[72]

Several of these poets seemed to have had a kind of masochistic enjoyment of the pain of love. The trouvère Blondel de Nesle sang, 'Love is killing me with a martyrdom so pleasant.'[73] But Raimbaut d'Orange was no masochist, he was afraid it might kill him to put his true feelings into his song.

> I would willingly make up a little song, simple to say, but of it I fear that I'll die; so I'll make it such that it conceals its sense.[74]

The central aesthetic focus for most of these poets was the listener: the song must be understood.[75] A song by Borneil explains, 'I have made an effort for you to understand the type of songs I am composing.'[76] For Ventadorn, this was the very definition of a good song.

> The verse is perfect and well-written and good if one understands it well.[77]

---

[70] 'Si'm sentis fizels amics,' in Ibid., 185.
[71] 'Si soutils senz,' in Sharman, *The Cansos and Sirventes of the Troubadour Giraut de Borneil*.
[72] 'Amics Bernartz de Ventadorn,' in Nichols, *The Songs of Bernart de Ventadorn*, 46.
[73] 'Mout se feist bon tenir de chanter,' in Goldin, *Lyrics of the Troubadours and Trouveres*, 371.
[74] 'Una chansoneta fera,' in Ibid., 109.
[75] A few troubadours, such as Arnaut Daniel, were known for songs which were difficult to understand.
[76] 'Non puesc,' in Sharman, *The Cansos and Sirventes of the Troubadour Giraut de Borneil*, 220.
[77] 'Chantars no pot,' in Nichols, *The Songs of Bernart de Ventadorn*, 82.

Whether the song was serious or just for fun, the highest form of this aesthetic was universality. A song by Peire Cardenal (1180–1278), who was worried about greed, begins,

> I want to recite my song to all peoples in common, and if they deign to hear it and understand it and can construe it, each will be able to distinguish good from evil.[78]

Finally, the repertoire of the troubadours mention prevalent styles from time to time, especially the virtues of the so-called simple style versus the complex style. Raimbaut d'Orange notes in one poem that 'he is liked more and more esteemed who [writes] plainly and simply.'[79] At the same time, he saw that the style had changed and that he, too, must learn this style.

> Since the plain style is in such demand, it will be very hard for me if I don't excel in it; for it seems right that he who composes such words as were never before spoken in song should be able, if he so wishes, to say at another time those which are said and sung every day.[80]

The troubadour Guiraut Riquier (1230–1292) seemed puzzled by the change in the style favored by the court and doubted whether he was suited to compose light songs.

> Never more will a man be in this world thanked for well composing fair words and pleasant melodies, nor for being eager for esteem, so much is the world come to its decline. For that which used to inspire merit, approval, and praise, I hear blamed as the utmost folly; and that which one used to criticize and blame, I see upheld, and hear it praised by all.[81]

Another who had difficulty in adjusting to the new popular style was Borneil. He describes working an entire day just trying to get started. By a later poem he seems to have convinced himself, saying, in effect, 'Well, one should not be serious all the time!'

> I hardly know how to begin a 'vers' which I want to make light and easy, and so I have been thinking since yesterday how to compose it on a theme which would be easy for everyone to understand and easy to sing, since I am composing it just to give pleasure.
>
> I could certainly make it less explicit, but a song does not have perfect merit unless everyone can enjoy it. Whoever else this may annoy, I am glad when I hear hoarse and clear voices vying with one another to sing my song, and when I hear it being taken to the well.
>
> Few can reach my level, I think, if ever I wish to sing in the difficult style, and so I must indeed compose a light love song; and it seems to me that it requires as much wit to sustain a [single] theme as to weave together [rich and unusual] words.[82]

---

78 'Mon chantar,' in Press, *Anthology of Troubadour Lyric Poetry*, 285.
79 'Ara'm platz,' in Ibid., 117.
80 'Pos trobars plans,' in Ibid., 119.
81 'Ja mas non er hom,' in Ibid., 315.
82 'A penas sai comenssar,' in Sharman, *The Cansos and Sirventes of the Troubadour Giraut de Borneil*, 197. In 'Era'm platz, Guiraut de Borneill,' this poet creates a dialog on the pros and cons of the simple style.

On Performance

Taking for granted inspiration, intent and skill in composition, these composers, as now, understood that it was in performance that their song must succeed or fail. This is surely what Borneil had in mind when he made this observation regarding the audience's genetic ability to make a determination of a song's value.

> If a song is properly understood and if it were to promise merit and renown, why is it unseemly for a troubadour to praise his own song, once it is known?—Because it is clear from the performance whether it deserves praise or blame.[83]

These troubadours tell us in their songs the characteristics of an ideal performance. 'Eloquently, surely, I take up a fine song,' says Borneil.[84] In another song, he begins,

> Whoever is in the habit of singing and knows whom to sing about and believes that his pleasing service, his conversation and song may advance his case, let him sing graciously.[85]

The vocal style the troubadours distinctly objected to, they called 'braying.' Guillaume IX commands, 'sing this nicely, do not bray it out.'[86] And Peire d'Auvergne defends his work with this wish:

> With noble joy the poem begins which rimes fair words together, and there's no fault in anything therein; but it pleases me not that such a one should learn it whom my song does not befit. I've no wish that some wretched singer, the sort who ruins any song, should turn my sweet melody into braying.[87]

It was no doubt such a singer that Raimbaut d'Orange feared when he sought a messenger to take his song to his beloved. He wished for a singer, 'who can sing nobly, with joy, for [my song] befits no base singer.'[88]

There are a few references to a fine singer who finds himself, due to the passions of love, singing in a style he himself does not respect. Raimbaut d'Orange surely hints at this when he complains to his lover, 'you make me sing in joyful rage.'[89] Marcabru is much more outspoken.

> But what summons me to be an enemy is
> that this bitch *likes* to hear me roar and cry.[90]

---

[83] 'S'es chantars ben entendutz,' in Sharman, *The Cansos and Sirventes of the Troubadour Giraut de Borneil*, 427.

[84] 'Gen M'aten,' in Ibid., 112.

[85] 'Qui chantar sol,' in Ibid., 237.

[86] 'Farai chansoneta nueva,' in Goldin, *Lyrics of the Troubadours and Trouveres*, 43.

[87] 'Ab fina joia comenssa,' in Press, *Anthology of Troubadour Lyric Poetry*, 89.

[88] 'Ar resplan la flors,' in Ibid., 109.

[89] 'Escotatz, mas no say,' line 30, in Goldin, *Lyrics of the Troubadours and Trouveres*, 181.

[90] 'Aujatz de chan com,' in Blackburn, *Proensa*, 33.

An eloquent performance requires an appropriate atmosphere, which Borneil summarizes as follows.

> With love and gratitude, the occasion and the right moment, it is easy to sing well.[91]

These poets also give us hints which describe those atmospheres which are not conducive to fine performance. For Bertran de Born it is dinner music, 'repasts to the noise of viol and song.'[92] The Monk of Montaudon composed a song listing 'what annoys me most,' and includes having to wait for his performance.

> What gives me a rash is waiting too long
> at table, for the instruments to finish.[93]

Ventadorn reminds us that a proper psychological frame of mind is also necessary to a fine performance. He observes, 'Rarely will you see a singer sing well if things are going badly for him.'[94] He undoubtedly regarded this as a vicious circle—a singer needing to sing to be in a positive frame of mind—for in another song he complains,

> Everything has been unpleasant since I gave up singing, and the longer I remain mute, the more I contribute to my own undoing.[95]

---

91 'A ben chantar,' in Sharman, *The Cansos and Sirventes of the Troubadour Giraut de Borneil*, 123.
92 'Mon chan fenisc,' in Goldin, *Lyrics of the Troubadours and Trouveres*, 231.
93 'Fort m'enoia, so auzes dir,' in Blackburn, *Proensa*, 179.
94 'Pois preyatz me,' in Nichols, *The Songs of Bernart de Ventadorn*, 147.
95 'Estat ai com,' in Ibid., 92.

Music of the French Romances

THE PURPOSE OF THE MUSIC described in the French Romances and Chansons de geste seems to have been simple joy and delight. No more poetic description of this joy can be found than that in the famous 'Romance of the Rose,' where the very name given the musician is 'Gladness.'

> This noble company of which I speak
> Had ordered for themselves a caroling.
> A dame named Gladness led them in the tune;
> Most pleasantly and sweetly rang her voice.
> No one could more becomingly or well
> Produce such notes; she was just made for song.
> She had a voice that was both clear and pure;
> About her there was nothing rude, for she
> Knew well the dance steps, and could keep good time
> The while she voiced her song. Ever the first
> Was she, by custom, to begin the tune;
> For music was the trade that she knew best
> Ever to practice most agreeably.[1]

Even the performance of the narrative Chanson de geste was for the purpose of delight. The following lines from Marie de France are also interesting in their reference to separate sung and written versions of the same tale.

> With a glad heart and right good mind will I tell the Lay that men call Honeysuckle; and that the truth may be known of all it shall be told as many a minstrel has sung it to my ear, and as the scribe hath written it for our delight.[2]

Wace takes the point even further, noting that in the retelling by scribe and singer as an art work, the factual aspect of the tale has long been lost.

> I know not if you have heard tell the marvelous gestes and errant deeds related so often of King Arthur. They have been noised about this mighty realm for so great a space that the truth has turned to fable and an idle song. Such rhymes are neither sheer bare lies, nor gospel truths. They should not be considered either an idiot's tale, or given by inspiration. The minstrel has sung his balled, the sto-

---

[1] Lorris, Guillaume de and Jean de Meun, *The Romance of the Rose*, trans. Harry Robbins. New York: Dutton, 1962, III, 142ff.

[2] 'The Lay of the Honeysuckle,' in Marie de France, *French Mediaeval Romances from the Lays of Marie de France*, trans. Eugene Mason (London: Dent, 1924), 102.

ryteller told over his story so frequently, little by little he has decked and painted, till by reason of his embellishment the truth stands hid in the trappings of a tale. Thus to make a delectable tune to your ear, history goes masking as fable.[3]

There are two interesting references in this literature to the power of art. The first, in Layamon's 'Brut,' a reworking of the Wace tale, Merlin relates to King Arthur what he describes as an ancient truth.

Yes, lord king, it was of yore said, that better is art, than evil strength; for with art men may hold what strength may not obtain.[4]

The second has its roots in one of the most familiar of Greek myths, that of Orpheus taming the wild beasts with music. This charming invention reappears in a thirteenth-century collection of fables known as *Gesta Romanorum*. Here an emperor, faced with a wild elephant in his forest, finds two beautiful virgins who are musicians and sends them naked into the forest to tame the elephant. Sure enough, their music causes the elephant to fall asleep, with his head on one of the girls lap (!), whereupon the other girl cuts it off![5]

We should note that while the music theorists of the thirteenth century denounced the ancient concept of the 'Music of the Spheres,' it still surfaces in the literature of that period. In the 'Romance of the Rose,' for example, the character, 'Nature,' says of the spheres,

Sweet harmonies they make,
Which are the source of all the melodies
And divers tunes that we in concord set
In all our sorts of song. There is no thing
That would not chant in unison with them.[6]

One of the characteristics which we believe is synonymous with art music is the attentive, contemplative, listener. One of the most extraordinary twelfth-century accounts of an art performance, in the *Roman de Horn*, includes such an audience, which 'marvels' at what it heard.

Then he took the harp to tune it. God! whoever saw how well he handled it, touching the strings and making them vibrate, sometimes causing them to sing and at other times join in harmonies, he would have been reminded of the heavenly harmony. This man, of all those that there are, causes most wonder. When he has played his notes he makes the harp go up so that the strings give out completely different notes. All those present marvel that he could play thus. And when he has done all this he

---

3   Robert Wace, *Roman de Brut*, trans. Gwyn Jones (London: Dent, 1962), 56.

4   Ibid., 158.

5   *Gesta Romanorum*, trans. Charles Swan (London: C. and J. Rivington, 1824), II, 128.

6   *Romance of the Rose*, LXXXI, 187.

> begins to play the aforesaid lai of Baltof, in a loud and clear voice, just as the Bretons are versed in such performances. Afterwards he made the strings of the instrument play exactly the same melody as he had just sung; he performed the whole lai for he wished to omit nothing.[7]

In the case of art music performed at a banquet, such descriptions are usually accompanied by some reference to the tables being cleared first, to distinguish music to listen to rather than to eat by. Both of these features are found in the description of a performance in the Romance, 'The Lay of the Thorn,' by Marie de France.

> After supper, when the tables were removed, the King seated himself for his delight upon a carpet spread before the dais, his son and many a courteous lord with him. The fair company gave ear to the Lay of Alys, sweetly sung by a minstrel from Ireland, to the music of his rote. When his story was ended, forthwith he commenced another, and related the Lay of Orpheus; none being so bold as to disturb the singer, or to let his mind wander from the song. Afterwards the knights spoke together amongst themselves.[8]

Another Romance[9] by this writer describes a lay as 'sweet to hear, and the tune thereof lovely to bear in mind,' which perhaps suggests the expectation of a listener attentive enough to actually remember the melody.

A thirteenth-century epic, *Hervis de Metz*, includes a performance of art music, again with the author carefully specifying that the performance was *after* the meal.

> Hervis says: 'Noble minstrel, you are welcome!'
> He had him brought to the banquet, and after the meal he
> began to play the fiddle at once and to sing *sons d'amours*
> in a beautiful and sweet way; Hervis, courteous and
> noble, listened to him.[10]

One of the tales in the *Gesta Romanorum* involves an impromptu performance after a banquet. First, a king requests his daughter to play.

> She commanded the instrument to be brought, and began to touch it with infinite sweetness. Applause followed the performance, 'There never was,' said the courtiers, 'a better or a sweeter song.'

A visiting knight, named Apollonius, then volunteers to perform.

> Apollonius retired for a few moments, and decorated his head; then re-entering the Triclinium, he took the instrument, and struck it so gracefully and delightfully that they unanimously agreed, it was the harmony not of Apollonius, but of Apollo.
> The guests positively asserted, that they never heard or saw anything better.[11]

---

7   An Anglo-Norman work, in French, quoted in Christopher Page, *Voices and Instruments of the Middle Ages* (London: Dent, 1987), 4.
8   Marie de France, *French Mediaeval Romances from the Lays of Marie de France*, 140ff.
9   'The Lay of Graelent,' in Ibid., 148.
10 Quoted in Page, *Voices and Instruments of the Middle Ages*, 31.
11 *Gesta Romanorum*, Ibid., II, 251ff. Later in this same tale the daughter again 'sang to an instrument, with such a sweet and ravishing melody, that Apollonius was enchanted.'

We include as art music the love songs characteristic of the troubadours and trouvères. Among the references to similar love songs in the 'Romance of the Rose,' there is a description, although ostensibly of birds singing, which we believe reflects Art Music.

> Sweetly and pleasantly they sang of love
> And chanted sonnets courteously and well.
> In part songs joining, one sang high, one low.
> Their singing was beyond reproach; their notes
> With sweetness and contentment filled my heart.[12]

The most remarkable reference to love songs in this Romance, however, is more in the spirit of the satirical songs of the Goliards. A character says sending love songs to a lady is not nearly so effective as being rich!

> Someone may ask if it is not worth while
> To make and send to charm and hold his love
> Fair verses, motets, ballads, chansonettes.
> Alas, one gains not much from such pursuit—
> He need not pain himself to poetize—
> Perhaps the poem's praised, but that is all.
> But ample purse, filled and weighed down with gold,
> Will make them run to him with open arms
> When ladies see him draw and open it;
> Their desperation has become so great
> That they pursue naught but full pocketbooks.
> Once, to be sure, 'twas different; times are getting worse.[13]

After the organ was accepted into the church, gradually the rest of the instruments, for which the organ was only a surrogate, began to appear. A charming reference to the use of string instruments in the service in the thirteenth century is found in the works of Gautier de Coinci (ca. 1218–1236).

> When the mouth is working hard the heart should so strive, and so press upon the strings of its viele, and so tune them up, that with the first word the bright sound ascends without delay to Paradise. Then their singing is pleasing to God. But there are many [church singers] who have such a viele that will go out of tune all the time unless it is tuned up with strong wine.[14]

In chapter eight the reader will find the extraordinary trumpet references of the 'Song of Roland' which is associated with the literature of this period. In this same work we might add that drums are mentioned, without description, and more interesting, singing on the battle

---

[12] *The Romance of the Rose*, III, 124. Other references to love songs are found in XI, 62 and L, 135.

[13] Ibid., XL, 106ff.

[14] *Les Miracles de Nostre Dame par Gautier de Coinci*, ed. V. R. Koenig (Geneva, 1955–1970), IV, 184.

field. It is an understandable prejudice that the allies *sing* their battle cry, while the pagans *bellow* theirs.[15] We wish we had more information in the two references to the victors singing 'mocking' songs to the defeated.[16]

There are in this literature a number of passing references to music of a more functional nature. The most extensive account of entertainment music in this literature is found in Wace's *Roman de Brut*. Here, for a banquet of King Arthur, in addition to story-tellers, chess and dice games, the guests were treated to an extraordinary variety of entertainment.

> Now to the court had gathered many tumblers, harpers, and makers of music, for Arthur's feast. He who would hear songs sung to the music of the rote, or would solace himself with the newest refrain of the minstrel, might win to his wish. Here stood the viol player, chanting ballads and lays to their appointed tunes. Everywhere might be heard the voice of viols and harp and flutes. In every place rose the sound of lyre and drum and shepherd's pipe, bagpipe, psaltery, cymbals, monochord, and all manner of music. Here the tumbler tumbled on his carpet. There the mime and the dancing girl put forth their feats.[17]

A similar festive gathering of musicians is found in the Romance, 'Erec and Enide,' by Chretien de Troyes. In this case the musicians are visitors, attracted by a wedding hosted by King Arthur. The celebrations lasted fifteen days and the musicians were richly rewarded, even by today's standards!

> All the minstrels were pleased with their excellent wages that day. Whatever had been due them was paid, and many beautiful gifts were presented to them: clothes of spotted fur and ermine, of rabbit and of purple cloth, and of rich gray wool or silk. Each man received his desire, whether a horse or money, according to his skill.[18]

---

[15] *The Song of Roland*, trans. Robert Harrison (New York: Mentor, 1970), 1793 and 1921.

[16] Ibid., 1014 and 1517.

[17] Wace, Robert, *Roman de Brut*, trans. Gwyn Jones (London: Dent, 1962), 69. The reference to the monochord here suggests that the writer was naming every instrument he knew, whether he had ever heard it or not!

[18] *The Complete romances of Chreien de Troyes*, trans. David Staines (Bloomington: Indiana University Press, 1993, 27.

The Music of the Minnesinger

LIKE THE BETTER KNOWN TROUBADOURS AND TROUVÈRES of France, the German Minnesingers ('love singers') performed in an aristocratic environment and were themselves representatives of all levels of society, some aristocrats and some representatives of the broad class of traveling entertainers known as jongleurs.

The best known of the Minnesingers was Walther von der Vogelweide (ca. 1170–1230). He apparently traveled widely ('from Mur to Seine … from Po to Trave')[1] seeking permanent employment and one song tells us he resented always being the guest and wished that he could be the noble host.

> Guest and lodging ofttimes make one sore ashamed.
> Ah, might I but receive a guest, and take
> As host the bows that he would have to make!
> 'Stay here tonight! Tomorrow's fare!'—
> What life is this, the jongleur's?[2]

Another song, composed upon his securing employment in a court, reflects on his less fortunate days and provides a description of what must have been the fate of many of his wandering colleagues.

> I've got my fief, everybody, I've got my fief!
> Now when it's cold I don't have to fear for my toes,
> I will beg a little less at stingy masters' doors—
> I have fresh air in the summer, in winter my fire roars,
> and the noble king, the sweet king, is the one I have to thank.
> My neighbors find me a much more presentable man—
> they don't look at me as though I were a scarecrow any more.
> I hated being poor, and I was poor too long—
> my mouth was so full of reproaches, my breath stank.
> Now the king has sweetened my breath—and my song.[3]

A song composed at the end of his life[4] reveals that he had been a Minnesinger for forty years. Earlier, he says, he sang with joy, but now he gets nothing from it and continues only in the hope for his listener's good wishes.

---

[1] 'Wealth more than Honor,' in *Selected Poems of Walter von der Vogelweide*, trans. W. Alison Phillips (London: Smith, Elder, & Co., 1896), 85.

[2] 'Host and Guest,' in Ibid., 77.

[3] 'Dankspruch,' in Frederick Goldin, trans., *German and Italian Lyrics of the Middle Ages* (Garden City: Anchor Books, 1973), 109.

[4] 'Ir reinen wip, ir werden man,' in Ibid., 131.

One Minnesinger of the thirteenth century, Tannhauser, had been a noble, but upon losing his fortune lived a life similar to that described by Vogelweide.

> The way things used to be with me the best of men would say
> that I was welcome everywhere; my kin were kind before.
> But now who once was glad to see me turns and looks away,
> and since I've lost my property none greet me anymore.
> I have to step aside for him (so altered is my state)
> who rightly yielded once to me, but now I have to wait.
> Who once along with me were guests have houses now, I know,
> but my condition is the same as twenty years ago.
> For I'm a guest and never host, my life's an errant one,
> and those who think it isn't hard should live as I have done.[5]

Among his former possessions was a villa in Vienna,[6] and perhaps the loss of his fortune may have been related to his complaint in one song that Vienna has too many lawyers![7] This same song describes what he has seen in his travels, which seem to have included most of Europe, North Africa, and Jerusalem.

Another song complains that he too is no longer welcome at court and in so doing he mentions the main themes of which all Minnesingers sang: Love, Nature, Spring, Summer, dances with music, and religion.

> I ought to be at court, you know, so they could hear me sing.
> The trouble is that no one gives me pretty melodies.
> If I had some, then I would tell of every courtly thing:
> of lovely ladies I'd sing well—and better far—with ease.
> I'd sing about the meadow and the foliage and of May;
> I'd sing about the summertime, of dance and roundelay.
> I'd sing of chilling snow and rain, and what the winds have done;
> I'd sing about the father, mother, and their infant son.
> Who will redeem my pledge? Alas, how sad that I have none.[8]

Of these themes, it is the singing of love songs with which these poets are most associated, as their very name signifies. Vogelweide has left a song which is an elegy for a Minnesinger known as Reinmar (ca. 1150–1210), whom he felt exemplified this duty most nobly.

> Alas, that wisdom, and youth,
> and the beauty of man, and his craft
> cannot be handed down when the body dies away.
> A man who has lived can mourn for this,

---

5 'Hie vor do stvnt min ding also,' in *Tannhauser: Poet and Legend*, trans. J. W. Thomas (Chapel Hill: University of North Carolina Press, 1974), 161.

6 'Ze wiene hat ich eine hof,' in Ibid., 173.

7 'Der kvnig von marroch,' line 59, in Ibid., 133.

8 'Das ich ze herren niht,' line 10ff, in Ibid., 171.

who is awake to human hurt.
Reinmar, what great art dies with you.
You've the right to rejoice till the end of days
that you never lost the taste, not once,
for singing noble women's praise.
They ought to thank your tongue forever.
If you had sung but the one theme—if that were all—
'Joy to you, Woman, how pure a name,' with that alone you would have striven
so for their praise's sake, let every woman pray for mercy on your soul.[9]

The late twelfth-century *Nibelungenlied* has a character, Folker, who is described as a 'noble minstrel,' and was sufficiently wealthy that he traveled with thirty of his own knights and squires.[10] This same work includes an account of a tourney hosted by Siegmund which describes a number of visiting minstrels who played all day without rest and were rewarded so freely with gold, clothes, and horses that one would have thought the nobles hadn't another day to live.[11] A similar reference to traveling minstrels being richly rewarded is found in Wolfram von Eschenbach's (ca. 1170–1220) *Parzival*.[12]

The literature of this period never describes the details of where in the noble residence the art songs were sung. One passing reference to dinner music, in *Parzival,* does mention, 'At the foot of his table sat his minstrels.'[13] In the case of art music, we may assume that a performance at such a banquet was given 'after the tables were cleared,' a common description indicating music to be listened to, rather than to eat by. Indeed, such a phrase is used in the account of an outdoor banquet in the anonymous thirteenth-century Romance, 'Laurin.'

> After they had eaten and drunk and the tables had been cleared, the princes sat there and listened to the singing and recitation that was performed before them. This was followed by music from so many stringed instruments that the entire mountain resounded.[14]

The majority of Minnesinger art songs are songs sung for aristocratic ladies, songs which Vogelweide says, brought 'the glow of rose and lily to their cheeks.'[15] The Minnesinger, Ulrich von Liechtenstein (1198–1276), tells us that these songs in praise of ladies were as familiar to court life as clothes themselves.

> There is so much honor in the praise I sing,
> it passes well in court

---

9 'Owe, daz wisheit unde jugent,' in Goldin, *German and Italian Lyrics of the Middle Ages*, 129.
10 'Twenty-fourth Adventure.'
11 'Second Adventure.'
12 Book II, 101.
13 Wolfram von Eschenbach, *Parzival*, trans. Helen Mustard and Charles Passage (New York: Vintage Books, 1961), Book I, page 20.
14 'Laurin,' trans. J. W. Thomas, in *The Best Novellas of Medieval Germany* (Columbia, S.C.: Camden House, 1984), 72.
15 'Rome's Lord,' in *Selected Poems of Walter von der Vogelweide*, 78.

and belongs there, without shame,
more than the raiment of a king.[16]

Gottfried von Strassburg (fl. 1200–1210) provides a touching description of the role these Minnesingers (here 'Nightingales') played in aristocratic life. Of particular interest in this passage is the reference to aesthetics, in the reaction of the listeners to these songs.

> 'Nightingales' there are many, but I shall not speak of them, since they do not belong to this company. Thus I shall say no more of them than what I must always say—they are adepts at their task and sing their sweet summer songs most excellently. Their voices are clear and pleasing, they raise our spirits and gladden our hearts within us. The world would be full of apathy and live as if on sufferance but for this sweet bird-song, which time and again brings back to any who has loved, things both pleasant and good, and varied emotions that soothe a noble heart. When this sweet bird-song begins to tell us of its joy it awakens intimate feelings that give rise to tender thoughts.[17]

Sometimes we are told that the Minnesinger has been hired to sing on behalf of some lover.[18] More often, as in the case of the troubadour and trouvère repertoire, these songs are personal, reflecting the love of the Minnesinger for a noble lady. A song by Vogelweide begins,

> Never before had I such hope of bliss!
> And hence it comes that I perforce must sing.
> Hail to the maid who shall requite me this!
> To her pure worth it is my song I bring.[19]

In a time when aristocratic marriages were made of political purpose and not love, this was allowed the Minnesinger. On the other hand, one song by Vogelweide mentions that he was criticized for singing songs of praise 'of one not nobly born.'[20]

These love songs were often sent by messenger who sang them on behalf of the composer. Ulrich von Liechtenstein, in his *In Service of Ladies*, tells of one extraordinary case in which a Minnesinger chops off his finger and sends it with the song, as a demonstration of commitment.[21] We often read of the messenger, but almost never of how the song is received by the lady. Liechtenstein gives us a rare view of the other end of this process, in this case a rejection of the Minnesinger's love.

> I was a faithful messenger

---

[16] 'Wizzet, frouwe wol getan,' in Goldin, *German and Italian Lyrics of the Middle Ages*, 185.

[17] Gottfried von Strassburg, *Tristan*, trans. Arthus Hatto (Harmondsworth: Penguin Books, 1960), 106ff. In this same passage he speaks of a rare lady Minnesinger, who specializes in the songs of Vogelweide, while accompanying herself on a small organ.

[18] 'Iarlang blozet sich der walt,' line 13, in *Tannhauser*, 151.

[19] *Selected Poems of Walter von der Vogelweide*, 48.

[20] 'God be with thee, dearest maid,' in Ibid., 22.

[21] Ulrich von Liechtenstein, *In Service of Ladies*, trans. J. W. Thomas (Chapel Hill: The University of North Carolina Press, 1969), lines 440ff. One of the Minnesinger songs from this work was used by Mendelssohn in his Op. 19.

> and told her that you loved her best,
> more than yourself and all the rest.
>
> I said much more; before I closed
> I [sang] the song which you composed.
> Then spoke your charming lady fair,
> 'It really is a pretty tune,
> but one he might as well have kept;
> his service I cannot accept
> and want to hear no more of this.
> The topic we shall now dismiss.'[22]

Songs which bemoan the disappointment of lost love nearly always result in the poet contemplating the futility of further singing, as in this example by Neidhart von Reuental (fl. 1210–1237).

> The lady has my heart so in her power
> I must waste my days without joy.
> All that I have sung for so long now—it does no good,
> I could just as well be silent from now on.[23]

Vogelweide, finding himself in the same position, has left a song in which he tells us he stopped singing, but was enticed into resuming. He supports his self-esteem with the notion that if he stops singing her praises her status in the court will be adversely affected.

> To be long silent was my thought:
> now I shall sing once again as before.
> Gentle people brought me back to it:
> they have the right to command me.
> I shall sing and make up words,
> and do what they desire; then they must lament my grief.
>
> Listen to this wonder, how I fared
> for all my hard work:
> a certain woman will not look at me—
> and it was I that brought her up to that esteem
> which makes her so high-minded now.
> She does not know: when I leave off singing,
> her praise will die away.
>
> Lord what curses she'd endure,
> were I to stop my song!
> All those who praise her now, I know
> They'll rebuke her then—against my will.[24]

---

[22] Ibid., 73ff.

[23] 'Sumer, diner suezen,' in Goldin, *German and Italian Lyrics of the Middle Ages*, 165.

[24] 'Lange swigen des hat ich gedaht,' in Goldin, *German and Italian Lyrics of the Middle Ages*, 117.

A song by Ulrich von Liechtenstein is quite different. Here the Minnesinger is bemoaning the fact that he has been dismissed from a lady's service. He regrets he was never properly paid for his services to her, but nothing can make him give up his art of singing.

> Oh to lose and to regret
> that which I cannot forget
> evermore!
> Joy and all my better days—
> gone with melancholy lays.
> Wounded sore,
> I must bear
> life given o'er to grieving care:
> death is less than such distress
>
> There my service was to be
> with such constant loyalty
> through the years.
> Still no pay will she accord
> and no prospect of reward ...
>
> Many years, I see with pain,
> I have squandered all in vain
> for someone
> who can never fully pay
> me for just a single day ...
>
> But I could not neglect my art
> nor leave off singing women's praise.[25]

Of course, songs in praise of the noble himself were another common theme. Tannhauser sings,

> I'll sing the prince's fame
> that all will know his name.
> His greeting and his laughter
> can bring me joy thereafter.[26]

The Minnesinger repertoire contains few hints regarding their compositional process. We find one comment by Vogelweide referring to his composition as 'toil,'[27] and Ulrich von Liechtenstein has a Minnesinger tell a messenger, who was taking a song to a lady, that he had worked a long time on the song and 'with all my skill.'[28]

---

25 'Twenty-first Dance Tune,' in Liechtenstein, *In Service of Ladies*.
26 'Ich mvs clagen,' lines 144ff, in *Tannhauser*, 147.
27 'I sang her praise,' in *Selected Poems of Walter von der Vogelweide*, 47.
28 Liechtenstein, *In Service of Ladies*, lines 1110ff.

The Music of the Minnesinger 153

We can assume the better Minnesingers were proud of their art, as seems apparent in a song by Vogelweide.

> But, lady, understand one thing:
> no other man can sing your praise so well.[29]

The versatility which some of these singers must have had can be seen in the representation of a minstrel, in *Tristan*, who knows a variety of forms[30] and accompanies himself as he sings in several languages.

> He played so beautifully and went with his music in so masterly a fashion that the [listener] was amazed. And at the appropriate places, sweetly and rapturously, the accomplished youth would wing his song to meet it. He sang the notes of his lay so beautifully in Breton, Welsh, Latin, and French that you could not tell which was sweeter or deserving of more praise, his harping or his singing.[31]

Finally, during the thirteenth century there are complaints by the Minnesingers of a decline in aristocratic support and interest in their art. Tannhauser protests that, 'he who would restore good manners is not honored as before.'[32] Vogelweide composed an entire song on the subject of this decline in courtly manners.

> Alas, courtly singing,
> that uncouth strains
> should supplant you at the court.
> God bring dishonor on them soon.
> Alas that your dignity should be laid low.
> All your friends are sad.
> It must be; let it be:
> Lady Vulgarity, you have won.
>
> Should any man restore our courteous
> and gentle joy,
> Oh how well we'd praise him
> every time we spoke of what he did.
> That would be the soul of courtliness,
> I shall always hope for it,
> it would suit lords and ladies well.
> Oh sorrow no one does it.
>
> Those who drown out the good singing—
> There's many more of them
> than those who want to hear it.
> But I still follow the old teaching:
> I shall not set my music to the mill,

---

29 'Saget mir ieman,' in Goldin, *German and Italian Lyrics of the Middle Ages*, 117.

30 Strassburg, *Tristan*, 71.

31 Ibid., 90.

32 'Dank habe der meie,' in *Tannhauser*, 175.

> for the stone goes round so raucously
> and the wheel has such awful melodies.
> Notice who would harp there.
>
> Those who make their shameful noise
> make me laugh with anger,
> they're so pleased
> with such gross things.
> They're like frogs in a pond
> who like their own croaking so much,
> the nightingale loses heart,
> though it gladly would sing more.
>
> If anyone commanded vulgarity be silent,
> drove it away from the castles
> so that it oppressed these happy few no more—
> what joys we'd sing about.
> If it were barred from the great courts
> that would all be as I wish.
> I'd have it lodge with peasants;
> That's where it came from.[33]

Strassburg must have known musicians and performances similar to those which he describes. To begin with, perhaps we may have, in Tristan, a view of the training of the most gifted performers. We are told that, in addition to languages and extensive reading of books, he studied all the string instruments for seven years, practicing all day long, beginning at age seven.[34]

From the perspective of aesthetics, by far the most interesting and valuable contribution of Strassburg is his attention to the listener. Our contention is that it is only in the listener that aesthetics is capable of meaningful discussion. It was here, in the listener, that Aristotle focused his definition of aesthetics when he founded this separate branch of philosophy.[35] In the following descriptions of Tristan's listeners, notice not only their emotional reaction to the music, but the lengths to which Strassburg goes to establish them as *intently* listening. These performances are not mere 'background music.'

Tristan is given a small hunting horn which he blew so splendidly and so entrancingly, that all who rode with him could,

> scarcely wait to join him for *sheer joy*.

They enter the castle and fill the castle with music, this 'skillful' and 'strange' hunting music.

---

33 'Owe, hovelichez singen,' in Goldin, *German and Italian Lyrics of the Middle Ages*, 127.

34 Ibid., 69, 91. He played harp, fiddle, organistrum, rote, lyre and sambuca.

35 *Poetics*.

The king and his household, never having heard such music, were *shocked to the very marrow*.[36]

After supper, Tristan hears a harpist playing, 'correctly and with sad passion.' Tristan then takes the harp and plays 'preludes and phrases, fine, sweet, and haunting.' Then he tunes, 'adjusting pegs and strings, some up, some down, until they were to his liking.' He begins to play again, haunting, sweetly and melodious.

The [listeners] '*all came running up, one calling another.*'

Now Tristan begins to play 'excellent sweet music in the Breton style.'

> *Many a man sitting or standing there forgot his very name. Hearts and ears began to play the fool and desert their rightful paths ... Nor was there sparing of eyes: a host of them were bent on him, following his hands.*[37]

Tristan arrives at the shore of Ireland in a boat. Those listeners on the shore heard 'sweet strains of a harp' playing softly,

> *to their hearts' delight*.

Tristan was singing so 'enchantingly' and 'most marvelous' that the listeners,

> *were rooted to the spot* as long as he harped and sang.[38]

Here Strassburg interrupts his story to make one of the most important statements on aesthetics in music of the Middle Ages. His definition is relative to Truth in performance, the honest intent of the performer to communicate genuine feelings.

> But the pleasure they had from him was short-lived, since the sounds that he made for them with hands or lips did not come from the depths—his heart was not in his music. For it is of the nature of music that one cannot play for any length of time unless one is in the mood. Although it is a very common thing, what one plays superficially in a heartless and soulless way cannot really claim to be music.[39]

Strassburg returns to the performance he was discussing above.

The listeners on the shore relate hearing Tristan to others, saying, 'God himself would love to hear it in His heavenly choirs.' Others come to the shore to listen, Tristan plays,

> and he *moved them all to pity*.[40]

---

[36] Strassburg, *Tristan*, 84.

[37] Ibid., 89ff.

[38] Ibid., 141.

[39] Ibid.

[40] Ibid., 143.

Now Tristan plays before Isolde for the first time. 'He was playing better than he had ever played before, for he played to them not as a lifeless man, [but] with animation, in the best of spirits ... In a brief [period],

> he *won the favor of them all.*'[41]

Isolde now becomes a student of Tristan and, in spite of her accomplishments, made much improvement. She is called to perform before her father and his guests, who found 'no Lady ever struck strings more sweetly.' In response to her performance,

> *many hearts grew full of longing; because of her, all manner of thoughts and ideas presented themselves. No end of things came to mind.*[42]

Next, she sang openly and secretly, in through ears and eyes,

> *to where many a heart was stirred.*

The song which she sang openly in this and other places was her own sweet singing and soft sounding of strings that echoed for all to hear through the kingdom of the ears deep down into the heart. But her secret song ... stole with its rapturous music hidden and unseen through the windows of the eyes into many noble hearts and,

> *soothed on the magic which took thoughts prisoner suddenly, and, taking them, fettered them with desire!*

Later, Tristan plays his harp for Isolde, striking 'a lay of such surpassing sweetness' that it stole into Isolde's heart,

> *and pervaded her whole consciousness to the point where she left her weeping and was lost in thoughts of her lover.*[43]

The impact on the listener here is Aristotelian aesthetics, pure and simple. At the same time it is clear that Strassburg could not have written such descriptions had he not been familiar with serious artists performing art music, and not casual entertainment music, before attentive listeners.

While to this point we have emphasized the Minnesinger music heard in the court, the literature of these musicians also includes some songs which give us a glimpse of the use of music heard outside the palace by the general population. There are, for example, some interesting reports of music used for signal giving purposes, such as the 'blast on a horn' to call Siegfried's hunters back to camp in the *Nibelungenlied*.[44]

---

41 Ibid., 145.

42 Ibid., 148.

43 Ibid., 217.

44 'Sixteenth Adventure.'

We know that by the Baroque Period it was a common practice for a noble to have his personal trumpets precede him, announcing him, as an aural symbol equivalent to the use of the coat of arms as a visual symbol. Ulrich von Liechtenstein provides an early example of this practice, which is interesting because the trumpets play not just a 'blast,' but an actual melody for this purpose.

> My buglers played a melody,
> a pretty tune in a treble key,
> and thus they told all people near
> that I was shortly to appear.[45]

Given the nature of these 'love singers,' it is no surprise that the watchman-musician on the tower, who plays during the night as a surrogate clock, is frequently mentioned in this repertoire. It was a custom to play a special melodic signal, called the *Aubade*, just before dawn, to warn lovers to run back to their own houses before first light. One example of several by Wolfram von Eschenbach goes,

> At daybreak you have always sung
> the dirge of secret love,
> the bitterness following on the sweet.
> No matter what you urged upon them
> when the morning star was rising,
> those who received love and woman's favor
> in such a way
> that they had to part,
> Watchman, be quiet,
> sing of that no more![46]

The use of music for battle is also a familiar theme, as well as for the music of the tourney, which was in part a form of practice for battle.

> Then the trumpets were blown lustily, and the noise of drums and flutes was so loud that Worms, the wide town, rang therewith.[47]

The Romance, *Erec,* by Hartmann von Aue, reveals that in the case of personal combat between knights, the winner had the right to play a horn signal announcing to all his victory.

---

45 Liechtenstein, *In Service of Ladies*, lines 580ff.

46 'Der helnden minne ir klage,' in Wolfram von Eschenbach, *Titurel and the Songs*, trans. Marion Gibbs and Sidney Johnson (New York: Garland Publishing, 1988), 83.

47 *Niebelungenlied*, 'Thirteenth Adventure.'

> 'Sir, you should now get up and go blow the horn joyfully, for it is there if anyone should defeat me so that he can immediately announce this to the people by blowing three times. It has hung there unblown much too long for me, for as long as this has been my home.' Now he took it from the post and asked Erec to blow it. He immediately put it to his mouth. The horn resounded loudly, for it was long and large.[48]

Wolfram von Eschenbach's epic poem, *Willehalm*, a Romance of chivalry dealing with the campaigns against the Saracens, includes some extraordinary descriptions of actual battle music. In one place he describes the 'heathen's' use of the modern-type metal trumpet (eight hundred of them!), which we know the Western armies brought back from the crusades.

> Eight hundred trumpets the king ordered to blow 'Advance at the gallop!' It is still a known fact that trumpets were invented in his country; they were brought from Thusi.[49]

In another place he mentions the roll of a thousand drums![50]

In *Parzival*, it is the sound, rather than the numbers, of these same heathen musicians, which is meant to impress us.

> He rode up with six banners, in front of which fighting began in early dawn. Trumpeters sounded ringing blasts, like thunder rousing fear and dread, and drummers beat a lively accompaniment to the noise of the trumpets.[51]

Finally there are some interesting references to the use of music in the processions by which nobles traveled, including string players playing on horseback! Ulrich von Liechtenstein gives the entire order of such a procession, including knights, cooks, men carrying banners, etc. When he comes to the musicians, we read,

> A flutist was the next to come
> who beat with skill upon a drum.
> Four squires were riding after him
> in uniforms of modish trim
> and each had brought three spears along,
> well-made and large, which with thong
> were bound together. One could praise
> these bearers for their courtly ways.
>
> Two maidens rode behind the squires
> and every bit of their attires
> was gleaming white from head to toe.
> The both looked very pretty so.
> A fiddler rode behind each maid;

---

[48] Hartmann von Aue, *Erec*, trans. Thomas Keller (New York: Garland, 1987), 133.
[49] Wolfram von Eschenbach, *Willehalm*, trans. Charles Passage (New York: Ungar, 1977), 202.
[50] Ibid., 231.
[51] Eschenbach, *Parzival*, 203.

> my heart was happy when they played,
> and when the two would fiddle high
> a marching tune most pleased was I.[52]

Wolfram von Eschenbach provides the details of a similar procession.

> After these rode trumpeters, who are still required today, and a drummer kept hitting his drum and swinging it high in the air. The master would not have thought much of the lot if flute players had not been riding along with the rest, and three good fiddlers.[53]

Gottfried von Strassburg also describes some of the entertainment music which might have been heard in court during the thirteenth century: 'at night here at home we shall sustain ourselves with courtly pursuits, such as harping, fiddling, and singing.'[54] On special occasions, such as the visit of a noble from a distant country, there must have been a much broader range of entertainment. We have a glimpse of an elaborate outdoor entertainment in the anonymous Romance, *Laurin*.

> The noble guests saw many beautiful things and were treated very well. They were seated on golden benches that sparkled with precious stones, and the best of wine and mead was poured for them. There was much entertainment of different kinds for them to watch. On one side there was singing; on the other men were jumping and engaged in tests of strength; then came the spear throwing and stone throwing, with several events going on at the same time; riders charged into each other right in front of them, and many spears were broken in jousts; they heard a large number of skillful musicians: fiddlers, harpers, and pipers.
>
> Later two short fiddlers, delightful dwarfs in rich and elegant clothing, came before the princes. The fiddles they carried were of red gold, glittered with jewels, and were worth more than a country. Their strings made sweet music. The princes enjoyed the fiddling, and time passed quickly ...
>
> Afterwards two fine singers and narrators appeared and sang many courtly tales to amuse and charm the guests ... Anyone who was well-versed in song would have forgotten all his sorrow.[55]

Gottfried von Strassburg makes a clear aesthetic division in entertainment between musicians and entertainers such as magicians and story tellers. This last type of entertainer offers nothing to delight the heart, they are, he says, like a tree without leaves.

> Inventors of wild tales, hired hunters after stories, who cheat with chains and dupe dull minds, who turn rubbish into gold for children and from magic boxes pour pearls of dust!—these give us shade with a bare staff, not with the green leaves and twigs and boughs of May. Their shade never soothes a stranger's eyes. To speak the truth, no pleasurable emotion comes from it, there is nothing in it to delight the heart. Their poetry is not such that a noble heart can laugh with it.[56]

---

[52] Liechtenstein, *In Service of Ladies*, lines 485ffr. The first musician mentioned here is the 'one-man band' known as the pipe and tabor player.

[53] Eschenbach, *Parzival*, 12.

[54] Strassburg, *Tristan*, 92.

[55] Thomas, *Novellas*, 71ff.

[56] Strassburg, *Tristan*, 105.

There are also a number of interesting references to banquet music in the Minnesinger repertoire. In *Parzival* we read of some of the squires playing fiddle after dinner. But apparently their level of performance was not satisfactory, 'their mastery did not go beyond playing old-fashioned dances,' so a call goes out for any visiting minstrels who may be in court.[57]

Accounts of court festivities often mention that these visiting minstrels were well paid. The anonymous Romance, *Duke Ernst*, describes a wedding banquet for the emperor and the lavish gifts he gave his knights and ladies in attendance. The visiting musicians were included in this largess.

> The host of wandering minstrels there also received plenty of gifts, so they too were joyous.[58]

Hartmann von Aue tells of a similar wedding festivity in which he assures us there were no fewer than three thousand visiting musicians!

> A dance began as soon as the meal was finished and lasted until nightfall. Sadness vanished. If they had been unhappy, their joy was now as great. They went to the ladies who received them warmly. There the entertainment was good. In addition they were delighted by sweet string music and other pastimes—storytelling and singing, and lively dancing. All types of skills were presented, and each by a master in his field. There were easily three thousand or more of the very best minstrels in the world there, who were called masters. Never was there greater splendor neither before nor since than at this celebration.[59]

In the *Nibelungenlied* we read of a minstrel who was not so fortunate. Playing for a banquet, he was caught in a scene of slaughter.

> He saw a minstrel sitting at Etzel's table, and sprang at him in wrath, and lopped off his right hand on his viol: 'Take that for the message thou broughtest to the Burgundians.'
> 'Woe is me for my hand!' cried Werbel. 'Sir Hagen of Trony, what have I done to thee? I rode with true heart to thy master's land. How shall I make my music now?'
> Little recked Hagen if he never fiddled more.[60]

Associations of music and dance are common in all literature, but in the Minnesinger repertoire one often finds dance with singing. Among several such references in *Tannhauser*, we find this recommendation to youth:

> Come, young folks, taste it, life is sweet!
> And since God gave us voice and feet,
> We'll seize this chance to sing and dance.[61]

---

57 Book XIII, 639.
58 *Duke Ernst*, trans. J. W. Thomas and Carolyn Dussere, in *Medieval Tales* (New York: Continuum, 1983), 27.
59 Aue, *Erec*, lines 2142ff.
60 'Thirty-Third Adventure.'
61 'Uns kvmt ein wunneklichu zit,' in *Tannhauser*, 103.

Many of these songs with dance are seasonal and outdoors, such as for May Day. But there is also some indication that they were performed during any festivity. Such a dance occurs after jousting, for example, in Wernher der Gartenaere's Romance, *Meier Helmbrecht*.

> When they had finished with the lance
> They trod the measures of a dance
> Accompanied by dashing song.
> To no one did the time seem long.[62]

---

[62] Wernher der Gartenaere, *Meier Helmbrecht*, trans. Claire Hayden Bell, 62.

The Music of the Goliards

STANDING APART FROM THE ARISTOCRATIC POETRY of the twelfth and thirteenth century Minnesingers, troubadours and trouvères is a smaller body of work reflecting the lower side of society and a group of people we call, collectively, the Goliards.[1] While the former poetry was sung in the new indigenous languages of German and French, the latter is in Latin, the language of both cleric and student.

A number of these Goliard poets were disaffected clerics, the result of a period of questioning caused not only by the bitter struggles between emperor and pope, but by important new heresies, in particular the Albigensian heresy. It follows that an interesting common thread in the Goliard poetry is a return to references of pagan gods.

One of these former Churchmen, a cleric turned harpist singing in taverns, was the poet, Walter of Chatillon,[2] one of only two Goliards we know by name.

> In the tavern let me die,
> That's my resolution,
> Bring me wine for lips so dry
> At life's dissolution.
> Joyfully the angel's choir
> Then will sing my glory:
> 'Sit deus propicius
> Huic potatori.'[3]

One scholar refers to these wandering clerics as the 'ecclesiastical equivalent of jongleurs,'[4] and indeed the song of one of them suggests the same impoverished existence.

> I, a cleric on the loose,
> Given to tribulation,
> Am for toil and travail born,
> Poverty's my ration.
>
> For the arts and literature
> I possess a yearning,
> Still, my indigence compels
> Me to cease from learning.

---

[1] From Golias, a variant of Goliath, or perhaps gula (gullet). By the thirteenth century the term had become one of reproach.

[2] First known as 'Gualtherus ab Insulis,' Walther was born in Lille and became canon in Reims. While part of the chancery of Henry II, of England, he was present when Thomas a Becket was murdered. He enjoyed a great reputation as head of the cathedral school of Chatillon. The other, Hugh of Orleans spent his life as a genuine vagabond, always broke and generally being evicted from some house because of his sharp tongue.

[3] 'The Vagabond's Confession,' in *Vagabond Verse*, trans. Edwin H. Zeydel (Detroit: Wayne State University Press, 1966), 63, 'May God be well-disposed to this old drunk.'

[4] George Whicher, *The Goliard Poets* (George Whicher, 1949), 4.

> All my clothing that I wear,
> Frail it is and torn;
> Oftentimes I suffer cold
> Since of warmth I'm shorn ...
>
> Take St. Martin's attitude,
> Never mean or shoddy,
> Give the pilgrim-scholar clothes,
> Cover up his body.[5]

Some of these disaffected poets were students, as is evident in the song which begins, 'Cast aside dull books and thought; Sweet is folly, sweet is play.'[6] They dropped out, or traveled from school to school, and we associate with them especially the Latin repertoire of German songs known as the 'Carmina Burana.' One of these, in fact, is composed by a person who identifies himself as a student from Paris, and one skilled in singing,

> with other men
> who are skilled in singing
> various songs and in giving
> their joys to spring.[7]

In another song, a German student also mentions Paris and his desire to study philosophy there.

> Dear my fatherland, to you,
> Sweet Swabian Swabia, adieu,
> Beloved France to which I roam,
> All hail! Philosophy's your home!
> Take the foreign student up
> To your bosom, please,
> And when the time's ripe, send him back
> Well trained like Socrates![8]

Some Goliards, like the anonymous poet known as the Archpoet of Cologne, drifted in and out of the court environment, probably never adjusting to the demands of that life-style.

> Public life, there's no mistake,
> Certain poets find irking;
> Courts they willingly forsake,

---

5   'Exul ego clericus,' in *Vagabond Verse*, 73.

6   'Quittamus studia,' from the Carmina Burana literature, quoted in John Symonds, *Wine Women and Song; Mediaeval Latin Students' Songs* (New York: Cooper Square Publishers, 1966), 99.

7   'Si de More,' in E.D. Blodgett, trans., *The Love Songs of the Carmina Burana* (New York: Garland Publishing, Inc., 1987), 221. Codex latinus 4660, in the Bavarian State Library, this manuscript came from the monastery of the Benediktbeuren, south of Munchen, where it had been kept in a secret cabinet of 'forbidden' books. The manuscript contains 131 love songs, 55 moral, satirical or historical songs, 35 vagabond songs and 6 religious plays.

8   'Hospita in Gallia,' in *Vagabond Verse*, 77.

In seclusion lurking;
There they study, drudge, and wake,
No endeavor shirking,
Hoping one great poem to make
Ere they cease from working.

Starveling rhymesters, when they thirst
Water is their potion!
City din they count accurst
And the crowd's commotion.
Foundlings by the Muses nursed,
Fame's their only notion:
Fame they sometimes win, but first
Die of their devotion.[9]

Like their more noble cousins, the Minnesingers and troubadours, the Goliards sing of the seasons,[10] especially Spring, and of love. Whereas the former sang of aristocratic ladies and the most noble forms of love, the Goliard sings of peasant girls[11] and makes love the subject for satire. In one example, the poet suddenly finds himself disagreeing with what he had been singing.

Stop, this song displeases me
That I've recited,
My opinion contradicts
What I've indited.

For punishment, he recommends that the young lady lock him up in her bedroom![12]

While the troubadour hoped to win his lady through the quality of his song, Hugh of Orleans says, no, the women are mainly interested in food, not music!

Dinner they love far more than music, whatever the type.
When the aroma approaches their nose, they will relish tripe
Or a plateful of rubbish, but music, it has no appeal.[13]

In only one Goliard song, from the Carmina Burana collection, do we find the genuine expression of pain felt by an unhappy lover.

---

[9] 'Estuans intrinsecus,' known as 'The Confession of Golias,' in Whicher, *The Goliard Poets*, 111.

[10] One of the Carmina Burana songs, 'Quocumque More Motu Volvuntur Tempora,' begins,

Whichever way the seasons turn in their movement,
Accordingly I beat my trusty, well-tempered drums.

[11] Only one Goliard song, 'Nahtegel, sing einen Don mit Sinne,' from the Carmina Burana collection, refers to an aristocratic lady.

[12] 'Volo virum vivere,' in *Vagabond Verse*, 139.

[13] 'Quid luges, lirice,' in Ibid., 237.

> Grief, lament, sadness, anxiety
> have encumbered my quaking limbs all at once.
>
> For grief, as if it spoke in verse,
> my song abates: nothing remains but lament.
>
> To an awful fate my lyre is bound;
> despised, it mourns.[14]

In our favorite Goliard song a poet-musician tells us that wine brings feelings of love, and love feelings of music, but he would give up both wine and love before music.

> Bacchus wakes within my breast
> Love and love's desire,
> Venus comes and stirs the blessed
> Rage of Phoebus's fire;
> Deathless honor is our due
> From the laureled sire:
> Woe should I turn traitor to
> Wine and love and lyre!
>
> Should a tyrant rise and say,
> 'Give up wine!' I'd do it;
> 'Love no girls!' I would obey,
> Though my heart should rue it.
> 'Dash thy lyre!' suppose he saith,
> Naught should bring me to it;
> 'Yield thy lyre or die!' my breath,
> Dying, should thrill through it![15]

A number of surviving Goliard songs, like the above, attribute the inspiration of their music and poetry to wine. One poet says he drinks not for thirst, but for better thinking ability.[16] Another is somewhat more specific, contending that the quality of his poetry is dependent on the quality of the wine!

> Special gifts for every man
> Nature will produce,
> I, when I compose my verse,
> Vintage wine must use,
> All the best the cellar's casks
> Hold of these libations.
> Such a wine calls forth from me
> Copious conversations.

---

14 'Captus Amore Gravi.'
15 Quoted in Symonds, *Wine, Women and Song*, 162.
16 'Bacchic Frenzy,' in Ibid., 173.

> My verse has the quality
> Of the wine I sip,
> I can not do much until
> Food has passed my lip,
> What I write when starved and parched
> Is of the lowest class,
> When I'm tight, with verse I make
> Ovid I surpass.
>
> As a poet 'er can I
> Be appreciated
> Till my stomach has been well
> Filled with food and sated,
> When god Bacchus gains my brain's
> Lofty citadel
> Phoebus rushes in to voice
> Many a miracle.[17]

The wandering Archpoet of Cologne frankly tells us he writes from a different form of inspiration.

> And poems more sweet than tongue can tell
> I'll write you—if you pay me well.[18]

The Goliard literature reveals little regarding aesthetic purpose in music. Hugh of Orleans speaks of the ability of music to relieve grief, here the grief brought by Fate.

> Let us endure what cannot be changed, let's bear it serenely!
> Only the lyre assuages the grief that smarts ever keenly.[19]

One of the most famous of the Carmina Burana songs, 'The Wheel of Fortune,' seems to have the same meaning.

> Don't delay,
> Strike the lyre with grave intent;
> How our fate
> Fells what's great!
> Come ye, join in my lament.[20]

Another of the Carmina Burana songs not only gives the purpose of music to soothe, but to actually *change* the state of the listener.

---

[17] In 'Estuans intrinsecus,' in *Vagabond Verse*, 67.
[18] In 'Fama tuba dante sonum,' in Whicher, *The Goliard Poets*, 123.
[19] In 'Quid luges, lirice,' in *Vagabond Verse*, 237.
[20] 'O Fortuna,' in Ibid., 47.

> So the power
> of lyre-strings soothes the breast
> and change
> the heart that wavers
> from the plights of love.[21]

This repertoire of tavern songs, Church satire, and political protest never addresses the importance to man of engaging in emotional communication through music. Only in the most indirect reference do we find some hint that this universal facet of music was understood, such as in the song quoted above in which the compulsion to compose is described as the 'blessed rage of Phoebus's fire.'

With the Goliards we see the underside of society, the reflections of disaffected students and clerics. Their poverty necessitates their focus on such basic needs as food and shelter, and not philosophy or aesthetics. One, the Archpoet of Cologne, has some characteristics of a genuine nineteenth-century Romanticist as he curses city life and dreams of artistic fame.

It would be a long time before musicians enjoy artistic fame and social respectability of which this Goliard sings. Indeed, there may be some musicians even today who wonder if they are truly accepted as 'normal' members of society.

---

[21] 'Dum Diane Vitrea,' in Blodgett, *The Love Songs of the Carmina Burana*, 22.

Bibliography

CHAPTER 1 ON EARLY PERFORMERS

Aelianus. *On the Characteristics of Animals*

Ammianus Marcellinus. *Constantius et Gallus*. Translated by John C. Rolfe. London: Heinemann, 1935.

Aristophanes. *The Thesmophoriazusae*.

Aristotle. *Atheniensium Respublica*.

Aristotle. *Coming-to-be and Passing-away*.

Aristotle. *Politica*.

Athenaeus. *Deipnosophistae*.

Capella, Martianus. *Martianus Capella and the Seven Liberal Arts*. Translated by William Harris Stahl and Richard Johnson. New York: Columbia University Press, 1977.

Cicero. *Brutus*.

Diogenes. *Lives of the Eminent Philosophers*. Translated by R. D. Hicks. Cambridge: Harvard University Press, 1950.

Epic and Saga, Vol. 49, *The Harvard Classics*. New York: Collier.

The Greek Anthology. Translated by W. R. Paton. Cambridge: Harvard University Press, 1939.

Horace. *De Arte Poetica liber*. Edited by F. Vollmer. Leipzig, 1925.

Hucbald, Guido, and John on Music. Translated by Warren Babb. New Haven: Yale University Press, 1978.

John of Salisbury. *The Metalogicon*. Translated by Daniel McGarry. Berkeley: University of California Press, 1955.

Julian. 'The Heroic Deeds of Constantius,' in *The Works of the Emperor Julian*. Translated by Wilmer Wright. London: Heinemann, 1913.

Julian. *The Works of the Emperor Julian*. Translated by Wilmer Wright. London: Heinemann, 1913.

Marie de France. *French Mediaeval Romances from the Lays of Marie de France*. Translated by Eugene Mason. London: Dent, 1924.

Ovid. *Metamorphoses*.

Page, Christopher. *Voices and Instruments of the Middle Ages*. London: Dent, 1987.

Philostratus. *The Life of Apollonius of Tyana*.

Pickard-Cambridge, Arthur. *The Dramatic Festivals of Athens*. Oxford: Clarendon Press, 1953.

St. Paulinus of Nola. *The Poems of St. Paulinus of Nola*. Translated by P. G. Walsh. New York: Newman Press, 1975.

Sendrey, Alfred. *Music in the Social and Religious Life of Antiquity*. Rutherford: Fairleigh Dickinson University Press, 1974.

Sidonius. *Sidonius Poems and Letters*. Translated by W. B. Anderson. Cambridge: Harvard University Press, 1965.

Suetonius. *Lives of the Caesars*.

Xenophon. *Memorabilia and Oeconomicus*. Translated by E. C. Marchant. Cambridge: Harvard University Press, 1953.

CHAPTER 2 ON ANCIENT SINGERS

Adomnan. *Life of Columba*. Translated by Alan Anderson and Marjorie Anderson. London: Nelson, 1961.

Aristophanes. *Clouds*.

Aristotle. *De Anima*.

Athenaeus. *Deipnosophistae*.

Bede. 'Life of St. Cuthbert,' in *Two Lives of Saint Cuthbert*. Translated by Bertram Colgrave. New York: Greenwood Press, 1969.

Chappell, W. *The History of Music*. London: Chappell.

Davenport, Guy. *Archilochos, Sappho, Alkman*. Berkeley: University of California Press, 1980.

Diogenes Laertius, in *Lives of the Eminent Philosophers*. Translated by R. D. Hicks. Cambridge: Harvard University Press, 1950.

Dionysius the Pseudo-Areopagite. *The Ecclesiastical Hierarchy*. Translated by Thomas Campbell. Washington, D.C.: University Press of America.

The Greek Anthology. Translated by W. R. Paton. Cambridge: Harvard University Press, 1939.

Gregory of Tours. *The History of the Franks*. Translated by Lewis Thorpe. Harmonsworth: Penguin Books, 1974.

Herodotus. *The Histories*.

Hucbald, Guido, and John on Music. Translated by Warren Babb. New Haven: Yale University Press, 1978.

Jebb, Richard C. *Bacchylides*. Hildesheim, Georg Olms Verlagsbuchhandlung, 1967.

Juvenal. *Satires*.

Nagy, Gregory. *Pindar's Homer*. Baltimore: Johns Hopkins University Press, 1982.

Pliny the Elder. *Natural History*.

Plutarch. *Concerning Music*.

Strunk, Oliver. *Source Readings in Music History*. New York: Norton, 1950.

Suetonius. *The Twelve Caesars*. New York: Penguin, 1989.

Tacitus. *The Annals*.

Thucydides. *The Peloponnesian War*. New York: Modern Library, 1951.

Chapter 3 On the Ancient Rhapsodist

Apel, Willi. *Harvard Dictionary of Music.* Cambridge: Harvard University Press, 1953.

Bacon, Roger. *The Opus Majus of Roger Bacon.* Translated by Robert Burke. New York: Russell & Russell, 1962.

Capella, Martianus. *Martianus Capella and the Seven Liberal Arts.* William Harris Stahl and Richard Johnson. New York: Columbia University Press, 1977.

Couperin, Fraançois. *L'Art de toucher.*

Hooker, Richard. *Bureaucrats & Barbarians, The Greek Dark Ages* (1996).

Monteverdi, Claudio. *The Letters of Claudio Monteverdi.* Translated by Denis Stevens. Cambridge: Cambridge University Press, 1980.

Plato. *Ion.*

Plato. *Symposium.*

Pliny the Younger. *Letters of Plinius.* Translated by William Melmoth. Collier Press, 1909.

Strunk, Oliver. *Source Readings in Music History.* New York: Norton, 1950.

Chapter 4 On Women Performers of the Ancient World

Athenaeus. *Deipnosophistae.*

Chambers, E. K. *The Mediaeval Stage.* Oxford, 1903.

The Greek Anthology. W. R. Paton. Cambridge: Harvard University Press, 1939.

Hildegard von Bingen. *Divine Words.*

Hildegard of Bingen. *Hildegard of Bingen.* Edited by Fiona Bowie and Oliver Davies. New York: Crossroad, 1993.

Horace. *Odes.*

Horace. *Satires.*

Livy. *History of Rome.*

Ovid. *Metamorphoses.*

Ovid. *The Love Poems.*

Persaeus of Citium. *Convivial Notes.*

Plato. *The Anabasis of Cyrus.* Translated by Carleton L. Brownson. Cambridge: Harvard University Press, 1947.

Plato. *Gorgias.*

Plato. *Symposium.*

Plautus. *Epidicus.*

Plautus. *The Pot of Gold.*

Pliny the Elder. *Natural History.*

Pliny the Younger. *The Letters of the Younger Pliny.* New York: Penguin, 1985.

Plutarch. *Concerning the Cure of Anger.*

Propertius. *The Poems.*

Sendrey, Alfred. *Music in the Social and Religious Life of Antiquity*. Rutherford: Fairleigh Dickinson University Press, 1974.
Strassburg, Gottfried von. *Tristan*. Translated by Arthus Hatto. Harmondsworth: Penguin Books, 1960.
Tacitus. *Annals*.
Terence. *The Brothers*.

CHAPTER 5 ON ANCIENT CONDUCTORS

Athenaeus. *Deipnosophistae*.
Bottrigari, Hercole. *Il Desiderio*. Translated by Carol MacClintock. American Institute of Musicology, 1962.
David, Hans T. and Arthur Mendel. *The Bach Reader*. New York: Norton, 1966.
Farmer, Henry G., 'The Music of Ancient Mesopotamia,' in *The New Oxford History of Music*. London: Oxford University Press, 1966.
Herodotus, *Histories*.
Hildegard von Bingen. *The Book of Divine Works*. Edited by Matthew Fox. Santa Fe: Bear & Company, 1987.
Manniche, Lise. *Music and Musicians in Ancient Egypt*. London: British Museum Press, 1991.
Mattheson, Johann. *Der vollkommene Capellmeister* (1739). Translated by Ernest Harriss. Ann Arbor: UMI Research Press, 1981.
Nagy, Gregory. *Pindar's Homer*. Baltimore: Johns Hopkins University Press, 1982.
Ovid. *Tristia*.
Plutarch. *Laconic Apophthegms*.
Saint Gregory of Nazianzus. 'Concerning his own Life,' Translated by Denis Meehan. Washington, D.C.: The Catholic University of America Press.
Sendrey, Alfred. *Music in the Social and Religious Life of Antiquity*. Rutherford: Fairleigh Dickinson University Press.
Xenophon. *Memorabilia and Oeconomicus*. Translated by E. C. Marchant. Cambridge: Harvard University Press, 1953.
Xenophon. *Scripta Minora*. Translated by E. C. Marchant. Cambridge: Harvard University Press, 1956.

CHAPTER 6 ON THE ANCIENT AULOS

Athenaeus. *Deipnosophistae*.
Claudius Aelianus. *Of the Characteristics of Animals*.
Diogenes Laertius. *Lives of the Eminent Philosophers*. Translated by R. D. Hicks. Cambridge: Harvard University Press, 1950.
The Greek Anthology. W. R. Paton. Cambridge: Harvard University Press, 1939.
Herodotus. *Histories*.

Horace. *The Art of Poetry*. Translated by H. Rushton Fairclough. Cambridge: Harvard University Press, 1955.
Isidore of Seville. *Etymologiarum*.
Jebb, Richard C. *Bacchylides*. Hildesheim, Georg Olms Verlagsbuchhandlung, 1967.
The Letters of Abelard and Heloise. Translated by C. K. Scott Moncrieff. New York: Knopf, 1933.
Livy. *A History of Rome*.
Lucretius. *The Way Things Are*.
Marcus Varro. *On the Latin Language*.
Ovid. *Fasti*.
Ovid. *Fasti*.
Ovid. *The Art of Love*.
Philostratus. *The Life of Apollonius of Tyana*.
Pickard-Cambridge, Arthur. *The Dramatic Festivals of Athens*. Oxford: Clarendon Press, 1953.
Pliny the Elder. *Natural History*.
Plutarch. *Concerning Music*.
Plutarch. *Lives*.
Polybius. *Histories*.
Polybius. *The Histories*. Translated by W. R. Paton. Cambridge: Harvard University Press, 1954.
Propertius. *The Poems*.
Sendrey, Alfred. *Music in the Social and Religious Life of Antiquity*. Rutherford: Fairleigh Dickinson University Press, 1974.
Sophocles. *Ajax*.
Sophocles. *The Trachiniae*.
Strabo. *The Geography of Strabo*. Translated by Horace L. Jones. Cambridge: Harvard University Press, 1960.
Theophrastus. *Historia Plantarum*.

Chapter 7 On the Ancient Trumpet

Aeschylus. *The Complete Plays of Aeschylus*. Translated by Gilbert Murray. London: George Allen, 1952.
Aeschylus. *Eumenides*.
Athenaeus. *Deipnosophistae*.
Calpurnius Siculus. *Eclogue IV*
Euripides. *The Phoenician Woman*.
Horace. *Odes*.
Jebb, Richard C. *Bacchylides*. Hildesheim, Georg Olms Verlagsbuchhandlung, 1967.
Josephus. *Jewish Antiquities*.
Juvenal. *Satires*.

Livy. *History of Rome.*
Pliny the Elder. *Natural History,*
Pliny the Younger. *The Letters of the Younger Pliny.* New York: Penguin, 1985.
Propertius. *The Poems.*
Sendrey, Alfred. *Music in the Social and Religious Life of Antiquity.* Rutherford: Fairleigh Dickinson University Press, 1974.
Sophocles. *Ajax.*
Strabo. *On Geography.*
Suetonius. *The Twelve Caesars.* New York: Penguin, 1989.
Tacitus. *The Annals.* New York: Modern Library, 1942.
Tibullus. *The Poems.*
Varro, Marcus. *On the Latin Language.*
Virgil. *Aeneid.*

CHAPTER 8 ON THE MEDIEVAL TRUMPET

Bernardino Corio. *L'Historia di Milano volgarmente scritta.* Padoa, 1646.
Epic and Saga, Vol. 49, *The Harvard Classics.* New York: Collier.
The Exeter Book. Oxford University Press, 1958.
Kantorowicz, Ernst. *Frederick the Second.* Translated by E. O. Lorimer. New York, 1957.
Mizawa, S. *Nicholas Copernicus.* New York, 1943.
Otto of Freising. *The Deeds of Frederick Barbarossa.* Translated by Charles Mierow. New York: Columbia University Press, 1953.
Paris, Matthew. *English History.* Translated by J. A. Giles. London: Bohn, 1852.
The Song of Roland. Translated by Robert Harrison. New York: Mentor, 1970.
Stone, Edward, trans. *Three Old French Chronicles of the Crusades.* Seattle: The University of Washington Press, 1939.
Ulrich von Liechtenstein. *In Service of Ladies.* Translated by J. W. Thomas. Chapel Hill: The University of North Carolina Press, 1969.
Wace, Robert. *Roman de Brut.* Translated by Gwyn Jones. London: Dent, 1962.
Zeydel, Edwin H. *Vagabond Verse.* Detroit: Wayne State University Press, 1966.

CHAPTER 9 ON THE JONGLEUR

Chambers, E. K. *The Mediaeval Stage.* Oxford, 1903.
Duncan, Edmondstoune. *The Story of Minstrelsy.* Detroit: Singing Tree Press, 1968.
Faral, E., ed. *Mimes Francais du XIII siecle.* Paris, 1910.
Funck-Brentano, Fr. *The Middle Ages.* New York, 1923.
Geoffrey of Monmouth. *The History of the Kings of Britain.* Translated by Lewis Thorpe. Baltimore: Penguin Books, 1966.
Gerbert, Martin. *Scriptores ecclesiastici de musica sacra.* Saint Blaise, 1784.

Gibbon, Edward. *The History of the Decline and Fall of the Roman Empire*. Philadelphia: Coates.
Goldin, Frederick. *Lyrics of the Troubadours and Trouveres*. Garden City: Anchor Books, 1973.
Hillgarth, J. N. *The Spanish Kingdoms*. Oxford, 1976.
The Journey of Charlemagne. Translated by Jean-Louis Picherit. Birmingham, AL: Summa, 1984.
Three Lives of the Last Englishmen. Translated by Michael Swanton. New York: Garland Publishing, 1984.
Lorris, Guillaume de and Jean de Meun. *The Romance of the Rose*. Translated by Harry Robbins. New York: Dutton, 1962.
Lull, Ramon. *Selected Works of Ramon Lull*. Translated by Anthony Bonner. Princeton University Press, 1985.
McKinney, Howard D. and W. R. Anderson. *Music in History*. Boston, 1940.
Marie de France. *French Mediaeval Romances from the Lays of Marie de France*. Translated by Eugene Mason. London: Dent, 1924.
Page, Christopher. *Voices and Instruments of the Middle Ages*. London: Dent, 1987.
Saldoni, M. Balthasar. *Diccionario biografio-bibliografico de Efemèrides de musicos españoles*.
Sharman, Ruth. *The Cansos and Sirventes of the Troubadour Giraut de Borneil*. Cambridge: Cambridge University Press, 1989.
The Song of William. Translated by Edward Stone. Seattle: University of Washington Press, 1951.
Stone, Edward, trans. *Three Old French Chronicles of the Crusades*. Seattle: The University of Washington Press, 1939.
Vagabond Verse. Translated by Edwin H. Zeydel. Detroit: Wayne State University Press, 1966.
Wace, Robert. *Roman de Brut*. Translated by Gwyn Jones. London: Dent, 1962.
Whicher, George. *The Goliard Poets*. George Whicher, 1949.
Wilkins, Nigel, ed. *Two Miracles*. Edinburgh: Scottish Academic Press, 1972.

CHAPTER 10 ON THE MINSTREL

Chambers, E. K. *The Mediaeval Stage*. Oxford, 1903.
Chaucer. *House of Fame*.
Christine de Pizan. *The Book of the Duke of True Lovers*. Translated by Thelma Fenster. New York: Persea books, 1991.
Christine de Pizan. *Mirror of Honor; the Treasury of the City of Ladies*. Translated by Charity Willard. Tenafly, NJ: Bard Hall Press, 1989.
Crewdson, H. A. F. *The Worshipful Company of Musicians*. London: Knight.
Duncan, Edmonstoune. *The Story of Minstrelsy*. Detroit, 1968.
Goldin, Frederick. trans. *German and Italian Lyrics of the Middle Ages*. Garden City: Anchor Books, 1973.
Goldron, Romain. *Minstrels and Masters*. H. S. Stuttman Co.

Gosson, Stephen. 'An Apologie of the Schoole of Abuse,' in *The Schoole of Abuse*. Edited by Edward Arber. London, 1868.
Langland, William. *Piers Plowman*. Translated by E. Talbot Donaldson. New York: Norton, 1990.
Larner, John. *Culture and Society in Italy, 1290–1420*. New York: Scribner's, 1971.
Reese, Gustave. *Music in the Renaissance*. New York: Norton, 1959.
Sacchetti, Franco. *Tales from Sacchetti*. Trans;lated by Mary Steegmann. Westport: Hyperion Press, 1978.
Salmen, Walter. *Der Fahrende Musiker im Europaischen Mittelalter*. Kassel, 1960.
Skelton, John. 'The Bouge of Court,' in *The Complete Poems of John Skelton*. Edited by Philip Henderson. London: Dent, 1959.
Stevens, John. *Music & Poetry in the Early Tudor Court*. London: Methuen), 302.
Stubbs, Philip. *The Anatomy of the Abuses in England* [1583]. Edited by Frederick Furnivall. London: The New Shakespeare Society, n.d.
Villon, François. *The Complete Works of Francois Villon*. Translated by Anthony Bonner. New York: David McKay, 1960.
Woodfill, Walter. *Musicians in English Society from Elizabeth to Charles I*. Princeton, 1953.

CHAPTER 11 THE MUSIC OF THE TROUBADOURS

Blackburn, Paul. *Proensa*. Berkeley: University of California Press, 1978.
Bonner, Anthony. *Songs of the Troubadours*. New York: Schocken Books, 1972.
Dante. *Purgatorio*.
Goldin, Frederick. *Lyrics of the Troubadours and Trouvères*. Garden City: Anchor Books, 1973.
Nichols, Stephen. *The Songs of Bernart de Ventadorn*. Chapel Hill: The University of North Carolina Press, 1965.
Press, Alan. *Anthology of Troubadour Lyric Poetry*. Austin: University of Texas Press, 1971.
Sharman, Ruth. *The Cansos and Sirventes of the Troubadour Giraut de Borneil*. Cambridge: Cambridge University Press, 1989.

CHAPTER 12 THE MUSIC OF THE FRENCH ROMANCES AND CHANSONS DE GESTE

Gesta Romanorum. Translated by Charles Swan. London: C. and J. Rivington, 1824.
de Coinci, Gautier. *Les Miracles de Nostre Dame par Gautier de Coinci*. Edited by V. R. Koenig. Geneva, 1955–1970.
de Troyes, Chreien. *The Complete romances of Chreien de Troyes*. Translated by David Staines. Bloomington: Indiana University Press, 1993.
Lorris, Guillaume de and Jean de Meun. *The Romance of the Rose*. Translated by Harry Robbins. New York: Dutton, 1962.
Marie de France. *French Mediaeval Romances from the Lays of Marie de France*. Translated by Eugene Mason. London: Dent, 1924.

Page, Christopher. *Voices and Instruments of the Middle Ages*. London: Dent, 1987.
The Song of Roland. Translated by Robert Harrison. New York: Mentor, 1970.
Wace, Robert. *Roman de Brut*. Translated by Gwyn Jones. London: Dent, 1962.

CHAPTER 13 THE MUSIC OF THE MINNESINGERS

Aristotle. *Poetics*.
Duke Ernst. Translated by J. W. Thomas and Carolyn Dussere, in *Medieval Tales*. New York: Continuum, 1983.
Eschenbach, Wolfram von. *Parzival*. Translated by Helen Mustard and Charles Passage. New York: Vintage Books, 1961.
Eschenbach, Wolfram von. *Willehalm*. Translated by Charles Passage. New York: Ungar, 1977.
Eschenbach, Wolfram von. *Titurel and the Songs*. Translated by Marion Gibbs and Sidney Johnson. New York: Garland Publishing, 1988.
Goldin, Frederick, trans. *German and Italian Lyrics of the Middle Ages*. Garden City: Anchor Books, 1973.
Hartmann von Aue. *Erec*. Translated by Thomas Keller. New York: Garland, 1987.
Liechtenstein, Ulrich von. *In Service of Ladies*. Translated by J. W. Thomas. Chapel Hill: The University of North Carolina Press, 1969.
Strassburg, Gottfried von. *Tristan*. Translated by Arthus Hatto. Harmondsworth: Penguin Books, 1960.
Tannhauser. *Tannhauser: Poet and Legend*. Translated by J. W. Thomas. Chapel Hill: University of North Carolina Press, 1974.
Thomas, J. W. *The Best Novellas of Medieval Germany*. Columbia, S.C.: Camden House, 1984.
Vogelweide, Walter von der. *Selected Poems of Walter von der Vogelweide*. Translated by W. Alison Phillips. London: Smith, Elder, & Co., 1896.

CHAPTER 14 THE MUSIC OF THE GOLIARDS

Blodgett, E. D., trans. *The Love Songs of the Carmina Burana*. New York: Garland Publishing, Inc., 1987.
Symonds, John. *Wine Women and Song; Mediaeval Latin Students' Songs*. New York: Cooper Square Publishers, 1966.
Vagabond Verse. Translated by Edwin H. Zeydel. Detroit: Wayne State University Press, 1966.
Whicher, George. *The Goliard Poets*. George Whicher, 1949.

About the Author

Dr. David Whitwell is a graduate ('with distinction') of the University of Michigan and the Catholic University of America, Washington DC (PhD, Musicology, Distinguished Alumni Award, 2000) and has studied conducting with Eugene Ormandy and at the Akademie für Musik, Vienna. Prior to coming to Northridge, Dr. Whitwell participated in concerts throughout the United States and Asia as Associate First Horn in the USAF Band and Orchestra in Washington DC, and in recitals throughout South America in cooperation with the United States State Department.

At the California State University, Northridge, which is in Los Angeles, Dr. Whitwell developed the CSUN Wind Ensemble into an ensemble of international reputation, with international tours to Europe in 1981 and 1989 and to Japan in 1984. The CSUN Wind Ensemble has made professional studio recordings for BBC (London), the Köln Westdeutscher Rundfunk (Germany), NOS National Radio (The Netherlands), Zürich Radio (Switzerland), the Television Broadcasting System (Japan) as well as for the United States State Department for broadcast on its 'Voice of America' program. The CSUN Wind Ensemble's recording with the Mirecourt Trio in 1982 was named the 'Record of the Year' by The Village Voice. Composers who have guest conducted Whitwell's ensembles include Aaron Copland, Ernest Krenek, Alan Hovhaness, Morton Gould, Karel Husa, Frank Erickson and Vaclav Nelhybel.

Dr. Whitwell has been a guest professor in 100 different universities and conservatories throughout the United States and in 23 foreign countries (most recently in China, in an elite school housed in the Forbidden City). Guest conducting experiences have included the Philadelphia Orchestra, Seattle Symphony Orchestra, the Czech Radio Orchestras of Brno and Bratislava, The National Youth Orchestra of Israel, as well as resident wind ensembles in Russia, Israel, Austria, Switzerland, Germany, England, Wales, The Netherlands, Portugal, Peru, Korea, Japan, Taiwan, Canada and the United States.

He is a past president of the College Band Directors National Association, a member of the Prasidium of the International Society for the Promotion of Band Music, and was a member of the founding board of directors of the World Association for Symphonic Bands and Ensembles (WASBE). In 1964 he was made an honorary life member of Kappa Kappa Psi, a national professional music fraternity. In September, 2001, he was a delegate to the UNESCO Conference on Global Music in Tokyo. He has been knighted by sovereign organizations in France, Portugal and Scotland and has been awarded the gold medal of Kerkrade, The Netherlands, and the silver medal of Wangen, Germany, the highest honor given wind conductors in the United States, the medal of the Academy of Wind and Percussion Arts (National Band Association) and the highest honor given wind conductors in Austria, the gold medal of the Austrian Band Association. He is a member of the Hall of Fame of the California Music Educators Association.

Dr. Whitwell's publications include more than 127 articles on wind literature including publications in Music and Letters (London), the London Musical Times, the Mozart-Jahrbuch (Salzburg), and 52 books, among which is his 13-volume *History and Literature of the Wind Band and Wind Ensemble* and an 8-volume series on *Aesthetics in Music*. In addition to numerous modern editions of early wind band music his original compositions include 5 symphonies.

David Whitwell was named as one of six men who have determined the course of American bands during the second half of the 20th century, in the definitive history, *The Twentieth Century American Wind Band* (Meredith Music).

A doctoral dissertation by German Gonzales (2007, Arizona State University) is dedicated to the life and conducting career of David Whitwell through the year 1977. David Whitwell is one of nine men described by Paula A. Crider in *The Conductor's Legacy* (Chicago: GIA, 2010) as 'the legendary conductors' of the 20th century.

> 'I can't imagine the 2nd half of the 20th century—without David Whitwell and what he has given to all of the rest of us.' Frederick Fennell (1993)

About the Editor

CRAIG DABELSTEIN began studying the piano at age seven and took up the saxophone at age twelve. Mr Dabelstein has Bachelor of Arts (Music) and Bachelor of Music degrees from the Queensland Conservatorium of Music, where he majored in the performance of classical saxophone repertoire. He also has a Graduate Diploma of Learning and Teaching and a Graduate Certificate in Editing and Publishing from the University of Southern Queensland.

He has held the principal alto and tenor saxophone chairs in the Australian Wind Orchestra and has been an augmenting member of the Queensland Philharmonic Orchestra, the Queensland Symphony Orchestra, and the Queensland Pops Orchestra. For many years he was also a member of the Queensland Saxophone Quartet.

He has been a casual conductor of the Young Conservatorium Symphonic Winds, and has previously been a saxophone teacher at the Queensland Conservatorium of Music. He is a regular conductor of the Queensland Wind Orchestra, having served as their artistic director and chief conductor from 2004 to 2009.

Craig Dabelstein is a research associate for the *Teaching Music Through Performance in Band* series of books, contributing analyses to volumes 7, 8, 1 (rev. edn), and the *Solos with Wind Band Accompaniment* volume. He served as the copyeditor and layout designer of the *Australian Clarinet and Saxophone Magazine* from 2007 to 2009 and he has written many CD and book reviews for *Music Forum* magazine. He is the editor of the second editions of the books by Dr. David Whitwell including *A Concise History of the Wind Band*, *Foundations of Music Education*, *Music Education of the Future*, *The Sousa Oral History Project*, *Wagner on Bands*, *Berlioz on Bands*, *The Art of Musical Conducting*, and the *Aesthetics of Music* series (8 volumes) and *The History and Literature of the Wind Band and Wind Ensemble* series (13 volumes). From 1994 to 2012 he was a staff member at Brisbane Girls Grammar School. He now teaches woodwinds and conducts bands at St. Joseph's College, Gregory Terrace, Brisbane, Australia.

www.ingramcontent.com/pod-product-compliance
Lightning Source LLC
Chambersburg PA
CBHW080550230426
43663CB00015B/2787